Magic: A Life In More Worlds Than One
David Conway
(author of Magic: An Occult Primer)

First Edition published by Rose Ankh Publishing, Ltd, London 2020

Copyright © 2021 by David Conway

Cover Design © Peter Selgin

Chapter illustrations © Peter Selgin

Typeset by David Provolo in Garamond

Edited by David Haviland

Library of Congress Cataloguing-in-Publication Data
ISBN 9781913023072
ISBN 9781913023065

www.roseankhpublishing.com

Also by
David Conway

Magic: An Occult Primer

The Magic Of Herbs

Secret Wisdom: The Occult Universe Explored

"Reality is merely an illusion, albeit a very persistent one."

Albert Einstein

To
Philip Kewley

Pwy arall?

FOREWORD [1]

One little book changed my life. Writing it was easy, but finding a suitable title was not. In the end I settled for *Magic: an occult primer*, not because I particularly liked it, but because I could think of nothing better. (The same is true of the book you're now reading.)

That first book appeared in 1972. I was not yet thirty when I finished it, something commented on by many reviewers. Despite having done lots of other things since then, I am known even today as the man who wrote *Magic: an occult primer*. Indeed, many people overlook the intervening years and still refer to me as the young man who wrote *Magic: an occult primer*. That always makes me feel better about the rather awkward title.

A review in the *Sunday Telegraph* predicted I would become a cult figure among the young. I hadn't reckoned on that. My only aim was to promote the cause of magic, real magic that is, not the smoke and mirrors kind, by showing how its practice was compatible with common sense and reason. In those halcyon days, our minds filled with loving thoughts and gently fuelled by dope, there was much talk of occultism, mostly ill-informed, with astrology, runes, angels, tarot cards and crystals as popular as long hair, flowered shirts and flared trousers, not to mention the patchouli I wore to work each day, one of Her Majesty's less conventional Civil Servants. What information there was on magic tended to be vague and often strangely coy, with authors, perhaps eager to conceal their ignorance, hinting at secrets impossible to divulge to the uninitiated. Sadly, they admitted this only after you'd spent a fiver on the book and waded through page after page of cumbersome prose.

---

1 This Foreword appeared in an earlier, substantially different, version of this book, *Magic without Mirrors* (2011), now discontinued.

People deserved something better. Magic deserved something better.

The result was *Magic: an occult primer*, a title briefly changed twenty years later to *The Complete Magician* when a new paperback edition appeared, although the new title never caught on and the original title was quickly restored. From the outset my aim was both to provide helpful information to people already committed to magic, and to persuade sceptical readers that magic made sense. I hoped also to show that magicians, myself included, were neither mad nor bad, even if there have been one or two notable exceptions in the past.

What was altogether new was the practical advice on offer, something rarely, if ever, found in popular books on the topic, which is odd, because magic is nothing if not practical. I may have been right therefore to include the word 'primer' in the title for that is precisely what it was. (One reviewer compared it to a manual in the popular *Teach Yourself* series.) At the heart of the book were two complete rituals, one Egyptian and the other based on the Kabbalah, as well as full and detailed instructions on how to set about performing them. This enabled any reader willing to invest the necessary time and effort to try his or her hand at magic. And many of them did. Within a week of the book's publication scores of letters reached me, several from people far more famous than I, who reported with delight (and sometimes incredulity) that this or that had worked for them. The editor of a well-known magazine even confessed that after using one of the oils listed in the Appendix, she and her partner had enjoyed sex that was, in every sense, out of this world. Sadly, I forgot to ask which oil they'd used.

By then I was probably too busy enjoying my celebrity. There were television appearances and radio interviews, several with a well-known broadcaster named Jack de Manio, who liked having me on his afternoon show, because I prattled on effortlessly while he had a snooze, the effect of too much wine at lunchtime.

One American network even turned up to film me in a derelict London graveyard, the setting presumably chosen because of a perceived connection between tombstones and magic, the black sort especially. (The fee persuaded me to stifle my objections.) And then there were the press interviews, so frequent that back home in Wales my mother spent hours pasting cuttings in a smart new album she'd bought for that purpose. Her one complaint was that I looked scruffy in the photographs; scruffy and in dire need of a haircut.

For a long time I stayed flattered, sometimes dazzled, by the limelight, my only grumble being that Maxine and Alex Sanders, in those days witchcraft's most glamorous couple, sometimes edged me out of it. (Even magicians are human, especially when they've yet to turn thirty.) What eventually coaxed me away from its glow was a move to the Foreign Office and the chance to live abroad. (With full diplomatic status, I was assured, when offered the post.) It did not take me long to work out that as First Secretary in Brussels, the perks of the job far exceeded what the BBC paid me for spouting nonsense — and by then it was little more than that — while Mr de Manio had his forty winks. Even cult figures must eat.

What I did not grasp until recently was that after my departure abroad, *Magic: an occult primer* continued to influence people with occult sympathies, as well as arouse the curiosity of those with none at all. And, remarkably, it remains in print today.[2] Only when I chanced recently to type 'David Conway' and 'Magic' into Google did I realise how popular the book had become. I was more touched than flattered, especially as many contributors spoke of it with evident affection. (I noted too that American evangelicals quoted extensively, almost lasciviously, from parts of it.) "What happened to David Conway?" was the question people often asked. "He died," was the answer sometimes given.

Not true, happily, and the present book is proof of it, written not merely to confirm my survival, but also to pick up where I left off, after the final sentence of *Magic: an occult primer* was penned one October afternoon on a cold and all but empty Spanish beach. (A sudden squall

---

2 Magic: an occult primer, Jonathan Cape, London,1972 (revised and updated edition: The Witches' Almanac, Newport, Rhode Island, 2016)

later blew the pages away, forcing me to race after them, pursued by wild dogs and forlorn cries of "Helados!" from an ice-cream seller desperate for custom.) The fact is of course that the magic in my life didn't end when the book appeared close to half a century ago, any more than it started with the book's first appearance. It's been with me all the time, but hitherto I have kept the story to myself. Now, with my days of flowered shirts, flared pants and patchouli long gone — happily, I still have my hair although it's getting greyer by the day — the time seems right to put everything down on paper, enabling a new generation of readers, as well as those who read and enjoyed *Magic: an occult primer* in their younger days, to discover what went into the making of it, and into the making of its author as well. While this book is by no means a primer, I hope it too will inform as well as entertain. It is the story of my life, magical and otherwise, although in reality both were always one and the same.

Finally, I need to stress that nothing you will read here is imagined or invented. "All is true," proclaimed the French novelist Honoré de Balzac — in English — at the start of one of his best-known works, although as the book was a novel, then clearly all was *not* true. (By pretending otherwise, even in jest, the author doubtless sought to make the story credible.) Because much of what follows may beggar belief, I had better imitate Balzac and declare formally that everything you are about to read is true. By this I mean that the events described *did* happen and that the people mentioned were (and in some cases still are) every bit as real as you and me. I am not sure which is the greater challenge, to attempt what Balzac did and make fiction take on the appearance of fact or, as I must do, prevent fact from reading like fiction, a task made more difficult because the type of fiction my story resembles is not the sort that imitates life as most people know it, but something more fanciful and seemingly far-fetched.

By promising that all is true, I hope also to keep your disbelief at bay long enough to persuade you I am neither deluded nor dishonest. Sadly, many of those engaged in occultism have in the past been one or the other, at times even both, but then so have people involved in most other types of activity, no matter how respectable, the only difference being that when occultists go wrong, they do so more spectacularly or with more panache than anybody else. And so far as honesty's concerned, I am willing to place my right hand on whatever book you suggest — even the complete works of Aleister Crowley or Madame Blavatsky — and swear that what you are about to read is the truth, the whole truth, and nothing but that. What I cannot guarantee is that I am not deluded. It is something I am ill equipped to decide. Only you can do that.

And even you may get it wrong.

PART ONE

1

"Aberystwyth: a nostalgic yearning which is in itself more pleasant than the thing being yearned for.

Douglas Adams and John Lloyd (after Alfred, Lord Tennyson):
The Meaning of Liff (1983).

There are pretty babies and then there are the rest of us. Some babies are noisier than others. Mathonwy James was one.

Scarcely had he drawn his first breath than he began to squeal. Many babies do, but few have squealed so loudly or for quite so long. The year was 1885 and it was the first day of October, a Thursday.

"He doesn't like this wicked world," observed the midwife, a staunch Methodist whose own view of the world did not amount to much either. Universally known as 'Nurse', but with no formal claim to the title, she went about the countryside delivering babies, caring for the sick and laying out the dead, this last job being the one she relished most. It was her custom to sing hymns as she busied herself with her corpses, a kind of musical viaticum that always ended with *Lo, He standeth 'midst the Myrtles*, a favourite of hers. Sometimes she'd hint that she and its composer, Ann Griffiths, née Thomas, were somehow related through an uncle, himself a Thomas, who'd lived near the farm where Ann Griffiths grew up. Few took her seriously. Wales is full of Thomases.

No sooner had the baby's squeals been stilled than others, even louder, rent the crisp, autumnal air.

"It's the pig," Mathonwy's mother told the startled midwife. "We're killing it today." And with that she looked down at the baby she was holding and murmured something about one life ending and another about to begin. She'd grown rather fond of the pig. Every year there'd be a new one, although they all looked pretty much the same, and each year she'd get to know it well, feed it peelings from the kitchen until, before you knew where you were, October came around, and it was time to slit the poor thing's throat. If only they didn't make so much noise when it happened. Pigs, she reflected, were loth to quit the world Mathonwy had not wanted to come into. And with that it struck her for the first time that with his pink face and flat little nose he looked like a piglet himself. The thought made her smile.

"You can have a piece of hock when it's ready," she absently told the midwife. Or so the infant she was suckling would tell me many years later. How he remembered, I never thought to ask.

Mathonwy was a name she'd picked after coming across it in *Cyfaill yr Aelwyd* (Companion of the Hearth), a magazine popular the length and breadth of Wales.[3] She took to the name at once, unlike the minister who called to baptise the infant that same day. (With so many babies dying early, it was best to get the job done quickly: their 'ticket to Heaven' people called it.) He suspected the name might be pagan, not having met it until then. There was no Mathonwy in the Scriptures, that much he knew, but he was not, to his credit, a narrow-minded

---

3 The name appears in the fourth and final book of the Mabinogion, a collection of stories penned in the Middle Ages but dating from pre-Christian times. There we learn that Mathonwy's son, Math, did battle with a neighbouring ruler whose herd of pigs he stole on Mathonwy's behalf. Of course, it is mere coincidence, but one to be relished, that Mathonwy James came into the world as the Tanrallt pig was leaving it. The editor of *Cyfaill yr Aelwyd* was a former schoolteacher named Beriah Gwynfe Evans. He would later write a biography of David Lloyd George, as well as contribute articles to *The Occult Review*, having had a special interest in ghosts. Other contributors to the same magazine included Dion Fortune and Aleister Crowley.

man, so Mathonwy was the name he bestowed on the child, its face now pinker than ever, and its squeals even louder than before. Once formally endowed with a name, Mathonwy James stopped squealing, and lost much of his high colour. He even managed a smile. As if the world and its wickedness might well be to his liking after all.

It was a world his mother would leave one day short of her son's tenth birthday, the cause of death officially recorded as 'debility', a catch-all term popular back then. Escorted into the bedroom by Nurse Davies, her laying-out completed and hymns dutifully sung, the boy was enjoined to kiss the figure resting on the bed but he declined. Yes, the person lying there looked vaguely like his mother, but no more. To him it seemed a replica of her or, as he told me, savouring the word, a 'simulacrum', one impertinently wearing his mother's silk shawl, but whose grimace and sunken, rice-powdered cheeks were certainly not hers.

"She looks peaceful," volunteered Nurse Davies.

To Mathonwy she looked nothing of the sort, whoever the imposter might be.

His indifference shocked the nurse. Experience had taught her that bereaved infants could be relied upon to weep, often copiously, when confronted by a dead parent, a dead mother especially. In their confusion some would rush forward and fling themselves upon the corpse, a familiarity Nurse Davies discouraged lest it compromise her handiwork, but never in forty years had she met a child that stood there, as Mathonwy now did, gazing calmly at what, she heard herself reminding him, had been his mother until a few short hours before. Despite growing unease – he'd always struck her as different from other children – she followed her custom and began reciting the Lord's Prayer, eyes tight shut and hands devoutly clasped, confident that like everyone before him, he'd join in halfway through or, at a pinch, volunteer a muted 'amen' when she finished. But no, on opening her eyes she perceived that Mathonwy was no longer in the room.

"By then I was halfway up the bloody mountain."

Well, what he said was 'fucking' mountain, but in deference to

Nurse Davies, winner of the Thomas Gee medal for Sunday School attendance, I'll stick to 'bloody'. That's bad enough. You don't hear words like that among the myrtles.

What Mathonwy and I have in common is that neither was a pretty child. For if he came into the world looking (and sounding) like an irate piglet, then by all accounts I turned up looking like a grumpy tortoise, yellow-skinned and generously wrinkled.

"Are you sure that's mine?" my father reportedly enquired, when allowed to see me for the first time, much to the annoyance of my mother. Fortunately, within a day or two the wrinkles faded and my complexion turned a wholesome shade of pink. No longer could his paternity be doubted, not least because my ears stuck out with the same proud defiance as his own. (A piece of sticking plaster behind each soon taught them better manners, while a threepenny bit and an elasticated bandage did the same for a rebellious belly button.) I also had a lazy eye, cured by covering the good one and forcing its indolent partner to do the work of both.

Whatever my shortcomings, the miracle was that I'd turned up in person to exhibit them. For as my mother told anyone stopping to admire me — and she defied people not to — whenever she wheeled me down Aberystwyth promenade in my pram, she had lost no fewer than six previous babies.

"All of them boys" she would add.

When I grew older, she explained that this made me a seventh child. Indeed, thanks to six older siblings of her own, I was the seventh child of a seventh child.

The coincidence delighted a friend of my mother's, a woman whose interest in the supernatural bordered on the obsessive.

"He must have second-sight," enthused Mrs Caradoc Evans, her only disappointment being that I'd not also been born with a caul. As for my six stillborn brothers, these were thriving in the spirit world despite never having drawn a breath in this one. She claimed to have seen two such infants in the arms of a Scottish medium named Mrs

Duncan and, although made from ectoplasm, both were indisputably alive, even kicking. In fact, the tiny mites had never stopped bawling their lungs out. It struck me later that Mrs Duncan must be terribly psychic, seventh child or not, to produce wonders of this sort, for according to Mrs Evans, she could extrude — no one enquired how or from where — such quantities of ectoplasm that hordes of dead people took on form and substance in her presence, all every bit as real as they'd once been in the flesh. She even extruded pet rabbits and a parrot that answered to the name of Bronco.

There was something ectoplasmic about Mrs Evans as well. Unlike other women I knew, she did not so much as wear clothes as envelop herself in swathes of taffeta and silk, over which hung diaphanous layers of chiffon. These multi-coloured draperies, like her silver sandals and the rings on every finger, brought to mind a gaudy tropical bird blown off course by the wind and dumped among us dowdy sparrows. A bit like Bronco in fact. Meanwhile bracelets crawled sinuously up her bare arms, while beneath her generous chin hung row upon row of brightly coloured beads. Had it not been for a large floppy hat, black but enlivened with brooches, she might have stepped out of a painting by Alma-Tadema, part Roman matron and, with her nut-brown arms and shiny bangles, part Nubian slave.

Before a second marriage turned her into plain Mrs Evans, she had been Countess Barcynska, the widow of a Polish aristocrat. The name suited her better. That may be why she still used it when writing the romantic novels for which she was famous, few of them remembered today. Her second husband had also been a writer, disliked, even loathed, throughout his native Wales for the unpleasantness of his characters, most of them Welsh, and the robustness of his language. ('Pestilential' was the epithet applied by one critic to his best-known book, a collection of short stories called *My People*.) My father on the other hand quite liked his work and it was a supportive letter he sent him, by then living near Aberystwyth, that led to their acquaintance. After the author's death in 1945, his widow took to calling on us often.

The Aberystwyth I grew up in was a cheerless place. Not that this deterred the local guidebook, obtainable from the Town Hall in return for a large stamped-addressed envelope, from calling it the 'Biarritz of Wales'. Other resorts along the coast were understandably miffed and one, Llandudno, not to be outdone, alliteratively dubbed itself the 'Naples of the North'. Within a year the 'Biarritz of Wales', averse to challenge, had metamorphosed into 'Queen of the Welsh Riviera', a boast still heard from time to time today.

To be fair, the seafront was not unattractive, at least not when the tide was in and the weather bright and reasonably sunny. Its promenade curved agreeably enough, although the beach it curved around was composed entirely of shingle. At one end stood Constitution Hill, a rocky outcrop whose summit was accessible by funicular railway, while at the other rose a grassy elevation known as Pen Dinas, once a prehistoric hill fort, but crowned now by a structure resembling a factory chimney, and meant to represent the upturned barrel of a cannon. Erected to commemorate the Duke of Wellington's victory at Waterloo, the aim had been to top it with a likeness of the Iron Duke seated on his charger, but the statue got lost at sea while being shipped from Italy, and the squire who'd commissioned it never got around to ordering a replacement.

Even as a boy, I found the town dull, at least on all but the sunniest of days. The ubiquitous grey stone and slate of its buildings were partly to blame, these and an abundance of sombre Nonconformist chapels. People claimed the chapels outnumbered the town's public houses (and there was no shortage of those), for the pious a sign that the Devil, though a force to be reckoned with, had not yet gained the upper hand. Throughout the 1950s, the influence of the chapels remained strong, certainly strong enough to see off every secular challenge. It was this, I remember, that forced the Principal of the University to quit both his job and the town at short notice. Already suspect on account of his fondness for drink, his suede shoes, cravats and camel-hair coat, what did for him in the end was a series of articles he wrote for a Sunday newspaper about his friendship with the spies, Burgess and Maclean, newly defected to Moscow. Worse, one of the pair, Guy Burgess, had been both a drunk and a *homosexual.* Aberystwyth had a thing about unnatural vice.

To fit in, you had to conform. This was something I learned at an early age. It is why I resented being told I was psychic. That made me different. Only later would I realise that being different didn't matter, by which time I'd long stopped wanting to fit in.

By then, too, I was reconciled to the possibility that there might be some truth in what Mrs Evans had been saying. Not all that seventh child nonsense, but the possibility, and it was never more than that, of what she called second sight: a means of access, so to speak, to information outside normal empirical experience.

The first sign of it came shortly after my fifth birthday. One evening my mother had no sooner put me to bed and gone downstairs than two elderly ladies turned up from nowhere, and as I watched, more curious than afraid, advanced silently across the darkened room. Nothing about them was remotely sinister: the taller of the pair in a long skirt and lacy, cream-coloured blouse, a cameo brooch at her throat, and her hair tied back in a bun; the other, shorter and similarly dressed, with matching brooch, but whiter hair and wearing glasses. She, it was, who made a show of nodding and smiling and blowing kisses at me, none of it welcome, although being a well brought-up little boy, I probably smiled back.

On successive nights the two of them returned and slowly I began to take in more about them, noting small differences between the brooches, at first glance identical, as well as the incongruous black hair-pins the shorter woman wore to keep her white hair in place. True, their old-fashioned clothes seemed odd but not unduly so, as an elderly aunt of my mother's lived with us and dressed much the same way. As a result, long skirts and high-necked blouses, even lace cuffs and leg-of-mutton sleeves caused me no undue surprise,

Had my visitors left it at that, I might have dropped off to sleep. I might even have consented to call them by the names, preceded by 'Auntie', they kept pressing me to use. But their interest in me did not end there, for at some point — and I quickly came to dread it — the taller of the two would lean over the bed and tickle me. Now, I know that sounds harmless enough but in fact it was nothing of the sort, not when they turned up night after night and, chit-chat over, my tormentor would resume her tickling while I thrashed about, powerless to stop her. Throughout it all — and I remember how much this shocked me even back then — the woman's expression stayed blank, with no hint of a smirk or a scowl, just a mindless, unflinching resolve. I am told my screams could be heard outside in the street.

Night after night my parents, usually my mother, would assure me it was all a bad dream, that I should say my prayers all over again and put the whole silly business out of my head. The more I insisted I had *not* been asleep, that I *had* seen, while fully awake, two elderly women in my room, the more she sought to persuade me there was nobody, opening the wardrobe to show it contained only clothes (as if I expected anything else) and having me look under the bed to satisfy myself there was nothing there save my slippers, a few discarded toys and a potty.

Some weeks later she took me to see Dr Ellis. Her confidence in Dr Ellis knew no bounds for it was he who'd ended the succession of miscarriages, ensuring my safe arrival in the world, this "wicked world", as Nurse Davies would have put it.

"You say they talk to you?"

I told him they did. I went on also to describe their features, as well as the clothes they wore, the cameo brooches, the black hairpins and the tendency of one woman, the taller of the pair, to smother a persistent cough with the back of her hand. I even provided him with their names, as well as the diminutives, preceded by 'Auntie', they encouraged me to use.

When I finished, Dr Ellis asked the nurse to take me outside while he had a word with my mother. That night, on his recommendation, my bed was moved to another room and, to my relief, the mischief never recurred. Within days I lost the fear that my tormentors might return but I never forgot them. This account is proof of that.

Years would pass before my mother disclosed what Dr Ellis told her after I'd left them alone. Forty years before, he explained, at the start of his professional life, he'd attended two patients in what was now our home, elderly sisters, long dead. Not only had I described them in detail — the hair, the clothes, as well as the consumptive cough the taller woman kept trying to suppress — but given him their names, even the pet names each had used for the other.

A mystery, he called it. My mother, averse to mysteries, the psychic sort especially, put it down to coincidence. As for Mrs Caradoc Evans, she was told nothing, not a word, the fear being that, if apprised of it, she'd turn up with her crystal ball and ouija board. The best thing, decreed my mother, was to forget about the whole silly business and never speak of it again. The second of these was the easier by far.

Only after I got to know Mathonwy James did I find someone who would help me come to terms with, if not fully understand, what my five-year-old self had experienced. For he, too, saw things other people did not, something Nurse Davies would discover after she'd finished laying out the corpse of his mother.

She died, you'll remember, on the eve of his tenth birthday. That may be why his father did not scold him when he returned home after abandoning Nurse Davies. She, too, was not unsympathetic and when his father left the room, offered to make the boy a cup of tea. He helped himself to buttermilk instead.

"She was sitting where you are now," he told me years later, "in that very chair. Well, I think it was that one. In those days we had four. A set. Anyway, there she was, going on and on about Mam being up there with the angels, all nice and cosy like, until I told her she was not. Nor was she upstairs on the bed. No, she was in the room with us and not happy, not one little bit, with the way Nurse Davies, left to herself, had rummaged through the trunk underneath the wardrobe. She'd no business opening it, let alone taking out a roll of lace and stuffing it down the front of her blouse."

And that was how the nurse discovered Mathonwy James, as she'd begun to suspect, was unlike other children. This one had 'the gift'.

"You can see your mother?"

Just asking made her uneasy. Yes, such things were possible, but that didn't make them right. As Saint Paul told the Hebrews (or was it the Ephesians? She often got them mixed up), after death came the Judgement, not the chance to return to this life and tell tales. By then, too, she was half persuaded that she'd opened the trunk to look for a clean pillow slip, nothing more, and before she could account for the lace, the child spoke again.

"Mam says you'd already got all the pillow slips you needed," he declared, a froth of buttermilk around his mouth.

Now, dead bodies Nurse Davies could cope with. None had caused her a moment's unease. But being in a room with someone Mathonwy could see and she couldn't, someone who knew what she'd done and what was going on inside her head, that was different. As she told people later, careful not to mention pillow cases, let alone missing rolls of lace, she'd felt herself go cold all over, from the top of her head to the tips of her toes. And while at her coldest, there had come from outside a scream so terrible the blood all but froze in her veins.

The Devil himself!

"No", said the boy, "it's not the Devil. It's only the pig. Today's the day we kill it. My birthday. Don't you remember?"

The question went unanswered. By then Nurse Davies, too, was halfway up the fucking mountain.

2

> **"Still, around the corner, there may wait
> a new road or a secret gate"**
>
> J. R. Tolkien

It was in my Uncle Davy's shop — 'High-class Grocers and Confectioners' — that I first caught sight of Mathonwy James. By far the biggest man I'd seen up to then, his bulk was somehow magnified by the tweed suit he wore for his weekly excursions into Aberystwyth, its gingery brown vaguely unsettling until one became used to it. Taller than my father (himself fully six feet) and impressively broad shouldered, his head rested on a neck worthy of a stocky young bull. On top of it, whatever the weather, rested a bowler hat, also brown, and several sizes too small. It might have looked comical on anyone else, but on him it seemed just right, even oddly touching. His hands, coarsened and reddened by working outside in all weathers, were uncommonly large, even for someone as solidly built as himself, as were his feet in their smartly polished boots. On all but the sunniest of days, he carried over his arm a tightly rolled umbrella, and rolled-up it stayed, even when the rain was pelting down in buckets. For like the suit, the bowler hat, the polished boots and the silk handkerchief cascading from his breast pocket, the brolly was part of a disguise invented years earlier for these weekly expeditions. Since then he'd seen no reason to change it.

A cut above its rivals, Uncle Davy's shop stood on the corner of Market Street and Eastgate, with display windows in both and an entrance up three marble steps, flanked by Doric columns. 'The Fauchon of Wales' is how one customer, more widely travelled than most, once described it, although Uncle Davy misheard and thought she'd said Fortnum's. That pleased him every bit as much.

By the time I got to know him well, Uncle Davy had turned eighty, and retreated to a small office at the back of the shop, his days spent bullying commercial travellers and dreaming up new slogans for the firm, some of them quite clever, I thought. My favourite was 'Our cream can be whipped but not beaten', with 'Our bread can be buttered, not bettered' a close second. I could never understand why my father, by then running the business, didn't do as Uncle Davy wished and have them printed on the firm's bills and letterheads. Later he explained that none was original, my great-uncle having come across them while perusing a weekly paper called *The Grocer*, but immediately forgotten that he had.

In those days I was a puny child, in need, people said, of 'filling out'. I was also, my mother kept reminding me, far too pale, the way she said it implying the blame was somehow my own. By then she'd long been wondering if Saturdays spent with Mr James might put some extra flesh on me, as well as bring a wholesome dab of colour to my cheeks. The alternative was to enrol me in the Boy Scouts, but that appealed to her less. There was, she felt, something not quite right about middle-aged men in khaki shorts cavorting in the boscage with prepubescent boys.

To me neither prospect seemed appealing, but both were preferable to the Scott's Emulsion she'd been pouring down my throat up to then: made from fish livers, it tasted vile and, as she conceded, had done nothing to improve the way I looked. A spoonful of Virol at bedtime was more palatable but that, too, had been a disappointment.

"We'll soon build him up," promised Mr James.

The promise was endorsed by a friend of my father's, a medical doctor whose opinion carried extra weight. Originally from Llanelli and named after a sixteenth-century Welsh martyr, Tom Penry Evans had qualified in the 1920s but gone on to specialise in public health and nutrition rather than practise medicine full time. (For several months, a soy-based supplement he'd recommended was added to my cornflakes, supplementing the Virol and the Scott's Emulsion.) My memory of him is vague but I do remember that, like Dr Ellis, he questioned me about my 'nightmares', so my mother must have told him about the two old ladies and their unwelcome tickling. By contrast his wife, Anne, I do remember, possibly because she gave me a toothbrush holder modelled on one of Walt Disney's seven dwarfs: I think it was Happy. Somewhere in the attic, I still have it.

Mr James — I never called him anything else — and my father got on well. My mother, too, quite liked him, and each week would bake an apple tart or sponge cake for him to take home after he'd finished his shopping. And so it was decided among them that I'd spend my Saturdays with him on the farm. Only his use of bad language caused her unease, a vice impossible to overlook as the offending words were the only English ones in an otherwise mellifluous torrent of Welsh. Uncle Davy, a chapel elder, shared her concern.

"How rude are they, Jim?" he asked my father one afternoon.

"Let's say, I wouldn't use them."

"But you know what they mean?"

"I was in the army, remember. You hear words like that."

My mother, too, maintained she didn't understand them. She just sensed they weren't very nice.

"Young people can be led astray," Uncle Davy remarked a day or two later. "One must keep an eye on them."

It was a lesson he'd learned years before when his only son, Jim — not much to look at but by all accounts a sweet-natured lad — secretly fathered a daughter. The youthful misdemeanour came to light one Sunday morning when the child's mother, a housemaid of unmitigated plainness, turned up outside Gosen chapel to confront her seducer as he arrived with his parents for the ten o'clock service.

"She's yours, she's yours" the woman had shrieked, holding the infant aloft, its likeness to Jim so obvious it defied contradiction.

Hurried offers of financial provision were agreed, allowing Uncle Davy to dispatch mother and baby before fellow worshippers, already perplexed, could work out what was happening. After that, he lost no time in finding Jim a suitable bride, only for the groom to expire on his wedding night, presumably of a heart attack, although no one was tactless enough to speculate further, not even the coroner. Within the family there was general agreement that the cause of death was not what they referred to as 'you know what', if only because Jim, as the housemaid could testify, was no stranger to the 'what'. It was shortly afterwards that my father, also named Jim, was conscripted to help run — and later inherit — his uncle's flourishing business.

"Try not to listen when he swears," cautioned my mother, the first Saturday I set off for the farm, although even she must have realised that by doing so I'd hear next to nothing Mr James said. Given that the offending words meant as little to me as they did to Uncle Davy, I simply learned to ignore them.

The bike that conveyed me to Tanrallt (the name means 'Below the Hill') was a hybrid affair, cobbled together on the cheap by a man who repaired bicycles. A 'proper' bike, could wait until I'd stopped growing or at least begun to slow down. Mismatched its components might be, but the machine proved robust enough to convey me to my destination week after week in just under an hour, slightly more if the wind were blowing full on.

The outward journey was by far the harder because it was relentlessly uphill, with the landscape around me bleak and sullen on all but the sunniest of days. Of the few houses I passed, one was home to several nanny goats and their reclusive owner, rumoured to have been a dancer with the Ballets Russes, while the billy had a shed to himself at the back. So rank was the smell that I'd hold my breath when cycling past. Another cottage I remember because its elderly owner, never without a knitted balaclava on his head, would shuffle to the gate at my approach, keen to tell me German bombers had been flying overhead the night before.

"Bound for Liverpool, I expect. The docks."

"Or Manchester," I'd reply, not brave enough to tell him the war had long ended.

The final stretch was on the flat. That never failed to cheer me up. And as if to match my mood, everything around me seemed perceptibly less drab, the roadside bright with toadflax, marsh marigolds and vetch. Even the sheep looked more friendly. And then, all of a sudden, between two bends in the road, there opened up a cleft, so narrow, so unexpected, it might easily be missed. Still easier to miss was the track that plunged into it, accessible through an old wooden gate, with 'Tanrallt' crudely painted on the topmost bar and a biscuit tin nailed to one post by way of makeshift letterbox. Both gate and tin are long gone, the former replaced by an anonymous barrier of galvanised steel, the kind of gate you nowadays see everywhere in Wales.

Beyond was a small patch of asphalt, laid as a favour to Mr James when council workmen came to resurface the main road, but this quickly gave way to a twin-furrowed track, the width of a tractor's wheel span, with clumps of plantain and coarse grasses growing in between. Provided I steered carefully, one cautious hand on the brake, I could ride along the ruts and, apart from the occasional wobble, this was the part of the journey I enjoyed most, especially when the track suddenly veered to the right and there, as if by magic, a second valley opened up ahead of me. Nestling in it, no less magical, was the farmhouse, primly whitewashed and showing few signs of the many harsh winters it had lived through. True, its slatestone roof sagged in the middle but splashes of lichen, a bright mustard yellow, gave it an air of defiance, even sprightliness, as did the whitewashed walls and jaunty red front door.

All around it were the mountains, rumoured to be older than the Alps, and replete with peat bogs, streams, and tightly folded valleys.

Once upon a time, these hills had been home to Mathonwy James' fore-bears, descendants of more shadowy beings who, before history began, had travelled here to worship long-forgotten gods and build monuments to honour them. One such cairn, known as Clogwyn Bedwyr (Bedivere's Rock), is named after a knight at King Arthur's court, most handsome of them all, according to *Culhwch ac Olwen,* a text older even than the *Mabinogion.* To me it has always seemed that in this bleak, inhospitable place the mountains don't just clamber upwards to the sky, as they do elsewhere, but the sky comes down to them and, on all but the sunniest of days, tenderly envelops them in mist.

It is a place of eerie stillness, a stillness neither empty nor silent. At least not to those who remember how to listen.

3

Glendower: "I can call spirits from the vasty deep."
Hotspur: "Why, so can I, or so can any man; but
will they come when you do call for them?"

William Shakespeare, *King Henry IV, Part 1*

That Mathonwy James was known locally as *dyn hysbys* or 'magician' intrigued me from the start.

"He cures sick cattle," replied my father when I asked what type of magic he performed.

So did the vet. I had hoped for something better.

"And he helps people find things. Things they've lost. Money, jewellery, keys, that sort of thing."

An improvement, but not much. In Aberystwyth, missing objects usually turned up at the police station sooner or later. 'Finders keepers' was not the sort of behaviour its inhabitants condoned.

"What else?"

"People think he can see the future," volunteered my mother, the way she said it implying she was not among them.

"Can he see dead people?"

I was told to get on with my homework.

By then I'd developed an interest in Spiritualism, one my mother, mindful of the two old ladies, was doing her utmost to discourage. Not that it had gone beyond reading books — the municipal library had two shelves of them — by people like Harry Price, Sir Arthur Conan Doyle and a big favourite, Air Chief Marshal Lord Dowding, who'd spent much of the war helping dead airmen find their way into Heaven, although he called it something else. Summerland, I think. Only when I grew addicted to the musings of a Native American named Silver Birch, long dead but channelled by the editor of a weekly publication called *Psychic News*, did my mother grow anxious, less on account of what Silver Birch said — he was prone to homely platitudes [4] — than of the risk I might imitate his pidgin English. She need not have worried: Silver Birch's prose was impeccable. Suspiciously so, I might have realised, had I been older.

Only once, when staying with an aunt in North Wales, did I manage to attend a Spiritualist church, although I told the grown-ups I was off to the pictures.

"I've a gentleman here," declared the medium, a middle-aged woman in twinset and pearls who kept nodding vigorously, as if to acknowledge some confidence being whispered in her ear.

"He's giving me the name 'John'. Does anybody have a John in spirit?"

Three-quarters of the congregation did, judging by the flurry of hands that shot up.

"This John is a tall gentleman, very tall. With a lovely smile. And he's wearing glasses."

Down came a number of hands, their owners presumably acquainted with Johns who were short or grumpy, possibly both, and blessed with perfect eyesight.

"Now he's giving me an 'M'. I think it's for Mary. Yes, that's it, John's giving me a thumbs up. Thank you for that, dear."

Only two hands stayed aloft.

---

4 E.g. "Life is always a polarity. If there were no darkness there would be no light. If there were no trouble there could never be any peace. If the sun always shone you would not appreciate it."

"He tells me Mary – 'my lovely Mary' is how he puts it — has placed flowers in front of his picture. They're on the sideboard."

If by this detail the speaker hoped to eliminate one of the rival claimants, she was wrong.

"He liked his glass of beer," she ventured next.

Good try, but neither Mary yielded to the other.

"No, not beer," suggested the medium, now going for broke, "it was stout. A nice drop of stout."

Only one hand stayed aloft. A middle-aged couple in the same row as me started clapping but stopped when no one else joined in.

"Yes, I hear you, John. He tells me he was very partial to his Guinness. Oh! Now he's offering me a bottle of the stuff, the naughty boy."

"Mackeson," murmured John's widow. "He hated Guinness. Too bitter, he said."

A quick change of tack brought with it news that the deceased had died very suddenly and this time, to universal relief, his widow concurred.

Hand resting where the twinset covered her heart, the medium began to gasp.

"Perforated ulcer," said Mary quietly, "That's what got him."

"Exactly!"

The hand had moved from heart to solar plexus.

Such was my disappointment that I wrote a letter to *Psychic News,* a prominent Spiritualist weekly. Describing myself as a seventeen-year-old schoolboy — admitting to fourteen risked not being taken seriously — and already a committed Spiritualist, I complained that, 'The clairvoyance I have come across is an insult to the sacred nature of the faculty.' That I'd come across it only once I took care not to mention.

The letter was duly published, with my name and address printed, as was the custom back then, at the end of it. Not certain how she'd react, I showed it to my mother. To my relief she took it well. Mrs Caradoc Evans was of course delighted, even resurrecting all that seventh child nonsense, while a dozen readers of *Psychic News* sent me encouraging letters, among them a gentleman from Slough who asked for my photograph, preferably in swimming trunks. On Countess Barcynska's advice his letter was forwarded to the editor, the reference to swimming trunks underlined in red ink.

What my sudden fame did was embolden me to question Mr James about the supernatural, a word I'd only recently discovered but was already overfond of using. Until then the topic had never been mentioned between us. I even made a point of looking up the Welsh for 'supernatural' before setting off on my bike.

At the time, I remember, we were seated at the kitchen table, the horsehair stuffing in the seat of my chair pricking my thighs when I moved. (I'd yet to graduate to long trousers.) Before me stood a mug of greenish-grey liquid that Mr James kept pressing me to drink, insisting it would help me grow every bit as big as himself. I was not at all sure I wanted to. Normally we made do with ordinary tea.

"It's got chervil in it, as well as heather and a pinch of ginger, even honeysuckle. Everything a growing boy needs." Years later I'd discover it also contained a generous splash of sloe gin.

The room by then was dark but seldom was it anything else. Once through the door you entered a crepuscular gloom which two small windows tried in vain to lighten, not helped by the potted geraniums lined up in front of them, bereft of flowers and in dire need of pruning. Junk of all sorts lay everywhere: bits of harness, three or four shotguns, books, stacks of peat, old copies of the *Welsh Gazette* and *Farmers Weekly*, as well as earthenware jars containing what Mr James called his 'physics'. while from the ceiling hung bunches of herbs — broom, yarrow, wormwood, thyme and loosestrife — drying in their own sweet-scented time.

The house was small, no more than a living room and kitchen on the ground floor, with two bedrooms upstairs, one of them tiny. There was no bathroom and just an outside privy — *tŷ bach* or 'little house' in Welsh — but being too fastidious to use it, I never discovered if it was an earth closet or something more sophisticated. (I used to go to pee behind the barn.) There was also a loft, accessible by ladder, which again I never got to visit. For a long time, I suspected it was there that Mr James worked his magic.

Its practice was widespread throughout Wales until the second half of the nineteenth century. By then, however, it involved little more than telling fortunes, removing warts or peddling charms and herbal nostrums. Few witches were ever put to death in Wales, perhaps no more than three or four, the best documented case being that of Gwen ferch Ellis from Betws-yn-Rhos in Denbighshire, who in 1594 was accused of 'charming'. Court records show that Gwen, three times married, described herself as a healer, attending the sick, and dispensing salves and potions, her speciality being the treatment of children and livestock. In addition, she supplied charms to secure good fortune, and protect the wearer from harm.

It was one such charm that landed her in court, written on a scrap of paper and discovered at the home of Thomas Mostyn, a wealthy landowner, of Gloddaeth Hall near Llandudno. Believed to have been commissioned by his neighbour and sometime mistress, Jane Conway, the text was indisputably in Gwen's hand but, most damning of all, had been written backwards, a sure sign of malicious intent. Witnesses prepared to testify against the accused, five men and two women, were duly heard by magistrates and, on the basis of their testimony, Gwen was indicted for causing a child to go mad, and of securing the death of a man she'd been treating for jaundice. For good measure, she was accused also of having a spiteful disposition. Found guilty, she was publicly hanged in the small market town of Denbigh before the year was out.

Not until 1735 did the law change and, when it happened, the change was significant. Thanks to the Witchcraft Act of that year, it was the pretence of witchcraft, not its practice, that became a criminal offence. As a result, only persons claiming to have supernatural powers, now deemed fictitious, risked punishment, usually a fine or imprisonment, not those accused of possessing or exploiting them. The change would do little to inhibit Mr James' magical predecessors, still less halt the epidemic of table-turners, astrologers, palmists, and clairvoyants that burgeoned a century later, their successors no less prolific today.

I would learn from Mr James that one of the last people prosecuted under the Act was that self-same Mrs Duncan whose spirit babies had made such an impression on Countess Barcynska. Others might cheat, she'd reluctantly concede, but not Mrs Duncan. By all accounts, plenty of people thought likewise, with witnesses reporting how ectoplasm flowed from her by the yard, its appearance variously described as 'iridescent', 'pulsating', 'misty grey' and 'pastel coloured'. (It also had a rather yucky smell.) On one occasion a deceased civic dignitary turned up in the seance room complete with chain of office, followed by an Indian army captain who arrived still wearing his sola topi. A third visitor, this time an ex-policeman, even withdrew briefly to retrieve the helmet which, in his haste to materialise, he'd forgotten to put on. There was also a memorable afternoon in South Wales (where Mrs Duncan was always in demand) when a group of dead miners, still with coal dust on their faces, delighted everyone by singing hymns. In Welsh.

Party masks and cheesecloth scoffed the doubters. Harry Price, a well-known psychical researcher of the day, though less than completely honest himself, even suggested Mrs Duncan had a secondary stomach where she stored her props before coughing them up in the dark. It might explain the yucky smell.

Perhaps Victoria Helen Duncan was indeed the real McCoy, as Mrs Evans tirelessly maintained, at least some of the time.[5] But there were also times when her ectoplasm was not all it seemed. One was during an engagement at the Edinburgh home of Miss Esson Maule, an intimidating lady with a fondness for pin-striped suits, sturdy brogues and men's ties. It involved a spirit child, Peggy Hazeldine, a frequent,

---

5 Not only had Mrs Evans seen and touched ectoplasm, but she had also been permitted on one occasion to cut off a small piece from some spirit drapery and take it home in her handbag. (She stored it overnight in a jam jar, but found no trace of it the next morning. She was later told that she should have filled the jar with distilled water first.)

if at times irksome, revenant at Mrs Duncan's seances. (Her mother, invited to one of them, resignedly acknowledged it was indeed her late daughter.)

Given to showing off, this Shirley Temple of the au-delà insisted that night on entertaining the company with nursery rhymes, her favourite songs (*Loch Lomond* and *Ah Sweet Mystery of Life*), her frenetic skipping and her dancing. Whatever she was made of, she certainly livened things up. That evening, however, Miss Maule became increasingly persuaded that little Peggy, barely visible as she embarked on yet another jig, was in reality a towel or dishcloth being waved about in the dark. Determined to get at the truth, she lunged at the tiny figure, only to find herself clutching wads of Mrs Duncan's all too solid flesh. When someone turned on the lights, the medium was caught in flagrante trying to stuff a piece of white stockinette, later identified as a lady's vest ('outsize'), down the front of her dress, much as Nurse Davies had done with the lace. To her credit Mrs Duncan, though heavily outnumbered, managed to floor several of her persecutors in the ensuing fracas but could not escape the £10 fine imposed some months later at the Sheriff's Summary Court.

Her subsequent indictment for witchcraft happened in 1943 and the episode is worth reporting more fully.

It began when a young lieutenant in the Royal Navy Reserve, Stanley Worth, attended a demonstration Mrs Duncan gave at the grandly named Master Temple Psychic Centre in Portsmouth, in reality a drab room above a chemist's shop in Copnor Road. Admission was an exorbitant twelve shillings and sixpence, although for that price the ticket-holder did secure a front row seat. Once the lights were dimmed, Mrs Duncan's spirit guide Albert duly appeared and, assuming his customary role of compere, though by all accounts not on top form, languidly introduced the boisterous Peggy, who sang two verses of *Loch Lomond*, neither terribly well. A deceased parrot, possibly Bronco, showed up also, but didn't stay long. Next day, feeling cheated of his twelve-and-six, Worth lodged a complaint at Portsmouth Police Station.

While on the premises, he was persuaded to attend a second seance four days later, this time armed with a police whistle and standard issue torch. With him, at the suggestion of the police, was War Reserve Constable Rupert Cross. That afternoon the participants consisted of thirty people from this world and, it would transpire, four from the next, among them a reinvigorated Albert. For once even little Peggy sang in tune. No sooner had the fourth visitor materialised, however, than Cross leapt from his seat in the second row, barged through the row in front and tore aside a curtain to reveal a flustered Mrs Duncan struggling to conceal the bed sheet which, her accusers would claim, she'd been using to impersonate the dead. Meanwhile the owner of the premises, his Master Temple desecrated, was lashing out at Cross, while the treacherous Worth, his torch still beamed on Mrs Duncan as she struggled back into her shoes, blew his police whistle to summon two constables waiting on the staircase outside.

What ensued was not, as would normally happen, a routine appearance before the local magistrates, resulting in a modest fine and an order to keep the peace.[6] (The Vagrancy Act of 1824 was made for that purpose.) Instead the Director of Prosecutions in London, Sir Edward Atkinson, opted to apply the full rigor of the Witchcraft Act of 1735, with a trial that commenced at the Old Bailey on 21 March 1944 and lasted seven days. At the end of it, Mrs Duncan was found guilty and sentenced by the Recorder of London to nine months in jail, becoming the last person in Britain to be imprisoned for witchcraft. (The Prime Minister of the day, Winston Churchill, was reportedly furious at the waste of time and public money when the country was at war.) By 1951, following a campaign by Spiritualists and their sympathisers, the legislation had been scrapped, replaced by the Fraudulent Mediums Act

---

6 Mrs Duncan did in fact appear at Portsmouth Magistrates Court on 25 January, brought there from Holloway Prison, but proceedings were suspended while the Director of Public Prosecutions, intent on securing a custodial sentence, examined the available options. Conspiracy to defraud was eventually chosen, at least until someone pointed out that to secure a conviction, more substantial evidence was needed than a missing piece of bed linen. Finally, and in spite of widespread derision, recourse was had to the Witchcraft Act of 1735.

which since then has made it an offence *to claim falsely* to have commerce with the dead and to profit from the deception. Guilt became a lot more difficult to prove.

Mrs Duncan's defence had not been helped by the fact that her leading counsel, Charles Loseby, was himself a committed Spiritualist. He had reckoned on securing her acquittal by calling up to fifty witnesses who, though unconnected to the goings-on in Portsmouth, would testify that Mrs Duncan had in the past reunited them with deceased family members and friends. Not untypical are two such instances described to the Court by a Mr Alfred Dodd of Liverpool. They relate to two seances held four years apart, the first in Manchester in 1932.

"There came the living form of my grandfather. I knew it was him because he was a very big man. A very tall man, about six feet and one inch at least, and very corpulent. He looked round the room quizzically until his eyes met mine. He then strode across the room to where I was. He pushed the heads of two strangers that were before me on one side like that, and he put out his hand and grasped mine. He said as he grasped it 'I am very pleased to see you, Alfred, here in my native city.' I was very surprised to see him and looked at him closely and said 'Why, you look just the same.' He had on his smoking cap that he used to wear. He was dressed in a dark suit. He had on his donkey fringe that I knew so well, having been brought up with him from five years of age. His face was brown and bronzed in the same way, the same look in his eye, the same expression and tones I knew so well. He next said 'I am sorry you're having such a rough time.' (This was true.) He then touched upon a very personal matter, and concluded 'Ban is here.' Ban was the pet name of an old nurse of mine. Holding my hand all the time, he used some rather characteristic expressions like 'Keep your pepper up, old boy!' and 'Never say die while there's a shot still left in the locker.'"

Quite a different visitor turned up at a second seance, this time in Bootle.

"She stood there and she put up her hand to me and waved in

exactly the same way that she waved when I took her out to her last social . . . She stood there, dressed in a flowing white robe and over it was a fine curtain of net. I was so astonished that I stood up in my seat, which I ought not to have done, and called out to my wife, 'Why, it's Helen, it's Helen!' The girl did not come to me direct; she came right around the room from left to right, and she stood before me, a living, palpitating woman. The same that I had known so well, dark and ruddy hair, the same eyes, hazel; they shone with animation, her face the same ivory pallor on her cheeks. Then I heard her speak and she spoke with the same soft Scottish accent that I knew so well."

Helen had died in 1897. The question is, was the 'Helen' who came and chatted to him forty years later the person he took her to be, briefly endowed with substance, as well as form and speech? Or was she another Helen, the ungainly Mrs Duncan, all 17 stone of her, wrapped in a sheet? The jury would opt for the latter.[7]

The trouble was that no matter how impressive, at times moving, were the testimonies offered in court, they remained much of a muchness and a pretty depressing muchness at that. The Jury grew bored and, in the end, disgruntled. But worse was to follow. For by introducing character witnesses only too happy to reminisce about events prior to the debacle in Portsmouth, Loseby enabled the prosecution to divulge in court that Mrs Duncan had a previous conviction.

The 'Outsize' vest had come back to haunt her.

Robust sceptic that he was, what annoyed Mr James about such goings-on, genuine or not, was the assumption that they offered proof of survival. His view was that if a 'spirit' turned up in the seance room looking, for instance, like Mr Dodd's grandfather, complete with smoking cap and donkey fringe, there was no guarantee it was he. In any case, it was simplistic to believe that after death one's earthly personality stayed intact within a spirit world which, judging by the descriptions on offer, resembles Kew Gardens on a cloudless afternoon in May.

---

7 For a full transcript of the proceedings, see: C. E. Bechover Roberts (editor), *The Trial of Mrs Duncan*, Jarrold's, London. Part of *The Old Bailey Trial Series*, it is currently available online.

"The dead," he remarked gravely "have better things to do than entertain the living."

Or offer them bottles of stout, I might have added. Not that I didn't feel a wee bit disappointed on the bicycle ride home that evening. By then I'd grown quite fond of Silver Birch.

4

**"What the eyes perceive in herbs or stones or trees
is not yet a remedy; the eyes see only the dross."**

Philippus Aureolus Paracelsus

lthough Mr James was widely referred to as a magician or
dyn hysbys, few would have managed any better than my
parents, if asked to explain what that meant. 'Magician' is
the dictionary translation. Indeed *consiwrwr* ('conjuror')
was another word often used to describe him. That said, he was best
known locally for his knowledge of plants, not for practising the black
arts or raising the dead.

It meant that when Uncle Davy got shingles, he lost no time in
procuring the muddy-brown ointment – the sooner applied, the better
– Mr James provided to treat it. (The same ointment, give or take a few
ingredients, was said also to cure *dafad wyllt,* a type of skin cancer, with
the patient forbidden to touch the affected area except when applying
the salve, unil the malignancy finally dropped off — 'roots and all', as
sufferers gratefully reported.) By then he'd already rid me of worms;
caught, my mother suspected, from the family cat; while his cough
mixture, a blend of coltsfoot, elder flowers, ground-ivy and horehound,
was a trusted standby in our house throughout the winter months. Not

only did it taste good, but it also left you feeling warm and strangely comforted. Hindsight makes me think it, too, was probably laced with sloe gin.

According to my father, Mr James had inherited these skills from his grandmother, a detail he gleaned from Uncle Davy, who'd been told by none other than Mr James himself, or so my great-uncle maintained.

The trouble was that despite being a chapel deacon, Uncle Davy was not averse to telling fibs, even whoppers, when it suited him. Years earlier he'd practised a monumental deception, its intricacies beyond my grasp, that secured him first prize — a return trip to New York on the Queen Mary — in a competition sponsored by Thomas Hedley & Co, a well-known manufacturer of soap flakes. There exists a photograph of him aboard ship, dressed for dinner, complete with black tie and cummerbund, sipping what looks like a dry martini. And he a man so committed to teetotalism that he banned even tonic wine from the shelves of his emporium. Still, in claiming that Mr James got his knowledge of plants from his grandmother, he might well have been telling the truth.

The story is that soon after Mathonwy's mother died, her own mother moved into Tanrallt to care for his father and him; she being the niece, or some say daughter, of a physician named Rice Williams whose home, the census records of 1831 and 1841 reveal, was in Bridge Street, Aberystwyth. Little is known of Rice Williams, who died in 1842, but evidence suggests his paternal grandfather Rhys Williams lived in Myddfai, a village in Carmarthenshire, being the last of a medical dynasty active in the area for centuries. Two accounts exist of how the family business got started, the more credible rooted in the twelfth century when the Cistercian monastery of Strata Florida, a few miles south of Aberystwyth, was founded by a local princeling, known as Rhys Gryg or Husky Rhys (*gryg* means 'husky' in Welsh). Renowned for its apothecary garden, it soon became a popular destination for the sick, thanks largely to the medical skills of Rhiwallon Feddyg, personal physician to the prince.

Rhys Gryg died in 1232, having by then bestowed on his court physician hereditary lands in the parish of Myddfai. There, Rhiwallon and his sons continued to practise medicine, as did their descendants, harvesting their plants in nearby woods and fields. (To this day there are place names associated with them, among them a pretty hollow known as Pant y Meddygon or 'Physician's Dingle'.) A century and a half later, their remedies would be listed in *The Red Book of Hergest* (*Llyfr Goch Hergest*), a volume that also contains within its burgundy covers the four tales of the *Mabinogion*, as well as early examples of Welsh courtly verse. Today it resides at the Bodleian Library in Oxford.

Not until 1861, on the initiative of a William Rees were the remedies made known to a modern public. With help from a clergyman named John Williams, who styled himself 'ab Ithel' ('son of Ithel'), and John Pughe of Aberdovey, the former with MA and the latter FRCS after his name, the enterprising Mr Rees published a work entitled *The Physicians of Myddfai,* his own contribution being a fanciful alternative to the historical account, based, he would claim, on conversations he'd had with local people.[8] Of more interest is his assertion that the last physicians to practise in Myddfai were David Jones, who died in 1719

---

8 The second version tells of a widow and her only son, Gwyn. One morning the boy took his mother's cattle to graze beside a lake called Llyn-y-fan Fach. There he met a girl so pretty that he fell in love with her at once. For want of something better to say, he offered her some bread and cheese, but she declined the food and dived into the lake. Only then did he realise she was in fact a nymph. Back home the boy's mother recommended that on the next encounter he offer unbaked bread to his fairy sweetheart. This he did, at the same time asking her to marry him. She turned him down. The next day, Gwyn settled on a compromise, ensuring that the bread he offered was half-baked. With it came a renewed proposal of marriage, one she accepted, on the condition she would leave him, were he to strike her three times. Her name she told him, was Nelferch.

The couple made their home in Esgair Llaethdy, a farm near Llyn-y-Fan Fach, and there three sons were born to them. One morning, on their way to visit neighbours, Nelferch complained of tiredness so her husband suggested she catch a horse grazing nearby while he ran home to fetch some reins. On his return he found his wife where he'd left her, seemingly lost in thought, so gently tapped her on the shoulder. Thus was struck the first blow. The second followed when Nelferch grew tearful at a wedding. Again, it was no more than a consoling pat, but the damage was done. The third and final blow came at a funeral when she burst into hysterical laughter, and her husband, keen to restore her to her senses, slapped her on the cheek. With that she bade him farewell, kissed her three sons, now grown to manhood, and returned to the waters of the lake.

Only once did she reappear and that was to her eldest son, Rhiwallon. To him she disclosed that he and his male descendants would become physicians, handing him a bag of herbs and advice on how to use them. It was the start of the family business.

at the age of sixty-one, and his son John, who quit this life twenty years later, details which are confirmed by the parish records. He goes on to add that the last of the family line was the Dr Rice Williams mentioned above.

Of the cunning folk or *dynion hysbys* active throughout Wales, most would have claimed access to worlds other than this one and, by implication, their inhabitants, but few set out to traffic with the dead. Typical of them, as well as best recorded (their books and papers are held by the National Library of Wales) were John Harries and his son of Cwrt-y-Cadno, a village close to Myddfai where Rhiwallon and his successors had once practised medicine. So notorious were the Harrieses that in 1840 a writer in a Church of England monthly described John Harries as worse than any common thief, prompting the editor, in truth the unnamed author of the piece, to recommend he spend three months on the treadmill.[9] By then, however, John Harries, universally known as 'Dr' Harries, was dead so the object of editorial scorn was probably his son, Henry, back home after an apprenticeship in London under 'Raphael' (Robert Cross Smith), a popular astrologer of the day.

Throughout Wales and even beyond, father and son were esteemed for their medical and divinatory skills, as well as their ability to remove curses, secure good fortune, and recover lost or stolen property. How well they discerned the future, the most popular service on offer, we've no way of telling, but Mr James more than once told me how John Harries had a premonition he himself would not survive an accident on 11 May 1839. Keen to be proved wrong (and few would blame him) he prudently kept to his bed all day, only to perish that same night when the house around him caught fire.[10]

---

9 There is evidence that the editor, 'Brutus' (David Owen, 1795-1866), briefly harboured ambitions of becoming a cunning man himself. Lack of success may account for his animosity towards John Harries (see *Byd y Dyn Hysbys*, Kate Bosse Griffiths, Y Lolfa, Talybont, 1977, p.22 et seq.).

10 Not that there's any reference to this on his tombstone. There the inscription simply reads:
JOHN HARRIES
PANTCOY
Surgeon
Who died May 11 1839, aged 54 years.

It would be rash to say that Mr James had no confidence in astrology but when he spoke of it, he frequently did so in jest. A favourite anecdote — one of his vices, second only to bad language, was repetition — concerned a well known astrologer, Edward Lyndoe, who had lived in Aberystwyth in the nineteen-thirties. Author of a weekly column in *The People*, a popular Sunday newspaper, Mr. Lyndoe moved to London in 1937 and, shortly afterwards, confidently predicted that war with Germany would not happen. When it did, the disgraced prophet hurried back to Wales, keen to dodge the bombs about to fall on the capital. Happily, his reputation suffered no lasting damage, his readership apt to forget what he'd said from one week to the next, so with the advent of peace, back to London he repaired. Well into the 1960s he continued with his weekly forecasts until one morning, running short of stationery, he calmly ordered a fresh stock from his usual supplier, together with several spools of typewriter ribbon, only to quit this mortal life that same day, a calamity as unforeseen as the advent of World War II thirty years earlier.

What I do remember is that Mr James, sceptic or not, was never without his *Old Moore's Almanac*, although I've no grounds for thinking he read, still less took seriously, the predictions it contained, unlike an aunt of mine who at the end of each year delighted in ticking off those, the majority, that were wrong or remained unfulfilled. (It led us to wonder why she bothered buying the thing in the first place.) No, what Mr James looked for in its densely printed pages was the position of the moon and the planets, given that he grew his crops, largely cereals and root vegetables, in accordance with their phases or position in the sky.

For a time, I took this to be an idiosyncrasy peculiar to him, not unlike his preference for home-made fertilisers, on which I soon became expert, spending many a wet afternoon stirring, an important part of

---

Meanwhile, so far as I know, his home, Pantcoy, is still standing. Worth adding, as it illustrates the dynastic nature of the job, is that Harries' son, Henry Gwyn, born in 1822, followed in his father's footsteps after graduating from King's College, London, but died of consumption soon after his twenty-eighth birthday. A younger brother, John, seems also to have dabbled in astrology, but by all accounts was not very good at it..

the process, a home-made mixture of yarrow, dandelion, nettles and chamomile. (Fortunately, the cow dung he added to it came several stages later.)[11] Over the years, however, I grew to realise it was in fact part of his approach to the world, literally his *Weltanschauung*, as my Latin — and later German — teacher, Mrs Winkler, might have said. Without knowing it, I was being introduced to the kind of magical thinking I'd been so impatient to discover.

It is far from easy, even now and with hindsight, to describe what lay behind Mr James's approach to the natural world, partly because I was only fourteen when I discovered it, an age when children are willing, just, to accept on trust whatever grown-ups choose to tell them. In part, too, because for him the everyday reality we experience, belonged to something far bigger, being the particular manifestation within time and space of something that transcends, as well as accommodates, both. What I learned is that for Mathonwy James, the herbalist, the variety of plants around the farm was, paradoxically, a reminder of the unity implicit among them. Each was the particular manifestation of a common prototype, something Goethe called the *Urpflanze*, a kind of immaterial matrix from which they derived and to which they collectively bore witness. In Aristotelian terms they were the multifarious 'accidents' that express a common 'substance'.

Had he been familiar with modern cosmology, Mr James might have pointed out that the origin of plants, like everything else, from the stars in the sky to the skin at the end of our noses, was that single bundle of energy responsible for the Big Bang.[12] What he, the *dyn hys-*

---

11 Years later, I discovered that these same plants were among those favoured in biodynamic agriculture, a system based on guidelines offered by Rudolf Steiner. In this case, however, the plants are stuffed into specific animal parts e.g. red deer's bladder (yarrow), cow gut (chamomile) or skull (oak bark and nettles), and buried in the ground over winter. Disinterred, they are then added to a compost which again involves a lot of diligent stirring.

12 Not that he was necessarily unaware of the Big Bang theory, first proposed by Sir Fred Hoyle in 1949, although he had died before it became generally accepted, having by then ousted its rival, the so-called Steady State theory. Within esoteric cosmology both theories are compatible, notably in H. P. Blavatsky's notion of an expanding and contracting universe, described in her *Secret Doctrine* as the Law of Periodicity and compared to the sequential exhalation/inhalation of Brahma. (The Sanskrit root '*brh*' actually means 'to expand or to grow'.) I remember seeing Blavatsky's *Secret Doctrine*, all

bys, sought to discover and, where feasible, exploit, was the essential — 'ontic' might be a better word — oneness of these sundry parts, while as a herbalist he strove to identify the correspondence between specific plants and the medical condition they might cure. No doubt his predecessors, among them the Harrieses, father and son, of Pantcoy, did the same.

Recognising such correspondences depends on intuition as much as observation, something George Fox, founder of the Religious Society of Friends (the Quakers), acknowledged in his *Journal*. In it he describes how at the age of 24 he was privileged to see the natural world 'open up', as he put it, enabling him to perceive how certain plants bore what he called the signatures given to them 'according to their nature and virtue', an experience that briefly tempted him to study medicine. A hundred years earlier the same had been acknowledged by Paracelsus, at pains to point out that a good physician should not only focus on the composition of plants but also 'discern their powers and virtues in the signatures they carry about them', a notion his near contemporary Giambattista della Porta, would develop in his *Phytognomonica* (1588). Even the places where plants flourish could, it was suggested, alert the shrewd observer to their therapeutic worth, a good example being the willow, its bark formerly used to treat rheumatism, a condition aggravated, if not caused, by damp conditions, like those the tree seems to favour. The willow's affinity with water, its preferred habitat being river banks and marshy ground, was thus the correspondence that betrayed the tree's medicinal virtue. Only when chemists got around to investigating what made willow bark effective, did they discover it contained a glucoside which, under the name of salicin (from Latin *salix* = willow) was an important resource in the treatment of rheumatic conditions. Later a derivative of salicin, salicylic acid, became the chief constituent of aspirin.[13]

---

five volumes (plus a sixth comprising the index) on a shelf in Tanrallt, but paid no attention to it at the time.

13 Salicin (C13H1801) is found in other plants besides the willow, as is salicylic acid

Then there's the wild pansy (*Viola tricolor*), a native of heaths, moors and sunny banks. Its flowers are an attractive purple, speckled with white or yellow patches while, more importantly, its lower leaves are heart-shaped, like those of other members of the violet family (*violaceae*). This betrays their sympathy with that organ. As a result, the plant, popularly known as heartsease, was cherished as a cardiac tonic, particularly effective in the treatment of valvular disorders but above all endowed with anticoagulant virtues that have recently been demonstrated *in vitro*.[14]

Nor would Mr James have me overlook the lesser celandine, chief ingredient of an ointment he sold to people afflicted with haemorrhoids — Uncle Davy was a regular customer — the signature in this case being tiny nodules on the plant's roots. Indeed, the flower's other name is pilewort.

A final example, perhaps the most interesting, is mistletoe. Here it was the Austrian philosopher and 'spiritual scientist', Rudolf Steiner (1861–1925), founder of the movement known as Anthroposophy and, before that, official editor of Goethe's scientific writings, who advocated the use of mistletoe in the treatment of cancer, although its role in medicine goes back more than two thousand years. Revered by the Druids, as Pliny records in his *Natural History*, it was prized also by the Romans who, despite the plant's traditional association with Venus, scattered it on altars dedicated to Jupiter, mindful that the oak, a host tree favoured by the plant, was sacred to that deity. For the Druids, mistletoe was esteemed as a cure for infertility, the correspondence in this case being the plant's ability to flourish throughout the winter months while the tree to which it has attached itself gives every appearance of being dead.

(H0C8H4C000H), the latter notably in plants of the spiraea group. It is present also in birch bark and, abundantly, in wintergreen (*Gaultheria procumbens*), likewise a plant used in the treatment of rheumatism.

14 See Zhou, H. Y., Hong, J. L. et al. 2009, 'A New Dicoumarin and anticoagulant activity from Viola yedoensis Makino', *Fitoterapia* 80 Elsevier, 2009, pp. 283-5, and Yun Hee Jeong et al., 'Anti-inflammatory effects of Viola Yedoensis and the application of cell extraction methods for investigating bioactive constituents in macrophages', *BMC Complementary and Alternative Medicine*, 2016.

For Steiner, however, it was the plant's semi-parasitic nature that betrayed its primary role, this being to tackle cancer, itself an accumulation of rogue cells which, though attached to and dependent on a host organ, remain indifferent to its welfare. Such perverse behaviour is reflected in the way mistletoe grows perpendicularly to the branch it clings to, its leaves forming no discernible pattern and its berries impervious to cold. All this alerted Steiner to the 'correspondence' between mistletoe and cancer. Here again, scientific tests would confirm that the plant had cytotoxic properties likely to arrest the growth of cancerous cells, as well as immunomodulatory compounds that inhibit their wider diffusion to other parts of the body. Marketed under the name *Iscador*, an extract of mistletoe is widely used today in German hospitals not only to combat cancer but also to alleviate the side-effects of chemotherapy, the preparations sometimes differentiated according to the host tree (oak, apple, elm, pine etc.) the plant happens to have favoured. Much of the current research into mistletoe is conducted by the Verein für Krebsforschung at Arlesheim in Switzerland.

At no time did Mr James make a huge fuss about all this. Dismissive of anything redolent of what he called mumbo-jumbo, he might, if pressed, have even denied that how plants looked or the environment they favoured had a bearing on their curative potential. His real aim when talking about such things was to alter my perspective so that empirical reality, the evidence offered by our senses, might be viewed from within as well as without. At the same time, he did not shun orthodox medicine, still less deny its effectiveness, being like my parents a patient of the esteemed Dr Ellis. Indeed, according to my father, the two were good friends, although when the doctor retired, relations with his successor grew less cordial after Mr James refused to disclose what went into the mysterious brown salve he sold to people with shingles. Few would blame him: at five shillings a pot it kept him in Ringer's shag tobacco for the best part of a month.

His was a thriving little business. On many a wet afternoon, with a sheep dog beside me, I'd watch him prepare and mix his herbs: for Mrs

Price, whose legs swelled in hot weather, a pinch of larkspur, two each of nettle, broom and tansy, the lot to be infused in water and taken three times daily; for Moses Jones' tight chest, a mixture of coltsfoot, liquorice and honey; and by way of pick-me up for Lizzie Hughes some yarrow, chervil and a little rue, to be taken in a glass of milk each morning, with a raw egg added to the mix once a week. Throughout it all he'd tell me what he was dispensing, how much of it and why.

"You'll write a book on it before you get to my age," he predicted.

Twenty years later I did, mentioning in it Mrs Price, the asthmatic Moses Jones and the languid Lizzie Hughes.[15] The Harrieses of Pantcoy might have foreseen it. Mr Lyndoe probably not.

---

15 *The Magic of Herbs*, Jonathan Cape, London, 1972 (new ed. The Witches' Almanac, Rhode Island, 2019) Still alive when the book first appeared, Miss Hughes asked my mother to tell me it was a duck's egg Mr James had recommended: more nutritious than a hen's egg, according to him.

5

**"There is plenty to be learned even from a bad teacher:
what not to do, how not to be."**

J. K. Rowling

Some time after moving into Tanrallt to keep house for his father and him, Mathonwy's maternal grandmother decided the boy deserved a better education than that offered by the village school in Ponterwyd.[16] She accordingly arranged for him to attend Aberystwyth's well-regarded Board School instead, with week-day bed and four meals daily, two of them hot, provided by a cousin of hers who ran a temperance hotel near the railway station. The twelve-year-old had been there for no more than a month before a visiting inspector decreed he was bright enough for the local grammar school, an establishment which I, too, would attend sixty years later, indeed within a month of my first visit to Tanrallt.

That coincidence pleased Mr James. So much so that he never tired of questioning me about what went on at school and what I'd learned

---

16 Here she may have undervalued the quality of the teaching on offer. Fifty years earlier a pupil at the school, John Rees, went on to study Classics at Jesus College, Oxford, becoming an esteemed philologist. Knighted in 1910, he was appointed to the Privy Council a year later. Today the school in Ponterwyd is named after him, though the cottage he grew up in, Aberceirw, lies, sadly, in ruins.

the previous week, his motive in part to indulge his nostalgia but in part also, I suspect, to satisfy himself that academic standards, like so much else in the world, had declined since his own younger days.

He may well have been right. Certainly the school motto, *Nerth Dysg ei Ymdrech* ('Learning is powered by Effort'), could not have been more apt, given the effort needed to learn anything at all when the teaching was so poor. Even at eleven, I knew that when Miss Forster — "It's Forster, not Foster," — took us for Geography, there was more to Holland than windmills, tulips and cheerful blond people in clogs. Yet even that was preferable to Religious Instruction, a solid hour, twice a week, spent listening (or feigning to listen) while Mr Jenkins read aloud — I can still hear his weary monotone — from Bullinger's *Companion Bible*, first the sacred text then the commentary alongside. To forestall questions, he managed always to finish seconds before the bell so when he murmured "Any questions?" he was already halfway through the door. Only once do I remember a question being asked and that by a boy named Donald Evans, more precocious than the rest of us. "Sir," demanded Donald, "What exactly is a harlot?" (We'd been doing *Matthew* 21) "A bad woman," snapped Mr Jenkins, making sure he and Dr Bullinger were well away before Donald could respond.

More shocking to Mr James was that reading aloud from teaching aids was common practice among staff, especially favoured by Miss Mainwaring who took us for English Literature and, like Miss Forster, demanded to be addressed correctly: "It's Mannering, not Main-wearing". But whereas Mr Jenkins and others cheated brazenly, Miss Mainwaring concealed her crib behind a strategically placed hand-bag, lizard skin with several bald patches. One day, someone identified the book she was using so the entire class ordered copies from WHSmith, relying on it for exams instead of reading, possibly enjoying, the texts prescribed by the Welsh Joint Education Committee. That Miss Mainwaring, pronounced Mannering, never noticed our answers were, if not identical, then remarkably similar, shows how little attention she paid them.

No better was Georgie 'One Ball' Rowlands, so named after an injury sustained on the battlefield at Ypres, who also taught English. For months I'd wondered why my essays, regardless of their quality, earned a consistent seven out of ten, never more and never less. Something was clearly not right, and the fault not my own. In the middle of term, a new girl joined us, fresh from Cheltenham Ladies College, an institution where teaching standards were presumably higher, and it was she who rumbled what Georgie 'One Ball' was up to. His marks, she explained, were determined by how many pages we wrote, not by what we wrote on them. Ten pages — and no one managed more — got you a seven and fewer pages proportionately less. To prove her point she copied out the same page over two dozen times and some days later was handed back her essay with an unprecedented eight out of ten scrawled alongside. Having shown us the evidence, she carried it home to her father, manager of the local branch of Boots the Chemist, who in turn showed it to the headmaster.

It accomplished little. When next he turned up in class Georgie 'One Ball' gave us a lecture on integrity, lamenting its absence in one of our number, his or her identity withheld, who had sought to impugn his good name. And that was it. We continued writing our essays, now with duplicate pages tacked on, and the average mark went up from seven to eight. Everyone was happy except the manager of Boots who, so far as I recall, sent his daughter back to Cheltenham (motto: 'May she grow in Heavenly Light'). Of all my stories this was the one Mr James enjoyed most.

My favourite of our teachers by far was Gwyneth Winkler. Born and brought up not far from Tanrallt, she'd married a German national in the 1930s, and lived in that country throughout the war, returning home in 1945 with their two children. (Having elderly parents to support, her husband stayed behind in what would become the German Democratic Republic, rejoining his family in Wales only after both had died and he himself turned sixty.) White haired, with penetrating gaze and aquiline features, Mrs Winkler had a complexion so pink and glowing it seemed freshly buffed. With it went a fearsome temper. The most trivial misdemeanour risked provoking her wrath, and when that happened, she would hurl any missile within reach at the culprit, and dispense five-hundred lines on the spot, far in excess of the norm. Sometimes, gown flapping in her wake, she strode into the body of the classroom dispensing blows to left and right, regardless of the victim's sex or culpability. I have witnessed the toughest boys, heroes of the rugby field, cower at her approach, heads cradled in their brawny arms. I escaped her fury, as did a girl named Phyllis Manning, both of us, Mrs Winkler maintained, blessed with good speaking voices, my own reminding her of Lloyd George, a hero of hers and someone of whom she spoke often. Better still, when reading Latin verse — the Odes of Horace were a set text — we sounded like genuine Romans, or at least what Mrs Winkler thought genuine Romans sounded like, vowels open and every c and g percussively hard, as in Welsh or, come to think of it, German.

During lessons it was Mrs Winkler's habit to check that I'd grasped whatever grammatical point she was trying to explain, then, satisfied I had, move on to something else. It might have made sense, were I a backward pupil instead of one that normally managed to keep up. As it was, she and I advanced through the Latin primer with relative ease while much of the class lagged sullenly behind. Only once, when tackling the comparison of adjectives, did I let her down by giving the wrong answer. "Oh well," she sighed, "if you don't understand it, no one else does. We'll have to go through it all again."

"Dr Davies Latin would never do that," said Mr James when I told him, the "Latin", perhaps the 'Dr' also, intended to distinguish this particular Davies, after Jones the commonest surname in Wales, from other Davieses on the teaching staff. "He always made sure we'd got the point, even the dunces. I still remember my principal parts: *mitto, mittere, misi, missum*. And here's one you won't know: *pello, pellere, pepuli, pulsum*. And that's from sixty years ago."

At some point Mathonwy's father must have decided the boy's place was on the farm not in the classroom; one of the reasons, I discovered recently, being that the fifteen-year-old had got in with a gang of boys from Bedlam, the name popularly given to a huddle of bleak cottages overlooking Aberystwyth harbour, home not only to fishermen, caulkers and tanners but to the town's ne'er-do-wells also. It would account for the effing and blinding.

So far as concerns my 'magical' education, I'm hard put to say precisely when that started. For years I thought it happened one drizzly afternoon when I summoned the courage to ask Mr James if he'd teach me whatever magic it was that he practised. We were outside repairing fences at the time, and I'd just caught my finger on a piece of barbed wire. It bled, I remember, but I was told not to make a fuss. A bit unfairly, as I'd not intended making one. But Mr James could be like that. As if his mandate were to toughen me up, as well as bring a touch of colour to my pallid cheeks.

Today, I'm inclined to think my apprenticeship was already underway by then. Part of it may have been the mind games Mr James encouraged me to play, usually during our lunch break, although they seemed at the time to be just games, nothing more. I suspect now their true purpose was to help me 'think' in a novel, more imaginative way.

It began simply enough. I would be invited, for example, to gaze at something, then close my eyes and create a mental image of it in as much detail as I could muster. Having done that, I would open my eyes and check how successful I'd been. A matchbox is what Mr James chose for my first attempt, with him listening as I described what it looked like to my mind's eye. We then progressed to the packet of tobacco lying beside it. Next time it was back to the matchbox, with me now required to visualise it from whatever angle Mr James suggested, again describing what I 'saw' while mentally viewing it from, say, above or below or from any one of its four sides, even from all sides at once and, finally, from inside the matchbox itself.

The purpose of the exercise was to revive in me that pictorial way of thinking which comes naturally to young children, their mind effortlessly forming what psychologists call eidetic images. Nor did the technique apply to visual images alone. Within weeks I was encouraged to involve all five of my senses so that, for example, if told to imagine myself eating crisps, I had not only to 'see' them but also 'smell' and 'taste' them, even 'feel' them on my tongue and 'hear' my teeth crunching them. A more dignified exercise was to imagine myself walking along Aberystwyth beach on a breezy day at high tide, then inwardly 'see' and 'hear' the pounding of the waves, 'feel' the wind on my face, 'smell' the salt spray and 'taste' the brine upon my lips, the aim again being to 'objectify' a subjective experience, transferring what was inside my head to the world I was part of, thereby lending form and substance to what, of itself, possessed neither. It was, if you like, a voluntary hallucination, its purpose, as yet untested, to translate into the vernacular of empirical experience whatever extrasensory impressions — and this is the magical bit — I might eventually receive.

What all this supposes, of course, is that there exists a non-material reality, one which, by definition, is inaccessible to our senses, waiting for us to perceive it. Now, few people were less fanciful, let alone other-worldly, than Mr James — his language bore witness to that — yet he never doubted that reality extended beyond the particular manifestation registered by empirical experience. And more to us as well, given that we're part and parcel of the same caboodle.

The 1950s were coming to an end when Mr James was telling me all this. By then, scientists were starting to realise that subatomic structures, the building blocks of us and of everything around us, could no longer be viewed as 'objects' or, to put it another way, as discrete entities (what classical physicists labelled *res extensa*). Instead they were comprehensible only in terms of mathematical structures, implicit acknowledgement that ideas, not things, constitute the reality behind sensory phenomena. (One physicist Thomas Görnitz, has declared that matter, like energy, is essentially information and therefore 'spirit' — German

Geist — or, to use the more neutral word he coined, 'protyposis'.)[17]

But of course, mathematical structures are themselves abstractions of the human mind and, as such, have no reality per se. It follows therefore — if I were reading this, I'd be tempted to give up at this point — that there is never a quantum without a quale.[18] Yet although things are there because we observe them, they are no less real on that account, given that there is not only an implied reality hidden within the phenomena perceived, but also the reality that is the phenomena themselves. And Mr James, as befits an occultist — someone who by definition explores, even exploits, what is hidden — lost sight of neither.

For him, as for contemporary physicists, the components of matter straddle a frontier between the spatial-temporal world we inhabit and another, no less real, wherein time and space no longer exist. Such a reality, a pleroma, so to speak, lies not only beyond our understanding but beyond our imagining as well, nourished, as our imagination is, by the three-dimensional environment we occupy and nothing else. Only by analogy can we hope to make sense of what lies beyond, given that, though superficially different, both realities are intimately related, the two being part of a single whole. This, essentially, is what magic is about.

The next chapter is more fun.

---

17 The word *Geist* is more comprehensive than the English word 'spirit'. For much of this paragraph I am indebted less to Mr James than to Peter Heusser, author of *Anthroposophische Medizin u. Wissenschaft*, Schattauer GmbH, Stuttgart, 2011.

18 A 'quale' is the quality or property perceived or experienced by an individual and, as such, is essentially subjective but no less real because of it.

6

"Not a stone but has its history"

Marcus Annaeus Lucanus

Someone who'd been to Tanrallt before me and, by her own account, succumbed to its enchantment was Mrs Caradoc Evans, alias Countess Barcynska. On hearing where I spent my Saturdays, she disclosed that she'd visited Mr James twenty years before, having fallen prey to writer's block, unprecedented in an author as prolific as she, while her husband had a stubborn cough that neither Vick nor Gee's Linctus seemed able to shift. And so, one afternoon, the two of them set off to seek expert help.

According to her, the first thing she noticed on entering the house, presumably after her eyes became accustomed to the gloom, was a large chunk of rock, blue, multifaceted and having the vitreous appearance of quartz, lying on the hearth. Questioned about its provenance, their host reportedly told her it had come from Palestine or Egypt — Mrs Evans seemed never sure which — and been given to one of his ancestors for safe-keeping. Touching it, as the visitors were encouraged to do, was said to bring a variety of blessings, one presumably being that by the time they took their leave of Mr James, both were in far better spirits than when they arrived. Meanwhile on the back seat of their little Morris 8 rested the blue stone, vouchsafed to Mrs Evans by its hereditary custodian who, she boasted, had discerned what she called her karmic affinity to the relic. A new novel, *Angel's Kiss*, followed soon after.

Around my sixteenth birthday a change had come over Mrs Evans. Disposed to shun things she deemed mundane or frivolous, she'd enjoyed nothing better than talking about Life and Death — one could almost hear the capital letters in her voice — or, rather, about Life after Death. Few were the times she didn't call on us without bringing tidings from the Afterlife, mostly imparted by her late husband. (His predecessor, Count Barcynska stayed *stum*, but then the couple were already living apart when he died.) It was a surprise therefore when one day she turned up on the arm of an elderly gentleman, very much of this world, whom she introduced as Captain Hewitt, her seriousness replaced by girlish smiles and peals of tinkling laughter. The change, though disconcerting, was not unwelcome, my father putting it down to the advent of the captain. Aware that only majors and above keep their title in civilian life, he took the opportunity on next seeing Mrs Evans on her own, to enquire if Captain Hewitt had served in the Navy.

"No, he grew tea in Kenya," she replied, missing the point completely.

Within no time at all Mrs Evans went off to live with her beau at his home in Aberdyfi, ten miles up the coast, her metaphysical leanings replaced by a preoccupation with tea and the challenges of running a viable plantation. Instead of ectoplasm and astral bodies, her conversation was filled now with practical things like pruning, plucking and tipping, delivered with the authority of someone who'd spent years pruning, plucking and tipping under a hot tropical sun. No less impressive was her knowledge of soil temperatures, humidity levels and optimum rainfall. Once, she even showed us how to encourage more 'laterals' to grow, without explaining what these were, by, she maintained, tweaking the primary shoots growing above them. Most of all, however, she never tired of telling how Captain Hewitt had endeared himself to his native workforce in colonial Africa, respected and liked in equal measure. A Moses-like figure, was how she put it.

Especially cordial, it seems, were relations between him and his foreman, Songora, so cordial that one day the captain was invited to accompany him to his home on the slopes of Mount Elgon, an extinct volcano close to the border with neighbouring Uganda. There, the bwana was feted by tribesmen who, Mrs Evans liked to point out, were tall, slender and exceptionally fine-featured. C. G. Jung had similarly commented on their appearance after visiting the region in 1925.

"We may conclude," she assured us "that their forefathers came from an ancient civilization to the west of Africa, now drowned beneath the waves."

And to be sure we got the point, she added "This was of course Atlantis,"

At which point Captain Hewitt intervened, "East, my dear. The natives say their ancestors came from where the sun rises over Lake Baringo. That's east, not west." He was not the sort of man to muddle up his compass points.

"Better still," chirruped Mrs Evans, "They came from the island of Lemuria. It sank in the Pacific — that's east — long before Atlantis. You can read about it in Madame Blavatsky." Hers was a name we'd not heard for ages.

And with that she was off, my mother watching enviously as the Captain held open the car door for her to climb in. (My father was seldom that courteous.) Several months would elapse before we saw them again.

One of my reasons for leaving Tanrallt no later than five o'clock each Saturday, earlier still when the days grew short, was to reach home safely before it got dark. Another was to be in time to accompany my mother, sometimes my father as well, to the Little Theatre in Bath Street, home to whatever repertory company was in residence that season.

Built — on the cheap, it was said — by the town council just after the war, the Little Theatre lived up to its name, accommodating no more than three hundred people and having a slightly down-at-heel look which no amount of gilt or Wedgewood-blue distemper quite managed to dispel. Still, as my mother and others remarked, it was an improvement on its predecessor, well before my time, which by all accounts was barely more than a glorified shed behind the Queen's Hotel. It was there, from 1934 to 1936, that the Caradoc Evanses, no less, had put on plays, several by Countess Barcynska herself, while a son from her first marriage served as juvenile lead. Calling himself Nicholas Sandys ('Nickie' to family and friends), he shared with his mother a passion for silk scarves and was seldom seen around town without one or without a wide-brimmed fedora, charcoal-grey and neatly pinched. I'm told that in September 1939, with a defiant flick of scarf, he'd boarded the London-bound train, having assured a reporter from the *Cambrian News* that he'd never set foot in dreary Aberystwyth again.

In my younger days, the repertory company was run by a man, probably no older than thirty, named Jack Bradley and his partner, Maurice Neville, white-haired and said (but not widely believed) to be his father. Their weekly productions were consistently good. Only Mrs Evans thought otherwise. Forced by dwindling audiences to disband her own troupe of players, she resented Mr Bradley's success, a resentment compounded by his refusal to stage a play she'd written called *Hell Freezes*. It involved a group of dead people trapped in a kind of limbo where they bickered pointlessly for two long hours. Mr Neville told her Jean-Paul Sartre had done the same thing and done it better.

Not long afterwards Mr Bradley got into his first spot of bother. That summer was exceptionally fine and he'd taken to sunbathing naked on a river bank just outside town, his modesty, such as it was, protected by the reeds and rushes that grew there in abundance. One afternoon, however, he chose to stretch out on a patch of grass which, unknown to him or so he claimed, lay within yards of the railway line. As a result, the driver and fireman of the three-thirty train from Shrewsbury were treated to the sight of his manhood, as were a dozen affronted passengers in the carriages behind. The town was understandably shocked, the more so when the culprit showed no sign of remorse. On the contrary, he made light of the episode, even referring to it in the play being performed that same night.

"Did those snaps we took by the river come out?" enquired the leading lady apropos of nothing.

"Afraid not," replied Mr Bradley, "Over-exposed."

I remember my mother was among the few that laughed.

What got him into more serious trouble was an incident in the gentlemen's lavatories on the corner of Bath Street. Days earlier a mysterious hole had appeared, roughly waist-high, in a partition separating two cubicles and inside one of these Mr Bradley installed himself one Saturday during the hour between the matinée and evening performances. What he didn't realise, having been encouraged to think otherwise, was that next door two police constables were lying in wait. This was to be his undoing. For as the court heard in due course, one of the officers seized Mr Bradley's vital member as it emerged through the hole and held onto it while his colleague clambered over the dividing wall to apprehend its owner. This time there was no joking on his part. And the town or at least that section of it able to work out what had happened, took enormous pleasure in the scandal that ensued.

But not for long. For in court the defendant's barrister, Roderick Bowen Q.C., sometime Member of Parliament for Cardiganshire, confirmed bachelor and tireless advocate of flogging, was able to argue and, presumably, demonstrate to the satisfaction of the bench that the actor-manager's appendage, when aroused, was too large to pass through the hole, as the prosecution had claimed. The case was dismissed, and the accused became a legend overnight. That said, the damage to his reputation was irreparable, as well as bad for business, so shortly afterwards he, the enigmatic Mr Neville and the rest of the company moved to Royal Tunbridge Wells, a town five or six times bigger than our own. But, then, *pace* Mr Bradley, size isn't everything.

No one thought to patch up the hole.

In the meantime, a new company, run by a respectably married couple, Earl and Catherine Armstrong, had taken over the lease of the theatre and, somehow or other, they and my parents became friends. In little time their contribution to my social and cultural education would be second only to that of Mrs Evans so it was the more regrettable when she and the Armstrongs fell out. From then on care was needed never to mention the name of one protagonist to or even within earshot of the other, Mrs Evans being the more combustible by far.

Whatever play they staged, the Armstrong family (the couple had two daughters) saw to it that they kept the best parts for themselves, often to the resentment of others in the company. In the case of Mr and Mrs Armstrong, well past the first flush of youth, the result could be embarrassing, for they'd long outgrown the roles they'd formerly played in their prime. Vanity may in part have been to blame, but chiefly it was the reassurance that lines once learned were easier to memorise the umpteenth time around. One week Mr Armstrong, by then turned sixty, played the teenage villain in Emlyn Williams' *Night Must Fall*, fooling no one despite layers of Leichner No. 9 and mahogany-coloured hair. The hair was the same implausible colour both on and off stage and so, come to think of it, was his complexion.

The *casus belli* between them and Mrs Evans was nothing other than the chunk of rock she had received from Mr James.

As its official custodian, she suddenly felt compelled, so she claimed, to make it available to the world at large, or at least to that section of the world that was Aberystwyth. What no one thought to ask was why she'd allowed an object so precious — she now referred to it as the Miracle Stone of Wales — languish unremarked in her front porch for close to twenty years (next to the umbrella stand, according to my mother). To this day my belief is that news of my weekly expeditions to Tanrallt put the idea in her head, although she, true to form, invented a more romantic explanation.

According to her, the initiative stemmed from her first encounter with Captain Hewitt at a drinks party both had attended. Unknown to her at the time was an incident that happened in Kenya during the weekend the bwana had spent with his native foreman, Sonora, at the foot of Mount Elgon. While there, it now emerged, Hewitt was taken by his host to a cave deep inside the mountain, where the two eventually came upon a vast underground chamber, home to the Mhenge Mzouri, a blue, multifaceted rock held sacred by the local population. As it glittered in the flickering light of their torches, Sonora dropped to his knees and reverently touched the rock, signalling that his companion do likewise. It was then that Captain Hewitt noticed that a substantial chunk of it was missing.

On hearing the tale, Mrs Evans hastily invited her new friend to examine the stone Mr James had entrusted to her twenty years earlier, whereupon the Captain, sounding, it must be said, more like Countess Barcynska than himself, reportedly told her, "I looked closely at that stone and it seemed to be the like of the Blue Stone which is yours!" (Dialogue had never been her *forte*.)

Several months would pass before Mrs Evans, by then living with Captain Hewitt in Aberdyfi, resolved to exploit the miraculous properties of her Blue Stone, declaring for the first time that by touching it, the sick were healed, the dejected cheered up and those down on their luck assured of better fortune. And so one day, she sought out Mr Armstrong and bullied him into letting her exhibit the relic in a small room off the foyer of the Little Theatre. She proposed an admission fee of two shillings, but as this was the price of a seat in the auditorium, he felt it risked devaluing his weekly productions, so they finally agreed on one shilling, the proceeds to be divided equally between them.

Next came the matter of publicity. Still well regarded, though her laurels were by then far from fresh, Mrs Evans persuaded two local papers the *Cambrian News* and *Welsh Gazette*, to print a text submitted by her. At the same time an artist's easel bearing a hand-painted board showing the outline of Africa, with a blue blob in the middle, was placed on the steps of the theatre. The real treat, however, came the following Saturday when, at the end of that night's performance, the curtain no sooner came down than Mr Armstrong stepped out in front of it and invited us all to remain in our seats. 'Tabs' he called to someone in the wings and up once again went the curtain.

On stage, reclining in two bamboo armchairs, last seen in a production of Somerset Maugham's *Rain,* were Mrs Evans, introduced as Countess Barcynska, and the captain, she clad in lime-green organza and he, visibly ill at ease, in a white dinner jacket, with a jaunty red carnation in his buttonhole, while two potted palms conveyed a hint of Africa.

Prompted by Mr Armstrong, Captain Hewitt began a long-winded description of a planter's life in Kenya, until Mrs Evans cut him short and spoke about her trip to Pumlumon, the mysterious cave and, finally, the virtues of her blue stone.

At this point the object itself, covered by a paisley shawl, was wheeled out from the wings on a tea trolley, prompting an anguished cry from its owner as Mr Armstrong made as if to remove the shawl, thereby exposing to view something punters were meant to pay a shilling to see.

"The man's a fool," complained Mrs Evans at our house later, "and, as I've said before, no great shakes as an actor".

By then she and the captain had declined an invitation to stay overnight, to the relief of my mother who, not being privy to sleeping arrangements in Aberdyfi, was unsure whether to put them together or in separate rooms.

The stone remained on display for two weeks. On the final Saturday, shortly before that evening's performance, Mrs Evans arrived at the theatre to reclaim it and pocket her share of the takings. Asked about these, the girl selling tickets listlessly told her they amounted to eleven shillings. "Are you telling me" Mrs Evans shouted into the hatch "that only eleven persons came to see it? Eleven out of a population of ten thousand, double that number if you count the holidaymakers!?"

Urgently summoned from his dressing room, Mr Armstrong rushed to the front of the house where, according to those within earshot, the ensuing exchanges were terrible to hear, ending only after the impresario, his honesty impugned and Leichner running down his cheeks, handed over the full eleven shillings. He thereupon bundled Mrs Evans down the front steps to where the captain was trying to manoeuvre the stone into the boot of his car. Later Mr Armstrong admitted to my parents that he'd not had the heart to charge most of the sick and down-at-heel who'd bothered to turn up. But worse was to follow.

Intrigued by the miraculous stone and keen to learn more, I lost no time in telling the story to Mr James, only to elicit from him a stream of expletives, several new even to me, unlike anything I'd heard before. Somewhere among them was an assurance that he'd never set eyes on the object in his life, let alone given it house room. By the following week he'd instructed Mr Jessop, solicitor and some-time President of the Law Society, his office just across the road from Uncle Davy's shop, to write to Mrs Evans demanding a formal, indeed public, retraction, although by then my mother had already had a quiet word with her. As a result she amended her account, pleading that she'd got her conjurors mixed up: whereas Mr James had indeed given her some herbal nostrums, it was a rival of his in Llangurig, eight miles away, a man she referred to simply as 'Old Griff', who'd given her the blue stone, the donor sadly (but conveniently) by then dead and buried.

Not that she was discouraged. Within months the stone reposed in a grotto built for it by Captain Hewitt in his garden at Aberdyfi, while Mrs Evans set about writing a book called, unsurprisingly, *The Miracle Stone of Wales*. In this book, as well as talks up and down the county — Women's Institutes were always keen to have her — she described again how it comforted the bereaved, gave sight to the blind, cured deformities and restored the sick to perfect health. She even suggested the Captain's grotto was the Welsh answer to Lourdes. Meanwhile outside the house an ever-growing number of crudely painted notices urged passers-by to stop and pay a visit, their proliferation a sign that pilgrims were few and far between.

From then on, we began to see less of her, and in time she moved to a village in Shropshire, where she died in 1964. Buried beside Caradoc in New Cross, she reportedly bequeathed her blue stone to the Welsh

Folk Museum in Cardiff, although they were not at all sure where to put it.[19]

Mr James could have told them.

19 Now St. Fagan's National Museum. I should add that John Harris, biographer of Caradoc Evans (*Caradoc Evans: the devil in Eden*, Seren, 2018) tells me that according to one account, Nicholas Sandys, took the relic with him when he sailed to America in 1958, hoping to secure fame and fortune in Hollywood. Denied both, he returned to England nine months later, leaving the stone behind in San Francisco. Mr. Harris has further pointed out that the "Old Griff" Mrs Evans sought to pass off as the stone's previous owner, may have been Evan Griffiths (1854-1934) of Pantybenni, a farm some eight miles from Tanrallt. A *dyn hysbys*, like Mr. James, his family would cooperate by claiming to remember the stone (or one similar to it) formerly being used as a door-stop. Mrs. Evans' book, *The Miracle Stone of Wales* was published by Rider in 1957.

7

"Friends and acquaintances are the surest passport to Fortune."
Arthur Schopenhauer

That Christmas, Mr James gave me my first book on magic. It wasn't a new book, the scruffy cover attested to that, but at least it came wrapped in brown paper, secured with binder twine, while a blob of red sealing wax added a vaguely festive touch. It was the first book on magic — real magic, not the smoke-and-mirrors kind — I'd ever set eyes on, let alone owned. The public library drew the line at Silver Birch.

What I'd discover only later is that Dion Fortune, the book's author (whom I first took to be a man), had already impinged on my life, one of those coincidences that mean a lot to those they affect but, as statisticians never tire of pointing out, are less remarkable than they seem. For Dion Fortune, real name Violet Mary Firth, had been born, like my mother, in Llandudno, where her father ran the town's most prestigious hotel, the Craigside Hydro, although the family's roots were embedded in Yorkshire. My own grandparents and the Firths were on friendly terms despite living at opposite ends of the promenade, the former on a promontory called the Great Orme and the Firths on its smaller rival, the Little Orme, at the other end of the bay.

Based in Sheffield, the Firths were among the most important steel producers in the land, it being said that by the middle of the nineteenth century, every piece of artillery used by the British Army was manufactured by them. Recently I noticed that several of the knives in my kitchen drawer at home still have the words 'Firth's Stainless' engraved on the blade.

If the Llandudno Firths could boast (and by all accounts they frequently did) of being connected to the Sheffield branch, my grandmother could match them by declaring her kinship with the Wilsons of Hull. Such things meant a lot in those days. Her mother had been the sister, possibly niece, of Thomas Wilson who'd made his fortune in shipping. Owner of his first vessel at the age of twenty-seven, he went on to acquire an entire fleet, profiting from the boom in trade between Britain and the rest of the world that followed the Industrial Revolution. By the end of the century, the Wilson Line comprised no fewer than one hundred steamers, making it the largest private shipping company of its day, although by then the business had passed to two of his sons — he had fifteen children in all — who built on their father's success. My great-grandmother called her son Arthur after one of them.[20]

---

20 My great-uncle, he studied navigation after leaving school and would later serve as captain on various merchant ships, the last of them, the Cape of Good Hope. According to a North Wales newspaper, the vessel, bearing a cargo of nitrite, was approaching an unnamed French port in the summer of 1916 when fire broke out. To help the crew extinguish it, the captain jumped down into the hold but sustained grievous injuries as a result. Conveyed home to Pwllheli, he died shortly after and was buried with some pomp — the mayor and other civic dignitaries were present — in St Deinio's graveyard. (His tomb, white marble and topped with a life-sized anchor, is unmissable just beyond the entrance.) The report ends with a verse in Welsh:

By tymor'n hwylio'r heli — yn awr
Mewn bedd ca'dd angori —
Yn iach a llon uwch y lli
Glannodd yn nhir goleuni
For a time he sailed the seas, but now
Within a grave he hath dropped anchor —
And of good heart above the tide
Hath landed in the land of light

Among the pallbearers listed is a Captain Wilson, described as 'a cousin of the deceased'.

She had met her future husband after his ship docked in Hull. Born and bred in North Wales, my great-grandfather, Robert Jones, would also own ships but in his case never more than two or three at a time, and those more sloop than steamer. Perhaps that's why the nuptials took place, not with great pomp in Hull, but quietly in his hometown of Pwllheli, official records giving the bride's address as one of the better local hotels. According to family legend, the bridegroom spoke no English at the time of the marriage and his bride, less improbably, not one word of Welsh.

I have heard it said that the Wilsons, particularly Arthur, sent the couple money every now and then. They could certainly afford it. Unlike his older brother, committed to good works and Liberal politics, serving briefly as a Member of Parliament before being granted a peerage, Arthur had ambitions to be accepted by the landed gentry of his native Yorkshire. To that end he purchased over 3,000 acres of land, built himself a grand house, and got himself appointed Master of the Holderness Hunt. A measure of his success was that in 1890 the Prince of Wales, later King Edward VII, consented to stay at his home, Tranby Croft, during St Leger week at Doncaster racecourse. It was here during a late-night game of baccarat, that one of the royal party, Lieutenant Colonel Gordon-Cumming, who listed Charlemagne among his forebears, was accused of cheating. Despite attempts to hush up the scandal, news of it spread quickly to London, obliging Gordon-Cumming to take his accusers to court in order to redeem his good name. The subsequent trial, at which the Prince of Wales was called to testify, drew widespread attention and was extensively reported in the national press. In the event Gordon-Cumming lost the case. His honour irreparably damaged, he spent the remainder of his life, some forty years of it, ostracised by polite society and died in 1930 at his home in Scotland. Two generations later amends were discreetly made by Buckingham Palace, lending credence to my grandmother's claim that Gordon-Cumming was innocent all along, the real culprit being none other than the future king himself.

The Firth family motto (I'm not certain the Wilsons ever had one) was *Deo, et non fortuna* ('Through God, not by luck'). Suitably adapted, it was to provide Violet Firth with her pseudonym, when she began writing the books for which she is to this day revered in occult circles. It was also the motto she adopted for the practice of magic, the sort of magic which by then I wanted Mr James to teach me, the sort where, so far as I understood it, supernatural forces were evoked and rendered subservient to the will of the practitioner. For twelve years, Dion Fortune's partner of choice in the rituals she and her acolytes favoured, was her then husband, said to have a pagan rawness they lacked, who was familiarly referred to (but not in his hearing) as Merl, short for Merlin. His real name, however, was Thomas Penry Evans, the man whose opinion my mother had sought before entrusting me to Mr James.

It was Mrs Caradoc Evans who revealed that the author of my book was a woman, although, so far as I remember, she never divulged her real name. Perhaps she didn't know it. Had she said Mrs Penry Evans, then my father might well have linked it to his friend from South Wales, although that would not have enabled my mother to make a connection to the Firths of Llandudno. Mrs Evans knew more about the author than her gender, however, though not very much, having come across her years earlier through a spiritualistic friend she'd known in London while still married to her Polish count, although the couple were by then living apart.

The friend was the widow of Sir Vincent Caillard, sometime diplomat and director of several important companies, who had been just short of seventy when he married the studiously fragile Zoe Gertrude Maund (née Dudgeon) in 1927. Owner of The Belfry, a former Presbyterian church in Belgrave Square, Lady Caillard had by then converted the premises into what one society columnist called 'a wittily eccentric home'.

Lady Caillard had a passion for birds. Indeed 'Bird' had been her husband's pet name for her. (She in turn called him Big Fish.) The magazine piece went on to gush that 'what had earlier been the chancel now housed nearly a thousand china birds' while 'the new owner's bedroom was decorated with still more birds, these painted on aluminium panels'

Like Mrs Evans, Lady Caillard dabbled in Spiritualism, though wealth and idleness meant her dabbling soon turned into something more serious. Quick to exploit her enthusiasm was Maurice Barbanell, already the editor of *Psychic News* and a tireless social climber, as well as the mediumistic mouthpiece of my sometime hero, Silver Birch. To him we owe an account of a seance in which the late Sir Vincent materialised in a darkened room and, having summoned his wife from her chair, took her in his arms and kissed her, a public show of affection he would repeat shortly afterwards at a children's party, a *spirit* children's party, organised by Lady Caillard at her late husband's behest. It was *Psychic News* that printed Lady Caillard's account of these remarkable festivities:

'A few days before Christmas I was asked by my husband to arrange for a Christmas party on Christmas Eve. There was to be a Christmas tree for the spirit children, and I was to hang up my stocking. He said he would put something in it, even if it was only a clothes peg. The party was to be held at Mrs L. E. Singleton's house and only three of us were present — Mrs Singleton, B. E. Kirby[21] and myself. After our usual prayer, and before we had finished playing a Christmas carol on the gramophone, little Ivy came and asked Mr Kirby to stop it, meaning the gramophone. She told us the room was full of spirit children who had come to the party. One of the most wonderful things happened at the party. I was not going to write about it, because I felt it is too sacred. But Sir Vincent says he is so proud of being able to do it that he wished me to add it. He was able to put his arms around me and kiss me three times. I think it was the most wonderful party I ever attended.'

A wonderful time was had also by the children, thanks to the 'plated handbells' (which they dutifully rang), the 'special crackers',

---

21 The same Mr Kirby would resurface in 1944 as a witness for the defence in the Old Bailey trial of Helen Duncan (see pages 35-37).

and 'masses of toys'. Or at least things went wonderfully until a fight broke out, over a doll their hostess had purchased for Ivy, a 'negro spirit child', and one of her favourites.

'Jack Cornwell came and said "That black kid is awfully cheeky. She dug me in the ribs, and told me to get out because I touched her doll. I told her I would give her something when we got back this evening."'

Poor Ivy.

By then Lady Caillard had installed in the Belfry an instrument called the Reflectograph, a kind of elaborate typewriter which, its inventor claimed, could link the living and the dead. To do its job, however, it required a competent typist, not an ordinary Pitman-trained typist but one capable of generating the ectoplasm needed to depress its keys at the behest of the spirits. Not surprisingly, the job went to Mrs Singleton, at whose home little Ivy and her companions spent such a merry, if ultimately fractious, Christmas eve. Despite her best efforts, however, the Reflectograph failed to live up to its promise.

But it was a start. And lessons were learned, enough to make sure that when it's successor, the Communigraph, came into operation shortly after, it gave complete satisfaction. A handsome object, more ouija board than typewriter, it was mounted on an elegant stand, nicely varnished, and relied on the movements of a pendulum suspended above it. Such was its success that one of the communicators predicted that soon every home in England would own one, while Sir Vincent likewise expressed his approval, having earlier recommended that a prominent churchman, Archdeacon Wilberforce, pop in to bless the apparatus before it swung into action.

Within no time at all Sir Vincent, assisted by a motley crew of spirits, known as the Trianon Band, was transmitting word for word or, rather, letter by letter the contents of a new book he wished to see published under the title *A New Conception of Love*. It would, he confidently predicted, win over national leaders to the cause of peace and global amity. Week after week, usually on Wednesdays, a small group assembled in the drawing room at the Belfry, now reverently called the

Upper Room, while the pendulum swung complicitly back and forth. From time to time one of Mrs Singleton's more convivial familiars would drop in to jolly things up, a favourite being a Sergeant Murphy who entertained the company with quips and comic songs. A jolly sort of fellow, he never overstepped the mark.

Despite all the optimistic predictions, Sir Vincent's magnum opus did little to secure global amity. Nor did it do much for Bird. She fell ill and died on 17 January, 1935. The next day, the London papers displayed a picture of the Belfry, the large cross on its roof picked out by neon lights that remained switched on until after the funeral.

And what had all this to do with the book Mr James had given me for Christmas? I was beginning to ask myself the same question when Mrs Evans disclosed that in the weeks before her death Lady Caillard had sought a new tenant for the Belfry, preferably one sympathetic to her spiritualistic leanings. From several candidates her choice fell on Mrs Penry Evans, *née* Violet Firth and alias Dion Fortune, who'd recently come into money thanks to a bequest from a female admirer. With no time for the Communigraph, let alone Sergeant Murphy and his comic songs, Mrs Penry Evans exorcised the building before moving in. The china birds were presumably rehomed.

<h1 style="text-align: center;">8</h1>

"Listen to all, plucking a feather from every passing goose, but, follow no one absolutely."

Chinese Proverb

At some point, unremarked by me, my lunchtime chats with Mr James had moved from matchboxes to metaphysics, although the word wasn't known to me back then.

Not that there was anything overtly metaphysical, as I hope to have shown, about Mr James. For him the materialistic, even mechanistic, approach favoured by science remained the one best suited, at least most of the time, to understanding, as well as exploiting, the material world. What he recognised, however, is that of all the sentient beings inhabiting that world, we alone are conscious of being conscious, a privilege that both involves us in and detaches us from what we experience or observe. Thus, even when we think we're being objective or, if you like, 'scientific', our experience of ourselves experiencing means that we're not.

What it does mean is that as human beings we are uniquely equipped to transcend both the reality we experience and our experience of it. For Mr James magical practice (he'd have disliked the term and I'm not overfond of it myself) facilitated an awareness of this 'higher' consciousness and, more importantly, rendered intelligible whatever it might in the process encounter. Thus understood, magic became for him a kind of metaphysical Rosetta Stone, facilitating access to a reality beyond sense-derived experience as well as making it relevant to the here-and-now and, by an exercise of the will, adapting it to match our preferences. The last of these is what distinguishes the magical from the mystical and, even more, the downright fanciful. It is why Aleister Crowley defined magic as 'the science and art of causing change in conformity with the will'.[22]

Looking back, I can but marvel at how Mr James was able to explain all of this to the adolescent me, bright but not that bright, with by then thoughts and urges very much of this world, not of some other which, to be honest, seemed barely more than plausible at best.

Yet as the months, even years, passed, I kept going back week after week to Tanrallt, eager and sometimes impatient to learn more. Familiarity did little to diminish, let alone dispel, the kind of happiness I'd felt that first Saturday, when I saw the farm ahead of me and heard the dogs bark at my approach. Long after I'd grown up and left home, long after Mr James had died, the same enchantment persisted, ready to surprise me when I least expected it. Once, years later, I came close to tears during a revival of *Brigadoon* in London, so much did the notion of a place that was real but beyond the reach of time, remind me of Tanrallt.

"Give that f***er a kick," Mr James would yell, as an irate gander charged at me before I'd even got off my bike, its wings outstretched and honking balefully. (The bird must have changed over the years, but dislike of me was common to them all.) Reluctant to antagonise my assailant still further, I'd do nothing apart from making shooing noises or waving my arms about, often receiving a nip on the shin in return. It sometimes drew blood but not enough to make a fuss, certainly not in front of Mr James.

---

22 Dion Fortune, more circumspect. defined it as 'the art of causing changes in consciousness in conformity with the Will'.

The only other person allowed to call on Saturdays but not encouraged to stay beyond an hour, was Bronwen Humphries, universally known as Bronwen 'Llain' after the name of the cottage she lived in.[23] Monumentally stout, Bronwen could be found from Monday to Friday behind an ormolu desk at the Lexicon Library in North Parade, stamping books and collecting money from borrowers too fastidious to patronise the municipal library in nearby Corporation Street. She also kept an eye on the interior design shop next door whenever its owner, as flamboyant as the merchandise on offer, was away fitting curtains — regency stripes were all the rage back then — or silk bedspreads. My mother once commissioned a lampshade from him but, for reasons of her own, refused to let me go unaccompanied to collect it when he telephoned to say it was ready.

To strangers perceptibly astonished at her size, Bronwen liked to murmur, "It's my glands", then savour their remorse for having secretly blamed it on her appetite, although we all knew that this alone was the culprit. Once, during supper at my aunt's, the two being somehow related, she noticed that my Uncle George had not finished his meal. "Aren't you going to eat that, Mr Jones?" she enquired. Told he wasn't, she calmly tipped the food onto her plate, declaring it too good to waste. On a wall nearby my aunt, a staunch Methodist, had a framed text — 'Christ is the unseen guest at every meal' — so for months afterwards I wondered if Bronwen would have wolfed down her Saviour's leftovers as well.

Nothing Mr James gave her could make her lose weight. A mixture of chickweed, burdock, ginger and fennel, intended to suppress her appetite, seemed, perversely, to enhance it, while a diuretic blend of hawthorn, dandelion, horsetail and parsley was discarded after it left her spending more time on the lavatory than at her ormolu desk. (Her addiction to liquorice allsorts already accounted for several such

---

23 Identifying people by their address or job is common practice throughout Wales, given the prevalence of shared surnames. It enables 'Davies Snowdon Villa' to be distinguished from 'Davies the Milk' or 'Davies the Post'. In Holyhead there was an insurance salesman universally known as 'Jones Sudden Death' after the eventuality he urged potential customers to bear in mind.

absences throughout the working day.) Overweight even in her youth, she had, my father often recalled, been the ideal dance partner when both were young. "All fat girls dance well" he'd say, "they've got better balance", a claim my mother resented, being skinny and, like me, no great shakes on the dance floor.

It was on a Saturday in December, the last but one before Christmas, that I discovered Bronwen might have designs on Mr James. That morning she'd stayed away but in her place were the two Miss Davieses, always referred to as such, who were somehow related to Mr James, and came every year to help feather that season's crop of geese. (There was a third Miss Davies, but she'd run off to London fifty years before and not been heard of since.) Gander notwithstanding, I was rather fond of the geese. Earlier that year they'd surprised me by trotting into the yard with a gaggle of fluffy goslings in their wake, their arrival timed by Mr James to coincide, give or take a few days, with the Vernal Equinox, possibly one of Old Moore's recommendations. To ensure it happened, he'd put aside any eggs he found until they totalled twenty-six, at which point he gave each bird thirteen, more than recommended but a number deemed auspicious, to sit on. Once hatched, an abundance of fresh air and lots of exercise (but above all a generous supply of wheat) ensured that by December each gosling was plump and ready for the table.

That first Saturday I learned that the secret to feathering a goose is first to pour boiling water over it in order to soften the skin, then hang it up and pull downwards on the feathers. Before the Misses Davies started work, Mr James carefully removed the wings from several birds, explaining that Bronwen 'Llain' liked to use them as dusters.

"Never mind dusters, I hear she's made you new curtains," said the taller Miss Davies.

"Chintz," declared the other.

"What does she think I need curtains for?"

"You never know, she might come around after dark."

"Just when you're getting ready for bed," chortled her sister.

"Curtains would spoil her fun," quipped Mr James, prompting

more giggles until one Miss Davies nudged the other and nodded towards me. From then on there was no further mention of Bronwen 'Llain' or bedrooms or chintz curtains.

Later, one of the ladies reminded Mr James of the hamper which had turned up one Christmas at Tanrallt, delivered all the way from London.

"I still have the bowl you gave me. The one the plum pudding came in. It's got the name of the shop on one side. In blue."

"Fortnum and Mason," volunteered her sibling, "Fortnum and Mason of Piccadilly. Isn't that right?"

"It is indeed. A gift from Lord Tredegar."

"Very posh," chorused the pair, this time in English.

Now, as it happened, Tredegar was the name of a coal-mining town in South Wales where my father's uncle went looking for work on his return from France in 1918. Once the Miss Davieses had left us, I mentioned the coincidence to Mr James.

Tredegar House, home of Viscount Tredegar, he gently explained, was a good twenty miles away from Tredegar, the town; something he could say with confidence, having been a guest there in the 1940s, not once but twice. What struck me as remarkable on hearing it, was not that he'd been entertained by Lord Tredegar, however remarkable that also might be, but that someone as reclusive as he, someone who rarely ventured beyond Aberystwyth and was home well before dark when he did, had not only travelled that far but slept in a strange bed for three nights in a row. A fellow guest, he continued, had been Aleister Crowley, while on the second visit Mrs Duncan, no less, had entertained the company after dinner, presumably with Albert and the musical Peggy in tow. Did those names mean anything to me, he enquired? I told him I'd not heard of Aleister Crowley and he didn't mention him again.

Of greater interest to me were the exotic animals he'd found in the park around Tredegar House, among them deer, two zebras, several ostriches, some Barbary apes, and a kangaroo which the Viscount had taught how to box. Also on the premises was a tame macaw that accompanied its owner everywhere, even, legend has it, climbing up inside his trouser leg, in order to shock lady visitors by peeping out from between the buttons of his flies. Even at fourteen I found that hard to believe. A budgerigar, maybe, but not a bird the size of a macaw.

Like Lady Caillard, the Tredegars had a thing about birds, there being times when Evan's mother, *née* Lady Katherine Carnegie, was persuaded she was a bird herself. When that happened, she'd sally forth into the grounds, build herself a nest from sticks and mud then squat inside it, cooing prettily at any house-guests that happened to stroll by. Among those listed in the visitors' book are H. G. Wells, Aldous Huxley, J. B. Priestley and the painter Augustus John. The Caradoc Evanses, too, had stayed there at least twice, suggesting to me that talk of Mr James or the miraculous stone had secured him the hospitality of a man who was not only a Viscount but also Knight of the Sovereign Order of Malta, Knight of the Order of the Holy Sepulchre, Privy Chamberlain of Sword and Cape to Popes Benedict XV and Pius XI, not to mention Fellow of the Royal Society of Arts, the American Geographical Society, the Institute of Linguists and, more understandably, the Zoological Society of London. And as if these weren't honours enough, Aleister Crowley, scenting money and the chance of patronage, had named him the Adept of Adepts.[24]

"He liked the occult, that's for sure," chuckled Mr James.

It was the first time I'd heard him use the word 'occult', a favourite of Countess Barcynska ('esoteric' was another). I knew it referred to more exciting things than the mind games I'd been playing until then. Here was my chance to ask Mr James where to find them.

"No need to look," he replied, "they'll find you."

In bed that night, I dreamed that Mrs Duncan's parrot Bronco had got inside Lord Tredegar's trousers — better he, I suppose, than Albert or the musical Peggy.

---

24 A favourite also of Queen Mary who reportedly called him her 'favourite Bohemian', Tredegar worked for both MI5 and MI6 during World War II. Among his responsibilities, it is reported, was the department in charge of the carrier pigeons used to convey information to secret agents in occupied France. His bird-loving mother must have been delighted.

9

"Ah, poor ghost!"
Shakespeare, *Hamlet*, Act 1, scene 5

The winter that year was a hard one. By late September, the signs were there already, and for once Old Moore got things right and warned us to expect them.

Before the days grew shorter, Mr James began moving his sheep to low-lying pasture, finishing the job on what, appropriately enough, was the feast day of St Francis. Happily, conditions were not as bad as in that terrible winter of 1947 when, as he never tired of recounting, the snow had come early, well before the last stragglers could be rounded up and brought to safety. Off in search of them he went, accompanied by the dogs, with a spade to dig out any survivors they found buried underneath the drifts. Once, after clearing away the snow, he'd come across a fox and a ewe snuggled together for warmth, the two reconciled by their mutual need to survive. Welsh foxes are nothing if not cunning.

For me the onset of winter meant the journey to Tanrallt became more arduous, the wind doing its best to push against me as I pedalled away, sometimes through sleet and snow, with the lowest of my bike's three gears doing little to make the climb any easier. I might have felt less inclined to give up, had Mr James shown me how to 'experience' the supernatural for myself but so far that had not happened. Yes, he'd mentioned things like thought forms, even recommended exercises which, he claimed, would help me perceive them — a technique he called 'creative visualisation' (which sounds less pompous in Welsh) — but so far I'd seen nothing.

The purpose of these exercises, I've since come to understand, was to revive in me that pictorial way of thinking which comes naturally to infants, their mind effortlessly forming what psychologists call eidetic images. Part of it involved that business with the matchbox or an imagined stroll along Aberystwyth beach, the aim being to 'objectify' a subjective experience by imposing it on the world around me, lending form and substance to what, of itself, possessed neither. It was, if you like, a voluntary hallucination, one that might, with practice, be translated into the vernacular of empirical experience.

This all sounds terribly highfalutin. A few examples might better serve to show what's involved, even if they do suggest we're back with Mrs Duncan and that frisky 'Outsize' vest. In the next chapter, I shall describe my first encounter with — well, you'll see with what in due course — so I need now to persuade you to suspend your disbelief before we get there.

Let's start with an experiment conducted in the 1970s under the auspices of the Toronto Society for Psychical Research. It involved a group of friends, mostly academics, who set about creating an artificial entity, imagining for that purpose a character they named 'Philip Aylesford', a seventeenth-century landowner whose fictional biography would include a period spent fighting for the Royalist cause in the Civil War, as well as having a jealous wife and a gypsy mistress, later burned at the stake as a witch. The group met weekly in the hope that by concentrating on this narrative, they might induce their fictional hero to put in an appearance but, unsurprisingly, he did not.

After a year they stopped trying so hard and instead sat around a table chatting informally, even having the occasional singsong, while continuing to hope for the best. Still nothing. Then one day, quite unexpectedly, the table began to tilt and move independently around the room, while loud raps were heard coming from it. A code was hastily agreed and the agency responsible for the raps, calling itself Philip, went on to narrate a life history matching the one previously thought up on its behalf. Over time it went beyond this narrative and seemed increasingly to function independently of its creators. On one occasion a member of the group, Dr (later Professor) George Owen asked if Philip had ever come across Prince Rupert of Bohemia, commander of the Royalist cavalry in the Civil War. Philip said he had not. Knowing that his fictional biography included a grand tour of Europe, the questioner then asked if he'd ever visited Bohemia. The exchange, recorded by Owen's wife, Iris, proceeded as follows:

(Rap) "Yes."

"Did you know Elizabeth, the Winter Queen?" Dr Owen asked.

"Yes."

"That's odd," Dr Owen observed. "He says he knew Elizabeth, and yet previously he said he never knew of Rupert, her brother-in-law."

Dr Owen continued to maintain that Elizabeth was Rupert's brother-in-law, while an increasingly irate Philip continued, now with a series of double raps, to deny that he was. No one else present knew much about Rupert and Elizabeth, still less of their relationship to each other, so at that point Dr Owen went off to consult an encyclopaedia. In it he discovered that Rupert was not Elizabeth's brother-in-law. He was in fact her son.

Soon the movements of the table, now accompanied by other psychokinetic phenomena — technical terms like this help academics feel more comfortable — were being recorded on camera by the Canadian Broadcasting Corporation, and watched live by thousands of television viewers, as well as by a studio audience. Already it was evident that Philip had a touch of the diva about him, regarding himself, not unjustifiably, as the star of the show. Indeed, so determined was he to take centre stage that at one point in the broadcast the table tried to join the panel of independent experts lined up in the studio, roughly nudging them aside to make room.

The experiment was not unique. Other researchers grew curious to see if they could obtain similar effects. One group invented a World War II Resistance heroine they dubbed Lilith, creating a biography that ended with her being shot by the Germans, while another fabricated a medieval alchemist named Sebastian. Both characters were soon demonstrating the same verve and independence as the original Philip, although there was of course nothing original about them.

In occultism, such entities are often labelled 'thought forms' or, by Mr James, *delweddau creëdig*, best translated as 'created (i.e. objectified) images'. They have long been a feature of magical practice but as the following examples demonstrate, come not without a measure of risk.

A salutary account is provided by the Belgian-French explorer, Alexandra David-Néel (1868-1969) in the most famous of her several books.[25] In it she describes how, on a journey through Tibet, native sorcerers (*ngagspas*) taught her how to fabricate a thought creation (*tulpa*) of her choice. (In Sanskrit the process goes by the name of *kriyashakti*.) She opted for a fat and jolly monk who, after considerable effort on her part, became visible not only to her but to others in her party as well. Soon he could even be persuaded to perform simple tasks around the campsite.[26] As time went on, however, the little chap's good humour diminished and instead of being sweet-natured and compliant, he became increasingly self-willed, often truculent. Only with considerable effort was Madame David-Néel able to 'dismantle', as she puts it, her creation and despatch its 'elemental essence', whatever that means, to where it had come from. "My mind-creature," she ruefully observed, "was tenacious to life."

---

25 See *With Mystics and Magicians in Tibet*, a translation of her *Mystiques et Magiciens du Tibet*. (1929), published by Bodley Head (1936) and Penguin Books (1939). There have been numerous other editions, some with a slight change of title, since then.

26 "Un au pair de l'au-delà" as one of her more sceptical compatriots described it.

A similar experience awaited our friend, Dion Fortune, one that left her duly chastened also. This time it involved not a synthetic human being but — Mrs Penry Evans could seldom resist a touch of drama — a fully grown wolf. The animal turned up one afternoon as she lay on her bed, brooding over someone who'd earlier caused her offence. (I suspect she was easily offended.) While still in the foulest of moods, she had begun for no special reason to reflect on Norse mythology when, by her account, Fenris, 'wolf-horror of the North', flopped down on the counterpane beside her 'in well-materialised ectoplasmic form'. Grey in colour, the animal, she noted, had weight, for she could feel its back pressing against hers, 'as a large dog might do'.

Sensible woman that she was, she gave the intruder a poke in the ribs and, after a token snarl, down it jumped 'as meekly as a lamb', later withdrawing to a corner of the room. For several days it hung about the house, sometimes visible, sometimes not, until fearing it might turn nasty like Madame David-Néel's *tulpa*, its creator — the beast had emerged from her solar plexus and was still joined to it by a subtle umbilical cord — decided to reabsorb it into her body, however distasteful the prospect. Not that it promised to be a barrel-load of laughs for Fenris either.

On the big day the animal was lying on the hearth like a large Alsatian dog when, in her own words, Mrs Penry Evans 'began by an effort of will and imagination to draw the life out of it along the silver cord. The wolf form began to fade, the cord thickened and grew substantial. A violent emotional upheaval started in myself. The wolf form had now faded into a shapeless grey mist. This, too, was absorbed along the silver cord.'

Not surprisingly the narrator found herself 'bathed in perspiration' once the job was done.

Here, it is important to stress that for Mr James and, I suspect, both the Toronto group and Madame David-Néel, possibly Dion Fortune as well, the entities they conjured up had been invented by them, knowingly or not, and, as such, were artificial constructs. The same might be true also of the revenants described at Mrs Duncan's trial, at least of those, if any, not made of regurgitated cheesecloth and damp papier-mâché. Witnesses like Mr Dodds saw what they did, because, knowingly or not, they imposed a likeness of their choosing on whatever subtle matter Mrs Duncan, like Madame David-Néel, had generated. It might also explain the hymn-singing miners.

This procedure, often known to occultists as 'conjuring to visible appearance', was appropriated by the early Spiritualists, keen to persuade seance-goers that the dead not only survive but keep intact their former personality, even their tics and idiosyncrasies, well beyond the grave. Mr James, unsympathetic (as are most occultists) to Spiritualism, was keen to remind me that in the past even the cleverest people had been fooled by what went on in the seance room, one example dear to him — it never failed to make him chuckle — involving the scientist, Sir William Crookes (1856-1917), who investigated the mediumistic talents of a young woman named Florence Cook.

The case amused Mr James all the more because the spirit conjured up by Miss Cook and known as 'Katie King', was said to be Annie Owen Morgan, daughter of Captain Henry Morgan (1636-1688), a Welsh buccaneer and later Governor of Jamaica. Mr James had several Morgans in his family. But then, so do I. And so does half the population of Wales.

Temporarily restored to life, Katie was by all accounts more than happy to promenade around the seance room under the admiring gaze of those present, even to be photographed, her appearance eliciting fulsome praise from Sir William in his report of these remarkable events:

'Photography is inadequate to describe the beauty of Katie's face, as words are powerless to describe her charms of manner. Photography may indeed give a map of her countenance, but how can it reproduce the brilliant purity of her complexion or the ever-varying expression of her most noble features, now overshadowed with sadness when relating some of the bitter experiences of her past life, now smiling with all the happy innocence of a happy girlhood.

Round her she made an atmosphere of life.
The very air seems lighter from her eyes,
They were so soft and beautiful, and rife
With all we can imagine of the skies.
Her overpowering presence made me feel
It would not be idolatry to kneel.'[27]

So besotted was Sir William that he not only knelt before the win-some Katie but held her in his arms and lavished kisses on what, he assured his scientific peers, was a real person, not some 'phantom of a disordered brain'.

He was right. There was nothing phantom-like about the delecta-ble Miss King. Nothing ectoplasmic either, as a Mr Volckmann would discover when, persuaded she and the medium were one and the same, he grabbed hold of Katie's arm and refused to let go. In the ensuing fracas he suffered a bloody nose and lost several of his whiskers, 'a hir-sute ornamentation of which', we are informed, 'the owner... prided himself considerably'.[28] Florrie Cook, like Mrs Duncan, put up a fight when caught out.

It was Mr James' belief that ectoplasm, when not fraudulently produced, as in the example above, might be akin to the temporary 'substance' which, he maintained, subtle forces acquire when operating within space and time at the magician's behest — when, in the jargon of quantum physics, wave becomes particle and, as such, impacts upon the here-and-now.

In the past, parapsychologists have spoken of something not dis-similar, labelling it psychotronic or bioplasmic energy. That sounds impressive but leaves us little the wiser. The same is true of a variant, dubbed 'anthropoflux' by Professor Farney of the University of Zurich whose work in the 1930s attracted the attention of, among others,

---

27 Years later, Miss Cook would trade in Katie for another spirit, this one called Marie, but not long afterwards the new recruit suffered the same indignities as her predecessor, firstly at the hands of a Mr William Tipp, later at those, no more gentlemanly, of Sir George Sitwell, who grabbed her by the waist and, as he later testified, "felt her whalebone corset".

28 John Neville Maskelyne, *Modern Spiritualism*, Frederick Warne, London, 1876, p. 142.

C. G. Jung. More recently the Russian, Semeyon Kirlian (1898-1978), conducted similar experiments although the daddy of them all was our old friend, Sir William Crookes, inventor of something called the radiometer which, he claimed, detected a novel form of energy discharged by the medium Daniel Dunglas Home, a compatriot of Mrs Duncan but, unlike her, never caught cheating. Today, scientists believe such experiments reveal nothing that cannot be explained by environmental conditions, including temperature changes and moisture levels of the skin. Whatever ectoplasm is made of, it's almost certainly not this.

Neither, come to that, was the entity which — after all those Saturdays spent with Mr James, after all that cycling to and from Tanrallt, after all that manual work, all those swear words and all those mental gymnastics — would, finally, provide me with my first experience of magic, the more welcome, even credible, for being completely unexpected.

10

"I met a man that wasn't there"
William Hughes Mearns

Uncle Davy died that summer. For the best part of a year he'd been showing signs of what back then was called senile decay, which was less common than it is now, presumably because fewer people lived long enough to get it. My first inkling came one Saturday when, for reasons long forgotten, I'd not gone to Tanrallt, but spent the afternoon with him in his office at the back of the shop. Some time earlier, he'd expressed a desire to teach me double-entry bookkeeping, possibly with an eye to a day when I might take over the business. But that afternoon the debits and credits kept defying his efforts to get them to tally, while I made things worse by confusing the two. We were about to start all over again when the telephone rang. At the other end was Mrs Abraham-Williams, wife of the local auctioneer and a valued customer, the more so for being the owner of a compound surname. (A sometime Miss Williams, she'd consented to marry a Mr Abrahams only on condition they combine their names by deed poll. To her mind, 'Abrahams', *tout court*, sounded Jewish.) Now Mrs Abraham-Williams wanted to know if she'd left her umbrella behind in the shop.

"Is this the one?" asked my great-uncle, holding up a brolly found unattended by the bacon counter earlier that day, "If so, I'll send the errand boy with it at once."

"She can't see it, Uncle Davy," I whispered.

With that he turned to me, puzzled. "Mrs Abraham-Williams I have in my hand one lady's umbrella. Is this the one? Black with red spots. And an ebony handle. Excellent. I'll have it delivered."

Later he said to my father "Good job the boy was with me. No one told me Mrs Abraham-Williams had gone blind. What is it? Cataracts?"

Within a matter of weeks, he'd suffered a stroke. Able eventually to return to the shop, he never recovered fully and his right arm hung limply by his side. (I was warned not to stare.) His speech, too, was impaired, limited now to sounds no one could make sense of.

Keen for me to stay in his good books, my mother urged me to watch his face and pretend I understood what he was trying to say, then smile, nod or shake my head appropriately. But as Uncle Davy's face stayed the same at all times, another effect of the stroke, I never knew which to do, smile, nod or shake. In the end I played safe and kept my features every bit as immobile as his own.

In his will he left me £50, far less than people expected. I was told I should have tried harder.

After that, with school exams looming, not to mention entrance exams for Oxford and Cambridge, it was decided I'd thenceforth visit Mr James only every fourth Saturday. On the other three, I'd stay home and study, or else take the bus to Mrs Winkler's house a few miles out of town, close in fact to Bronwen Llain's cottage. By then, she'd offered to teach me German, a subject not on the syllabus at school, and so the pair of us would struggle through Kleist's *Erdbeben in Chili*, one of the set books for that year. Even when I read German aloud, she insisted that I sounded exactly like her hero, David Lloyd George.

Impatient though I was to see Tanrallt again, I didn't go there on the first Saturday after sitting the last of my exams. And that was because the circus was in town.

My 'thing for circuses', as my mother put it, matched, on occasion even surpassed, my infatuation with the supernatural. She viewed it with equal suspicion, sensing an overlap between the two, but unable to work out how or why. For her it was the more unsettling because it started long before I'd even heard of circuses, let alone seen one, none having visited Aberystwyth until my sixth birthday. (The last to do so, Chapman's Great London Circus, was there on September 2, 1939, the eve of World War II, when, by all accounts, the band defiantly played the national anthem not once but twice at the end of the final performance.) All that would change, however, when, as if to make up for lost time, two circuses arrived in quick succession: small, ramshackle affairs that failed dismally to match the promise of their rival posters, which I first glimpsed in a shop window in Chalybeate Street. I was still too young to take in what they said, but then I didn't need to, for the clown's face on one and prancing horses on the other told me all I needed to know. I can still see them now: Scott's Royal Circus ('the cream of circus talent', as my mother helpfully read out) and Dakota's Circus, the latter content merely to list the date and time of the performances.

The first of them was due in a fortnight, so from then on I insisted on being taken every evening to the showground, a good mile and a half outside town, to see if any wagons had turned up. In the event, they arrived no earlier than the date advertised, so for two weeks my hopes, immune to experience, were dashed on a daily basis, each successive disappointment no less brutal than the last.

Long before then, however, before I could even hold a pencil properly, I'd been drawing big tops, often surrounded by what looked like garden sheds on wheels, but presumably were caravans, on every scrap of paper I could find, leaving my mother puzzled not just by my choice of subject but because, when questioned, I seemed unaware of what I'd just drawn. It caused her less worry than the nightly visits from my two old ladies, but for a time my obsession with circuses, more puzzling than disturbing, caused her similar concern.

Anyway, the circus came and went, as did my final day at school. To celebrate the latter, I planned to stay overnight at Tanrallt, accompanied this time by Colin Samuel, my best friend for as long as I could remember. Our intention was to sleep outside in a tent I'd bought by mail order from an army surplus shop in London. What I'd forgotten to do, however, was order a groundsheet — perhaps my savings didn't stretch that far — and without a groundsheet to lie on, there was no way Mrs Samuel would let her Colin sleep al fresco, especially in a place as damp as Pumlumon. He was prone to coughs, was Colin, so much so that when he was small Mr James had urged his mother — she had the face of a Madonna, he once confided to my father — to rub goose grease on his chest in cold weather 'to keep the heat in'.

And so it was without Colin that I set off the following Saturday. Without my tent also, the business with the ground sheet having caused my mother to have second thoughts. Instead I took with me two clean sheets and a pillowcase, ostensibly to spare Mr James the chore of washing bed clothes after me, but in truth because she feared his own, even if clean, might not be properly aired.

"I don't want you catching rheumatic fever," she murmured, as she helped secure the package to the crossbar of my bike. And a poor job we made of it, the pair of us, for no sooner had I left than the parcel began tipping from one side to the other, all but causing me to fall off more than once. The bother of keeping one hand on the sheets and trying not to wobble meant, too, that the journey there took twice as long. Even the gander seemed relieved when I finally arrived.

That night, supper over and dishes left to soak in the sink, Mr James settled into his wing chair by the fire while I sat upright on the settle opposite. Snuggled up beside me was Nance, older of the sheepdogs, while her daughter Bet, endowed with one brown eye and another of the softest forget-me-not blue, slumbered at my feet, opening one or the other from time to time, as if to check I was still there, my usual departure time long past.

On the table beside us burned an oil lamp, its glow too weak to light up every corner of the room but enough for me to read the advertisements in an old copy of the *Farmers' Weekly* discarded on the hearth: Bibby's cattle cake, Massey-Harris tractors and, my favourite, Alfa-Laval, a name more exotic than the electric milking machines it referred to.

Mr James, meanwhile, was talking about plants held sacred by the Druids, the most important of them mistletoe. A symbol of wisdom, its juice extracted at the Winter Solstice was, he said, guaranteed to confer immortality on anyone who drank it in combination with five of the ten other plants favoured by the ancient Celtic priesthood. (These were wormwood, burdock, sage, heather, chamomile, wild orchid, ground ivy, couch grass, club-moss and pimpernel.) The trouble was, he continued, no one knew anymore which five were the right ones. And even if these were correctly identified, either by luck or by a process of elimination, there remained the need to combine them in the right proportions.

"You'd be dead before you found the recipe," he observed, adding that immortality was in any case more likely a curse than a blessing.

What prompted this conversation was a question I'd put to him about the medicinal uses of vervain, another plant the Druids held in high regard. Good at calming the nerves, as are other plants with blue or purplish flowers, it would, Mr James suggested, have been worth taking before my recent exams, for not only did it soothe jagged nerves but sharpened the wits while about it.

At this point he went over to turn down the oil lamp, pausing before settling back in his chair to put a match to some charcoal in a small terracotta bowl on the dresser, next to a regiment of Staffordshire figures. Until then, it had escaped my notice. Now, as the charcoal glowed briefly, he scattered over it some powder he removed from one of the drawers.

"Frankincense, lemongrass and storax — real storax not the rubbish you get nowadays," he informed me.

Frankincense I'd heard of, possibly lemon grass, but not storax. And

I'd certainly not have known real storax from any other kind.

"Vervain and mistletoe weren't the only herbs the Druids held sacred," he resumed after a pause during which I thought he'd nodded off. "No, they had eight others as well. For a start there was blackbane and what people call thorn apple, though it's too near bedtime to say much about those. You'd end up having nasty dreams. Now, clover, that's a nice one. They liked clover a lot, especially a five-leafed clover. It brought good luck. Let's see, there's also belladonna and a plant called lady's slipper" — *esgid Mair* in Welsh — "and of course St John's wort. Best thing for depression, St John's wort."

"That's six. You've forgotten two. "

"When you get to my age, you forget a lot of things."

I never discovered what the missing two were but keep meaning to find out. Fifty years on, I, too, forget a lot of things.

The Druids, continued Mr James, believed the sun had two faces. One is familiar to us as the celestial body that is our source of light, while a second, concealed from view, illuminates the 'other world'. Sometimes called the Akashic record, this mirrors and records everything that happens within space and time but, just as importantly, reflects also the perfected state that reality is slowly moving towards. Subsisting outside time, it is equipped to contemplate simultaneously both the progress of history and its ultimate consummation.

Mr James maintained that despite knowing the outcome of the process to which the universe is subject, the sun's hidden aspect was in no way superior to its visible or 'mundane' equivalent. On the contrary, the reality presided over by the latter possesses a quality absent from the other. For implicit in our unfinished and imperfect environment is a freedom not found elsewhere, one that empowers us to exercise our will by making choices that affect ourselves, other people and the world about us. Freedom of this kind, he continued, stands in contrast to the single-mindedness of other spiritual beings, the angels among them, whose commitment to their allotted function, however admirable, is bereft of moral worth, being determined by their nature rather than by choice.

Choice, he continued, was why the natural world could be as cruel as it is beautiful. This I'd heard from him before, since often when we were outside and he not in the happiest of moods, he'd tell me what a blessing it was to be deaf to the cries of the living creatures around us. Like our unhappiness, theirs was a consequence of the freedom prevailing everywhere, its purpose, although for them scant consolation, to allow human beings, possibly all sentient beings, to collaborate in bringing manifested reality to its ultimate perfection. When that happened, time would end and the sun's two faces merge into one.

"Why does God let bad things happen?" I enquired, too young to know the question was not new.

"Because we're free to do what we like. If God, whatever that means, interfered when things went wrong, intervening to help us here and there, where would it stop? There'd be no end to his meddling. Only by doing nothing can God make us responsible for what we get up to. That's why bad things happen. It's the price we pay for being free."

By then my eyelids were heavy. A cheese and pickle supper, the warmth of the fire and now the smell of incense made it hard to stay awake. The two dogs were still asleep, the one next to me whimpering from time to time as it dreamt of chasing rabbits, neither of them the least bit troubled by the wind which, restive all afternoon, had by now gathered strength and was beating against the walls of the house and rattling the window behind me. I was relieved to be indoors, warm and dry, not outside in my Army surplus tent which, once unpacked, looked far less sturdy than it did in the catalogue, not to mention being without a groundsheet.

Whether due to the racket outside or simple tiredness, I suddenly found myself unable to make out what Mr James was saying. It reminded me of being with Uncle Davy after his stroke. And then at some point I must have dozed off. To this day I'm not sure what constitutes a waking dream — hypnagogia is the fancy word for it — but what happened next makes me think I probably had one.

It began with a loud banging on the front door, and it took me several seconds to realise its cause was not the wind but someone outside, someone keen, presumably, to find refuge from the storm. Yet so far off the beaten track was Tanrallt that the chance of anybody turning up in the dead of night and on such a wicked night as this, seemed so remote that I began to feel uneasy. As did the dogs. At the first knock, the one beside me leapt to the floor and slunk off to the far end of the room, while the other retreated under the settle. Normally both would have stood their ground and barked. Only Mr James seemed unperturbed.

"Come in," he bellowed.

Now, not even a voice as powerful as his would have been heard by someone on the other side of that heavy oak door, let alone above the din of the wind and the rain. Yet heard it must have been, just as the door must have opened, although I never noticed it, to admit the man now standing in the middle of the room. With the assurance of someone familiar with his surroundings, he moved a bentwood chair closer to the hearth and sat down.

"We were talking about the Druids," said Mr James without preamble, "I can't remember why."

"Vervain," I heard myself say, "and you'd been saying how the Druids cut down mistletoe with a golden scythe. On the sixth day of the new moon."

"According to Pliny," murmured the stranger, "you'll find it in his *Natural History*."

"We didn't do Pliny in school, at least not that Pliny, only his nephew, Pliny the Younger. Most of the time we did Virgil. The Georgics. Oh, and Horace, too. We did lots of Horace."

He ignored my attempt to show off.

"There can't be much vervain in these parts. The ground's far too wet."

"You sometimes find it higher up," said Mr James, "a spot called Clogwyn Bedwyr."

"Have you been there?"

The stranger turned towards me and only then did I begin to realise there was something odd, something not quite right, about him. His eyes seemed different to start with, not just blue but archetypally blue, as if in them or, rather, beyond them, stretched an infinity of blueness, one I risked getting lost in, were I to gaze into it for too long.

"No, I've never been to Clogwyn Bedwyr."

"Then you shall," promised the visitor.

I felt disappointed yet also relieved when at that point Mr James declared it was long past my bedtime. Getting up from his chair, he lit a candle and, satisfied it was stuck firmly to its saucer, handed it to me, warning me to take care not to set the house alight. I remember walking to the bottom of the staircase then turning, well brought-up young chap that I was, to bid him and his companion a final goodnight. What strikes me now is how unsurprised I was to see Mr James alone in the room, with no sign of the visitor, and the bentwood chair back in its usual place. Before my head touched the pillow, I had time to notice that the wind had dropped to a whisper.

Or perhaps the whisper was a dying breath for no sooner was I asleep than I woke up again to find everywhere quiet, the room bathed in moonlight and, biggest surprise of all, myself by the dormer window gazing at the bed where someone suspiciously like me lay sleeping. Within seconds that suspicion was confirmed when I found myself transported, without perceptible movement — it was more an involuntary displacement — to the end of the bed and there compelled to acknowledge that the person lying in it was no trick of the moonlight but the real me.

No less real, however, was the other me that stood calmly taking stock of him. Indeed, of the two mes this one seemed the more real, having somehow become the custodian of my self-awareness. At the same time the sleeping figure was also unquestionably me, not some counterfeit version, even if my consciousness had chosen to desert it. The ambiguity might have alarmed me, had the mental exercises Mr James encouraged — displacing my consciousness into a matchbox or onto a windswept beach — not required a temporary dislocation of mind and body. What was disconcerting was to find myself contemplating the body my mind had so unexpectedly deserted.

Yet the detached but fully conscious me was not deprived, like some ever-smiling Cheshire cat, of all vestige of corporeality. Looking down I saw that I now inhabited a less solid version, indistinct and oddly translucent, of the body I'd seemingly vacated, though in retrospect that might have been an illusion designed to make me feel at ease, especially as I seemed also to be wearing a duplicate set of pyjamas. Possibly what I saw was ectoplasm, the stuff of Mrs Duncan's parrot, though I rather hoped it wasn't, but whatever it was, it seemed indifferent to the limitations to which physical objects are subject. This I discovered when, perhaps because it was the last thing on my mind before bed, I suddenly thought of Clogwyn Bedwyr and the vervain said to flourish there. The thought no sooner entered my head (or whatever now functioned in its place) than I found myself standing on an unfamiliar hilltop where clumps of sparsely leaved plants, more grey than green, an effect perhaps of the moonlight, were growing at my feet. From them rose tiny spikes bearing purplish or, rather, mauve flowers, not unlike heather but less densely clustered. I didn't need to be told what they were.

But told I was, all the same.

"Vervain. It doesn't look much, does it?"

Beside me, seemingly a lot more solid than I was, stood the man I'd seen or thought I'd seen earlier that night in Tanrallt.

"You know where you are, do you?

I believe I said I did. I know I meant to.

With that he talked about the journey which, according to him, I'd embarked upon since meeting Mr James, one that would lead me to what he called the innermost part of my being, a destination that didn't much appeal to me, at least not then, despite his assurance that I'd encounter there a portion of me which, though in the world, was not of it. By accepting it, I would become aware of a wider reality, eternal, immutable and timeless, with which I'd always been one, while never being less than myself. And in case I ever lost sight of it, there would be signs, as well as people, on the way to remind me.

When he'd finished my companion turned to me and smiled.

"Go on," he said (and I could swear he gave me a nudge) "pick some to take back with you. You might as well, after coming all this way."

The reminder of Tanrallt was again translated into action, this time propelling me back to the tiny bedroom where I'd just enough time to notice the iron bedstead, the rose-flecked wallpaper, even the damp patch on the ceiling, before being reunited with my body and falling asleep. The next thing I remember was waking up the following morning as sunlight cheerfully spilled in through the small dormer window, feeling contented and refreshed and disposed in the candid light of day to regard the previous night's adventure as the stuff of dreams, real enough while it lasted but essentially phantasmic, a moonstruck delirium, nothing more, brought on by too much cheese and pickle, and the unfamiliar incense (with its bona fide storax). Like those windswept seashores I'd walked along so often in my head, it must have been imagined. When the time came to push aside the bedclothes and get up, I was all but sure of it.

oOo

The author aged nine months

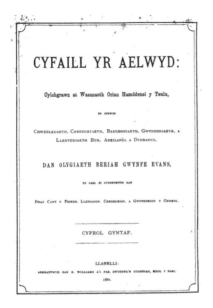

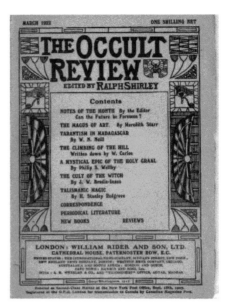

Cyfaill yr Aelwyd or "Companion of the Hearth" (1880-1891).
Its editor, Beriah Gwynfe Evans, would later contribute
to The Occult Review (1905-1952).

The author and proud parents
on Aberystwyth promenade
sometime in the nineteen-forties.

From "Aberystwyth Characters" *Sunday Graphic*, June 9, 1935
Countess Barcynska and her son Nick Sandys highlighted.

"a twin-furrowed track, the width of
a tractor's wheel span, with clumps of plantain
and coarse grasses growing in between."

Helen Duncan, Scottish medium (1897-1956),
and, below, with "spirits"

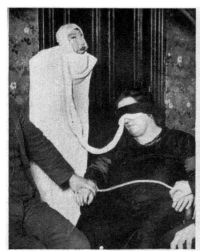

The author aged twelve, a school photograph

The Little Theatre

ABERYSTWYTH

EARL ARMSTRONG *presents his*
REPERTORY COMPANY
IN A SERIES OF

WEST END PLAYS

ONCE NIGHTLY
7.30 P.M.

SATURDAY
5.0 and 7.30 P.M.

BOX OFFICE OPEN DAILY
Monday to Saturday 10—12-30 — *Telephone* 423

Programme 3d.

The Little Theatre:
Earl Armstrong Repertory Company
programme (1955)

The Belfry, in Belgravia, London, now Mossiman's Club.

Viscount Tredegar (1893-1949), with Blue Boy, his infamous macaw, in 1935.

The author, aged fourteen, and his Welsh Terrier, Shelagh,
on the lake near Domen Bedwyr, Pumlumon.

PART TWO

11

**"I like the spirit of this great London which I feel around me.
Who but a coward would pass his whole life in hamlets; and
for ever abandon his faculties to the eating rust of obscurity?"**
Charlotte Brontë

"An out-of-the-body experience, OBE for short. They're not uncommon. Nothing supernatural about them, not a sausage."

The judgement came from a woman, softly spoken but unmistakably bored, whom I'd latched on to at a Freshers' party within days of arriving in London, my attention drawn to her by another student, also Welsh, who said he'd seen her picture in the *Evening News*. A junior lecturer in the Psychology Department of another London college, she was known to have a special interest in the paranormal and was currently investigating alleged poltergeist activity on a council estate in Shepherd's Bush, hence the picture, incentive enough for me to approach her when I got the chance. Within minutes, I was telling her about my experience two months earlier in Tanrallt, although with hindsight I can see it was a mistake. Too many people like me, each with a story to tell, accounted for the boredom now writ large across her face.

Suddenly aware of it, I was foolish enough to make things worse by trying to impress her with how much I knew, comparing my adventure with something I'd read in a book on Tibetan Buddhism. There, reference had been made to a ghostly duplicate of our physical body, known as the Bardo-body, into which our consciousness passes after death, sometimes during sleep. I even gabbled on about how a similar experience could be induced by meditation, adding that Buddhists disapproved of such practices, dismissing them as trivial and a hindrance to enlightenment.

"Yes, yes," murmured my listener, "and while you're at it, why not mention the Egyptians? They believed in a subtle body also, the ka or khu they called it. That doesn't make it any more real."

"Mine seemed real enough."

"Totally subjective. Were you drunk? I remember being drunk once and my discombobulated self was all over the place."

I sensed her attention was by then doing the same. Not that I blamed her.

Tanrallt seemed already far behind me, a different world, if not a different life. Aberystwyth felt equally remote, as did my parents and all my old friends. It wasn't just a matter of geography. Over the previous week I'd grown up, suddenly and to my surprise, but growing up meant growing away from people and things that once meant so much to me. Already they'd become, if not unimportant, then less important than they were. It was exciting, yes, but in a way rather sad.

The process started in my final term at school. Halfway through it I was lucky enough (or so people told me) to get offered a place at Oxford, but by July, a second glimpse at what life was like among the dreaming spires persuaded me to turn it down. Instead I found myself dashing off a late application to King's College, London, partly because its French Honours course was highly regarded but chiefly because, after consulting the *A to Z*, I'd worked out it took under fifteen minutes to walk from there to Regent Street.

Regent Street? Its attraction stemmed from an article I'd come across in the *News of the World*, a paper my parents disapproved of, about a police raid on a private club called The Mousehole, which, the writer helpfully explained, was 'off Regent Street' and patronised by men in thrall to unspeakable debauchery and vice. (Worse, some of them, like Mr Armstrong, wore make-up.) By then, I knew I was gay, and despite Aberystwyth's abhorrence of wayward inclinations, it didn't worry me one bit. Jack Bradley had been a good role model. Apart, that is, from the business with the hole in the wall.

It was in school, oddly enough, that I learned self-acceptance. Responsible for it was our English master, Georgie 'One Ball' Rowlands, the man who never bothered to read our essays. On the syllabus that year was Oscar Wilde's *Importance of Being Earnest* and before tackling it, though 'tackle' does the work an injustice, Mr Rowlands read aloud the introduction printed in our textbook version of the play. Largely an account of Wilde's life, it ended with a reference to 'the tragedy' that caused his downfall and, it was suggested, his eventual death.

Now, like others in the room, I knew what was meant so when one boy, the self-same Donald Evans who'd enquired about harlots, mischievously asked what the tragedy was, I dreaded what might follow. For a time Mr Rowlands said nothing, then, taking off his glasses, he began to speak. Gravely and very softly.

"Well, Donald," he said, "you know that most men fall in love with women. Now there are some men who fall in love with other men instead."

I no longer remember what followed. Perhaps I never heard it. In any case it had ceased to be important. What mattered was the word 'love'. That Mr Rowlands, never a favourite of mine, made no distinction between the love a man might feel for a woman and the love he might feel for a man brought me the reassurance I secretly craved. All of a sudden, my adolescent longings were exempt from guilt, even if there was fat chance of indulging them in Aberystwyth. Apart from the interior designer whose shop Bronwen Llain sometimes kept an eye on, I knew of no one else who was gay. True, there'd been talk of several local men, a town councillor among them, glimpsed trouser-less one night behind the golf club, but my father maintained they were Freemasons conducting lodge business al fresco. I believed him.

"I'll be fine," I assured my parents when the day finally came to leave home. Mr James said the same. The night before my departure I saw Mrs Caradoc Evans for what would be the last time. She'd turned up at the house with a Dupont cigarette lighter, tortoise-shell with gilt edging and, I suspect, no longer new, but neatly gift-wrapped, as well as a card bearing the address of the United Lodge of Theosophists in London.

"You'll miss your visits to Mr James," she declared, the two by then half reconciled, "and you'll miss his words of wisdom. These people will make up for it. The woman in charge is a friend."

She also brought with her a bottle of champagne, insisting we empty it there and then. Slightly squiffy, in her words, by the time Captain Hewitt came to collect her, she paused on the doorstep to warn me never to sit on the seat in public lavatories. A woman she knew had caught something unmentionable doing just that on Clapham Junction station.

The train next morning was the Cambrian Coast Express, leaving Aberystwyth at eleven o'clock and arriving in Paddington just after four. Mr James was already there when we got to the station but that didn't stop my mother shedding tears.

"When I left home my mother never cried," chided my father, "and don't forget I was off to war."

"It's not the same," she sobbed. "There were eight of you. I've only got the one."

"I'll be fine," I said for the umpteenth time.

And I was. By the time of the Freshers' Party I felt I'd been in London for months, if not years. No longer did I need to consult the map when travelling by Tube, and the bus routes I'd begun to memorise as well. And no snooty academic, *Evening News* or not, was going to blame what happened that night in Tanrallt on drink or self-delusion.

"I'm satisfied my OBE was real, not something I imagined."

Still looking bored but willing to indulge me, the lady parapsychologist asked what made me so certain.

With that I proceeded to tell how in bed the next morning, I too had tried to persuade myself the previous night's adventure was just a silly dream, a moonstruck fantasy brought on by a cheese-and-pickle supper and the incense Mr James had lit to make the room smell sweet. And yes, when the time came for me to push aside the bed clothes and get up, I was all but sure of it. But something had put paid to all that.

For as the sunshine spilled across the little bamboo table next to the bed, passing over the stub of candle in its china saucer, it seemed suddenly to pause. And there, in the candid light of day, not in fickle moonlight, lay the sprigs of vervain I had picked the night before, their grey-green leaves still wet with dew, their purple-lidded flowers half open. I touched them to make sure they were real.

My listener gave a patronising smile. The bored look suited her better. [29]

---

29 My 'disembodiment', real or imagined, is similar to the cases described by the Swiss neurologist, Dr Olaf Blanke of the Brain-Mind Institute at the Ecole Polytechnique de Lausanne, in an important article: 'Out of the Body Experience and Autoscopy of Neurological Origin' (*Brain*, vol. 127, Issue 2, February 2004, pp. 243-258). For the record, I should add that the lady academic to whom I recounted my adventure in Tanrallt would later write about the topic as well.

12

**"There are relative truths and we have to make
the best we can of them."**
H. P. Blavatsky

I never did find the Mousehole but it was not for want of trying. Forays into every alley and side street between Oxford Circus and Piccadilly were unproductive, and neither the telephone book nor Kelly's Directory was any help, while it seemed imprudent, even reckless, to approach a policeman. The final humiliation came when I plucked up the courage to ask a prostitute, least intimidating of the sisterhood gathered outside the Regent Palace Hotel, only to be told, not unkindly, to go home to my mother. With that I gave up.

My intention had been to rent a bed-sitter to begin with, then go on perhaps to share a flat with a couple of others from my year. Barely a week before term started, however, my mother took fright, alert suddenly to the immorality rampant, if not through London as a whole, then at least in those parts undergraduates were disposed to favour. (The daughter of a chapel deacon had recently moved from Chiswick to Chelsea, epicentre of the *vie bohème*, and stopped writing home every week.) In the end, through friends, she managed to find a respectable Welsh-speaking family in Clapham who undertook to provide me with a room, breakfast and evening meal, with full board at weekends and all my laundry done, for a modest sum. To her, the south side of Clapham Common seemed far enough from Chelsea.

Hospitable though my hosts were, within a month I'd found myself a bedsitter, really no more than a box room, at the top of a house in Onslow Gardens which, being in South Kensington, qualified — just — as one of those respectable parts of London my mother approved of. A gas ring made up for the absence of breakfast, evening meal and weekend board, while a launderette off Brompton Road took sporadic care of my washing. It wasn't quite the *vie bohème*, but it was close.

A reminder of home arrived days later, in a letter from my mother, reporting that Mrs Evans, or Countess Barcynska as she'd reverted to calling herself, was impatient to know if I'd been to see the Theosophists and passed on her regards to the woman in charge. And so with nothing better to do one Saturday, I found myself in Bayswater Road on my way to their headquarters in Queen's Gardens, not far, as it happens, from where Dr Penry Evans had once lived with Dion Fortune, magician and latter-day Priestess of Isis, at 3 Queensborough Terrace.

Nowadays the pavement from Marble Arch to Kensington Gardens is forever busy, never more so than at weekends, when amateur painters exhibit their works along the park wall, row upon row of woodland vistas, graceless nudes and dire seascapes where the waves are oddly static and sunsets too vermilion to be true. Back then, however, things were quieter, but no less colourful, thanks to the prostitutes lined up there from noon until dusk, many (and this always puzzled me) holding elegant umbrellas which, like Mr James, they seemed never to unfurl, not even when it rained. Listless and indifferent though they seemed, these ladies had about them an edginess, an air of defiance, which I relished. As a rule, they left you alone unless you happened to slow down or betray a flicker of interest, although a scruffy, duffle-coated student like me could usually walk by without being noticed, let alone accosted, as indeed happened that bleak November afternoon.

My destination turned out to be a substantial double-fronted mansion with steps leading up to a pillared entrance, reminiscent of Uncle Davy's shop, and with the same down-at-heel look as its neighbours, the cream walls in dire need of paint and the stucco peeling off listlessly in places. The building might have seemed unoccupied, were it not for a discreet noticeboard that assured passers-by they'd be welcome at any of the meetings listed. By no means reassured I rang the doorbell. 'Press hard' advised a handwritten card stuck beside it.

It took several minutes of pressing hard for anyone to answer but eventually the door opened a few inches and from within came a curt, interrogatory "Yes?"

The speaker, who showed herself only after I mentioned Mrs Evans or, rather, Countess Barcynska, was an elderly woman dressed all in grey and looking every bit as dilapidated as the building she took care of. On her feet were woollen bedroom slippers, likewise grey, with a coquettish red pompom on each. After allowing me inside, she locked the door behind me.

"One can't be too careful," she murmured. "This area went downhill after the war. Now it's all bedsits and," she nodded in the direction of Bayswater Road, "that sort of thing."

Facing me in the hall was a portrait of Madame Blavatsky, a scarf covering the back of her head and a central parting through what was visible of her short, crinkly hair. Peering straight ahead, one long-fingered hand cupping her chin, she looked monumentally fed up.

"Taken in 1888," I was told, "by Enrico Resta, the court photographer. He's managed to capture something of her mystery."

By then, I'd read enough to know that the only mystery surrounding the sitter was whether she was truly a miracle worker and 'the mouthpiece of hidden seers', as a sceptical report by the Committee of the Society for Psychical Research had put it, 'or merely a vulgar adventuress'. The same report, published in 1885, concluded she was neither but instead had 'achieved a title to permanent remembrance as one of the most accomplished, and interesting imposters in history.'

The recipient of this dubious accolade was born Helena von Hahn in Russia in 1831. A precocious self-willed child, she is said to have amused her playmates with her psychic powers and caused consternation among the superstitious servants looking after her. In 1849 she married Nikifor Blavatsky, eighteen years her senior, but not the doddery old man she'd later imply, possibly in order to justify having left him within a year — 'still' as she tactfully put it, 'a complete woman.'

By 1851, she and her father were in London for the Great Exhibition, and it was while both were ambling through Hyde Park that she first encountered a Rajput nobleman named Morya, one of the 'hidden seers' referred to by the Society for Psychical Research, though with consistency not among her strong points, she also claimed that her first encounter with 'the master of my dreams' happened one moonlit evening on the seafront in Ramsgate. Wherever it occurred, Morya invited her to visit him in Tibet.

According to her, the Master M, as she went on to call him, was 'someone so great that he towers above the rest of humanity for he has already attained the summit of ordinary human evolution'. As such, he belonged to a secret brotherhood whose members, no longer subject to the physical limitations we lesser mortals put up with, were active in promoting the moral and spiritual welfare of humanity. (Others involved in the enterprise include Confucius, Moses, Jesus, and, more surprisingly, Cagliostro.) Assisting Morya in this important work was another Master and fellow Sikh, Kuthumi lal Singh, familiarly known as Koot Hoomi, who would later play a significant role in Madame's life, although his day job was 'guardian of an Occult Museum in vast subterranean halls' near his home in Tibet. It was there that Madame Blavatsky claimed to have stayed when she finally made it into that country. Also in residence was Koot Hoomi's sister so the proprieties were duly observed.

Following her first meeting with the Master M, Madame Blavatsky spent the next seven years travelling all over the world, returning briefly to London in 1853 after a first unsuccessful attempt to enter Tibet from neighbouring Nepal. From there she journeyed to America, Japan and India before, now with luck on her side, managing to penetrate a few miles, but no more, into Tibet. Or so she maintained. More sceptical biographers contend that the only travelling she did was around provincial European opera houses, having by then become the mistress of an ageing bass named Agardi Metrowich. She is even rumoured to have borne him a child, a sadly deformed little boy, who died in 1867, although throughout her life she would insist she remained the 'complete woman' she'd been when she deserted her husband. What followed next is also disputed, with those sympathetic to her (and, to be fair, it's sometimes hard not to be) willing to accept her claim that, again in 1867, she was injured while fighting at Garibaldi's side at the Battle of Mentana, leaving shortly afterwards for yet another excursion to the Mystic East. This time, she claimed to have finally secured permission to enter Tibet.

One sympathetic biographer (who would later switch allegiance to Sai Baba) has offered this idyllic account of a typical day she spent there:

'Helena lifted her eyes from the old manuscript of Senzar characters that she was struggling to translate into English, and looked through the window. She never failed to get a great lifting of the heart from the mass of snow-capped mountains guarding the peaceful valley, from which no sound came save the occasional tingle of a distant cowbell or the warble of a bird from the trees behind the house. This, she thought, must be the abode of perfect peace and happiness. Sometimes she had to pinch herself to prove that she was really there in the flesh, and not suffering another of those double personality experiences, that she was actually in Shigatse, Tibet, living in the house of the Kashmiri adept Kuthumi Lal Singh. His sister and his sister's child were there too and, wonder of wonders, most of the time under the same roof as herself was the great Protector of her visions, the Master Morya.'[30]

30 Murphet, Howard, *When Daylight Comes*, Quest Books, 1998.

Alas, the harsh reality — even biographers need to pinch themselves from time to time — was that during this period Madame Blavatsky was traipsing with Metrowich from one seedy hotel to the next, the pair of them landing finally in Odessa where some of her kinsfolk were living. An observer noted that the couple looked a sorry sight, he 'a toothless lion perpetually at the feet of his mistress, an aged lady, stout and slovenly.' Stout she certainly was, as the picture in front of me suggested, perhaps a little untidy as well, but certainly not aged. After all, she'd yet to turn forty.

However much she might boast of meeting oriental sages not quite of this world or of visiting Tibet, the truth is that Madame Blavatsky began her occult career as an ordinary Spiritualist medium, even running her own *Société Spirite* in Cairo for almost two years before being forced to close it when evidence of wholesale fraud was uncovered. She had set sail for Egypt, still with Metrowich in tow, in 1871, but her companion was not one of the 16 out of 400 passengers, herself among them, rescued when their ship went down in the eastern Mediterranean, although she would always maintain he was poisoned by Jesuits after they had safely disembarked in Alexandria.

Nobody's fool, Madame rapidly became disillusioned with Spiritualism, although in her day the movement was relatively new. The craze had started in 1848 when the parents of two young girls, Margaretta (Maggie) and Catherine (Katie) Fox, of Hydesville, a small town in Wayne County, New York, heard rapping sounds coming from the room in which their daughters were supposed to be sleeping. On going upstairs, they discovered the girls sitting up in bed and conversing with the 'spirit' which, the children maintained, was responsible for making all the noise. The news spread rapidly and, now joined by curious neighbours, the adults devised a way for the spirit to answer simple questions by giving an appropriate number of knocks. By these means it identified itself as that of a pedlar murdered on the premises some years before. (Human remains were reportedly unearthed under the cellar at a later date.)

Within a short time, the girls were playing to packed houses in theatres and concert halls throughout the North East, now supported by an older sister, Leah, who, not to be outdone, had discovered that she, too, shared her siblings' lucrative talent. This being America, competition was not slow in coming and soon, with imitators springing up everywhere, the nation was gripped by a veritable frenzy of knocking, rapping and table-turning. The craze spread 'like a prairie fire,' as one commentator put it, yet in the 1850s, the flames still unquenched, Maggie Fox dismayed her devotees by confessing that the manifestations had been a hoax all along, the raps, she divulged, produced when the girls cracked the small joints in their fingers and toes. But far from ending their career, the admission gave it a boost. Now, the crowds that once flocked to marvel at the spirits, marvelled anew at the dexterity with which the ladies clicked their joints on command.

Until, that is, one sister declared that the earlier confession had been false and that the spirits did after all do the rapping. There followed a confusing series of confessions, retractions and still more confessions until, with two of the sisters hopelessly addicted to drink, it became impossible to determine where the truth lay. Not that it mattered, for rival mediums had in the meantime engineered phenomena more spectacular than anything so far accomplished by the Foxes, among them levitation, spirit photography, transfiguration (where the medium's features take on those of the departed) and, what would later become Mrs Duncan's stock-in-trade, full form materialisations. (To her credit, Katie Fox did have a valiant stab at these.)

Mired in controversy it might be, but the advent of Spiritualism was soon being proclaimed a turning point for humanity by supporters and spirits alike. Leah Fox herself called it 'the dawning of a new era', anticipating by half a century Sir Arthur Conan Doyle, for whom it constituted the 'New Revelation'. In 1853, five years before his death, the eminent social reformer, Robert Owen, born fewer than twenty miles from Tanrallt, was no less enthusiastic. His conversion followed a visit to Mrs Hayden, an American medium, who took London by storm, despite the tedium of her modus operandi: she handed her clients a card on which were printed the letters of the alphabet, then after putting a question to the spirits, they had to run a pencil down the letters until there came a rap. The corresponding letter was dutifully noted and after umpteen repetitions a reply of sorts would slowly begin to emerge.

Understandably, the big question for those stampeding to make contact with the spirit world was what conditions over there were like. In the event, few were disappointed even if, in Mrs Hayden's case, it took an awfully long time to find out. For virtually without exception they were introduced to a world reassuringly similar to this one but with none of its tiresome imperfections. The spirits, too, seemed much the same as they'd always been in life.

Typical was Michalko Guegidse, a Georgian manservant of Madame Blavatsky's family back home in Russia. By then living in New York, having left for America in 1874, she had travelled one day to a farmhouse in Chittenden, Vermont, after reading in the press about the mediumistic prowess of the farmer's two sons, William and Horatio Eddy. Their seances were nothing if not rumbustious and the visiting spirits more plentiful and certainly more colourful than anything later managed by the likes of Mrs Duncan, herself no slouch. Prior to Mr Guegidse's entrance, dressed in national costume and happy to play Caucasian dances on a guitar, participants were entertained by a native American named Sanctum and his squaw Honto, a splendidly attired Kurdish warrior and an African witch-doctor sporting a golden headdress but precious little else. Unfortunately, the impact made by the Georgian manservant turned out to be brief when, shortly afterwards, word reached Madame Blavatsky that he was alive and kicking (and presumably still strumming his guitar) back home in Russia.

Still, some good did come out of her visit to the Eddy household for it was during a break in the entertainment that she struck up an acquaintance with another spectator, there to write an article for the *Daily Graphic*, who was to become her closest collaborator and, despite an estrangement some years later, her lifelong friend. It started when he offered her a light for the cigarette she'd just rolled. ("*Permettez-moi, Madame,*" he'd chivalrously murmured, all but exhausting his knowledge of French.) Theirs, he later recorded, was a friendship which, although 'it began in smoke… stirred up a great and permanent fire.'

The man so ready with the matches was a lawyer named Colonel Henry Steel Olcott, the honorary army rank awarded for his success in uncovering fraud within the New York Mustering and Dispersing Service. Like Countess Barcynska's tea-planting captain, he continued to use his title in civilian life, and also like him, had an interest in plant husbandry, having written a book on the cultivation of sugarcane. Married, and the father of two boys, he was, in the words of Madame herself, 'a gay dog' who after his wife left him, spent his nights in drinking clubs, none of them gay in the Mousehole sense, but perhaps not entirely respectable for all that.

By then I'd been staring at Madame Blavatsky's portrait for a good five minutes, her limpid eyes reminding me, oddly enough, of those of the man I'd met on Clogwyn Bedwyr. Pleased by the interest I was showing, the woman beside me suggested we take a tour of what she called the public rooms. Largest of these was a lecture hall on the first floor, austere and filled with rows of plain wooden chairs, its walls painted an institutional eau-de-nil green and the only interesting feature a row of life-size portraits behind the lectern. I forget who most of them depicted but I do remember that Colonel Olcott, famous for his beard, was not among them.

From here we proceeded to the library on the other side of the landing, my guide's voice dropping to a whisper as we entered the room, even though it contained nobody and, to all appearances at least, had been empty, not to say undusted, for the past thirty years. At one end, facing the window, hung a portrait of Koot Hoomi, the work of a German artist who, I was told, perceived the sitter clairvoyantly. Madame Blavatsky had declared it a perfect likeness and ordered a companion portrait of Morya, also in the library but less conspicuously displayed.

There was no sign of either Mahatma on the evening of September 7 1875, when the idea came to Madame Blavatsky or to Colonel Olcott — neither could agree to whom it came first — of founding what would become the Theosophical Society, its purpose to 'diffuse information concerning those secret laws of Nature which were so familiar to the Chaldeans and Egyptians, but are totally unknown by our modern world of science.'

They and a group of friends, seventeen in all, had gathered in Madame's apartment at 46 Irving Place, Lower Manhattan, to hear a talk on 'The Lost Canon of Proportion of the Ancient Egyptians' by George F. Felt, an architectural engineer with occult leanings. Professing to be familiar with the secret laws of Nature the society aspired to make better known, Felt undertook to return at a later date to teach his listeners how to evoke elementals, pocketing 100 dollars to cover his expenses. But the elementals declined to be evoked and Felt, too, quickly scarpered.

By then, Madame Blavatsky, her attention focussed more on Ancient Egypt than Tibet, claimed to be receiving messages both telepathically and by letter (in gold ink on dark green paper) from a certain Tuitit Bey, Grand Master of the Brotherhood of Luxor, as well as from a colleague of his named Serapis, the majority of them addressed to Olcott. Flattered though Olcott was, to be the object of such attention, he found the communications so banal that even he voiced doubts about them every now and then. But Madame was too busy to care, having commenced work on her first book, *Isis Unveiled*, its expressed purpose 'to prove that underlying every ancient popular religion was the same wisdom doctrine, one and identical, professed and practised by the initiates of every country, who alone were aware of its existence and importance.' By way of evidence, she pointed to 'the prevalence of a system of initiation; in the secret sacerdotal castes who had the guardianship of mystical words of power, and a public display of a phenomenal control over natural forces, indicating an association with preterhuman beings.' Prominent among these preterhuman beings were

Tuitit Bey and Serapis, as well, presumably, as the as yet unannounced Morya and Koot Hoomi. All of them, the author would maintain, had collaborated extensively in the book's production, although one critic, William Emmette Coleman, identified no fewer than two thousand examples of plagiarism in the finished text. Plagiarised or not, the first edition sold out within days.

The turning point in Madame's fortunes would follow in 1877 when she and Colonel Olcott moved to India and eventually settled in Madras. Within a short time, the society (which more or less moved with them) had amassed a large membership, thanks to Olcott's missionary zeal and, even more, to Madame Blavatsky's ability to produce signs and wonders in profusion. Most common of these were the so-called Mahatma letters, ostensibly written by the Masters in Tibet, notably Koot Hoomi, either on demand, having been telepathically requested by Madame Blavatsky, or on their own initiative. Sometimes these missives arrived by post or, more impressively, turned up in unexpected places, even on occasion dropping from the ceiling onto the head of their intended — and presumably startled — recipient.

But letters were not the only things turning up from nowhere. Once, on a picnic attended by Madame Blavatsky near Simla, it was found that there were only six cups and saucers for seven people, an extra guest having joined the party at the very last minute. Our heroine calmly told a member of the group to dig at a spot nearby and there, sure enough, he unearthed a cup and saucer perfectly matching the six others. A second miracle occurred at a dinner party shortly afterwards when Madame urged her hostess to name a missing object, anything at all, that she'd like to have restored to her. This turned out to be a brooch which had passed out of the family's possession some time earlier. "It will not be brought into the house but into the garden, I am told by a Brother" declared the mouthpiece of the Masters, leaving those at table to rush outside to search for it. And, sure enough, there it was, neatly wrapped in tissue paper, lying in a bed of nasturtiums. Only later would it emerge that Madame Blavatsky had retrieved the brooch from a Bombay pawnbroker some months previously, having bought the ticket from an individual known to both the owner and herself.

In 1884 and in poor health, she returned to Europe. Among those left behind to run the society's headquarters in Adyar — they are still there today — was an associate from her days with the *Société Spirite* in Cairo, an English woman named Emma Coulomb, together with her carpenter husband. Resentful at not being put in sole charge of the premises, Emma turned up one morning at the home of a Reverend George Patterson, Presbyterian minister and editor of the *Madras Christian College Magazine*, bearing a bundle of letters. In them Blavatsky appeared to be soliciting the Coulomb's help in faking the miracles for which she was famous, help that included impersonating Koot Hoomi and fixing sliding doors behind a small wooden cabinet, respectfully known as 'the shrine', that hung against a wall between the so-called Occult Room and Madame's bedroom next door. An aperture in the wall made it easy to smuggle into it letters and other small objects, encouraging visitors who had been shown the empty cabinet seconds earlier to think the Masters had miraculously placed them there.

As if publication of these documents in the article ('The Collapse of Koot Hoomi') Patterson wrote for his magazine and in a subsequent pamphlet weren't trouble enough, the newly formed Society for Psychical Research now dispatched one of its youngest and brightest members, Richard Hodgson, from London to investigate the wonders reportedly taking place in Adyar. It was his negative conclusions, some of which have since been called into question, that led to Blavatsky being described as 'one of the most accomplished, ingenious and interesting impostors in history', She responded by threatening to murder the Society's bosses, but in the end contented herself with an irate letter to *The Times*. The editor declined to publish it.

"What is one to do?" she is said to have asked a compatriot, Vsevolod Solovyov, late in her life, though we've only his word for it, "when in order to rule men, you must deceive them, when in order to catch them, it is necessary to promise and show them playthings?

Why, suppose my books and *The Theosophist* [the Society's magazine] had been more interesting and serious, do you imagine I should have anywhere to live and any degree of success unless behind all this there stood 'phenomena'?"

It would take more than tribulations of this sort to finish off a woman who in her day had fought alongside Garibaldi, survived shipwrecks, travelled the world on her own and ventured deep inside the mountain fastness of Tibet. (At one point she'd even ridden bareback in a circus.) Indifferent even to the resignations pouring in from disaffected members of the Society, she pressed ahead with writing what her supporters rank as her crowning achievement, *The Secret Doctrine*, subtitled '*The Synthesis of Science, Religion and Philosophy*' which appeared in 1888. And it is for this that many would like her to be remembered, not for the serendipitous teacups, the missing brooches, the unexplained knocking that occurred in her presence or the invisible 'astral bell' that tinkled prettily on command. It is possible that early in her career she deemed it necessary to perform such sleights of hand, even to invent her Masters, Egyptian and Himalayan alike, then compose the letters attributed to them, inventing also the ancient texts in long dead languages she pretended her unseen Masters had shown her. (*The Secret Doctrine* purports to be a commentary on one such text, the Book of Dzyan, written in an unknown language, the precursor of Sanskrit, called Senzar.) Her deceptions were possibly intended to lend weight to the message she craved to present to the world, done in the knowledge that without them, few would have paid attention to a 'stout and slovenly' Russian exile with a questionable past.

Her final years were spent in London, first in the South Norwood home of the novelist Mabel Collins, then in Holland Park and finally with Annie Besant, well-known free-thinker and socialist, who became a convert after reviewing the *Secret Doctrine* for the *Pall Mall Gazette*. Meanwhile her enigmatic Masters remained discreetly in attendance and often the air around her was mysteriously filled with a fragrant scent of incense, a sure sign of their presence. Even the little astral bell tinkled prettily from time to time. But her health was failing and she died on the morning of 8 May 1891, two months short of her sixtieth birthday.

By now my guide and I, tour over, were again in front of Signor Resta's portrait, the date of its subject's death, like that of her birth, shown on a small card tucked into the base of the frame. Below it on a table covered with green baize rested half a dozen books and an assortment of pamphlets, all looking as if they'd lain there undisturbed for years. Although I could ill afford it, I felt morally bound to make a purchase so ended up buying a history of the Theosophical movement from its beginnings in 1875 to 1950.[31]

"It's a very balanced account," the owner of the pom-pom slippers assured me as she put it in a paper bag, adding a complimentary bookmark on which was reproduced a painting by Paul Klee, at one time a student of Theosophy.

"Klee described his work as taking a line for a walk," I volunteered.

"And she," — there was a deferential nod towards the portrait — "showed him the path to follow."

Her pert reply did full justice to the pom-poms.

---

31 *The Theosophical Movement* (1875-1950), The Cunningham Press, Los Angeles, 1951.

13

"Esprit, es-tu là?"

Having set out to conquer the world — well, conquer London for starters — I soon discovered there was no world out there waiting to be conquered. Or if there was, I'd not managed to find it. (I hadn't even found the Mousehole, for Heaven's sake.) On Saturday nights I would tramp around the West End searching for something, but never quite certain what. Love? Companionship? Sex? All three perhaps, preferably together, although just one would have done nicely. With that in mind, I'd loiter outside Cecil Gee's, a trendy menswear shop in Shaftesbury Avenue, affecting to study the window display but in reality hoping someone — anyone — who was male, not much older than me and reasonably good-looking, would sidle up and start chatting me up, then, chatting-up over, whisk me back to his place. (At that point things became vaguer.) In the event, no one did. Which may be just as well. We'd have both been disappointed.

At the end of that first year it was decided to test our progress by requiring us to translate, sight-unseen, a text from English into French, the one chosen being a dense piece by Kenneth Tynan, theatre critic of the *Observer*. All the more gratifying was it therefore that when Professor Cocking, his books on Proust still in print, turned up in person with our marked papers, I spotted mine on top of the pile. No sooner had I contrived to look self-effacing than the Professor announced he'd be proceeding in reverse order, the worst effort first. And that worst effort was all too plainly my own.

Back home I told Mr James. He advised me to learn from my disappointment, a tactful way of telling me to work (as he'd normally have put it) a fucking lot harder.

By then it was twelve months, almost to the day, since I'd stayed overnight at Tanrallt. To acknowledge the occasion, Mr James declared he had something to give me, something special. With that, he produced a book with a deep blue cover on which *The Equinox* was printed in red, and which I'd seen once before. On that occasion he'd read from it a Hymn to Pan composed in 1892 by Aleister Crowley. Now he proceeded to read again its opening lines, his rich baritone doing full justice to the poem's incantatory, quasi-magical, force:

'Thrill with me lissom lust of the light

O man! My man!

O Pan! Io Pan!

Io Pan! Io Pan! Come over the sea

From Sicily and from Arcady

Roaming as Bacchus, with fauns and pards

And nymphs and satyrs for thy guards...

"Don't believe everything you hear about Crowley," he cautioned when he'd finished. "He was bad enough but not as bad as he liked people to think."

"Those verses sound good."

"Not as good as they did at the old boy's cremation. They say you could have heard a pin drop when the chap reading them had finished. Wilkinson his name was. I met him once. He used to visit Cowper Powys in Blaenau Ffestiniog, skinny chap with dark hair. He put boot blacking on it."

With that he began wrapping the book up in brown paper.

"There's a piece by Blavatsky in it as well."

I'd earlier described my visit to Queen's Gardens.

"It's called *The Voice of the Silence*. Best thing she wrote, if you ask me."

Mr James seldom mentioned Aleister Crowley. One occasion had been when describing what magicians refer to as 'conjuring to visible appearance', by which they mean the willed displacement to our world of entities not normally resident in it. I suppose my adventure on Domen Bedwyr might be one such case, although no conjuration was involved, not on my part certainly. Another would be Mrs Duncan's cast of revenants or at least those not made of papier-mâché or regurgitated cheesecloth.

With mischievous relish, Mr James now proceeded to recount how Crowley, still only in his twenties but never one to duck a challenge, made his first attempt at conjuration, an exercise few magicians undertake lightly, by following a procedure set out in the Book of Abramelin. Composed in the fifteenth century, possibly earlier, the work is commonly attributed to Abraham of Worms. In it he recounts to his son Lamech, how he travelled to Egypt in pursuit of magical knowledge, finally coming upon the secret teachings of Abramelin, among them helpful instructions on how to get acquainted with one's Holy Guardian Angel.

Or perhaps not so helpful, given that the process is dauntingly cumbersome, requiring a full eighteen months of preparation, although in the corrupted version familiar to Crowley, based possibly on a text preserved at the Bibliothèque Nationale in Paris, these preliminaries are reduced to a third of that time.

In his *Confessions*, Crowley describes how he quit London for Scotland in pursuit of the recommended solitude, acquiring a house called Boleskine 'secure from observation and interference' on the shores of Loch Ness.[32] As instructed, he converted one of the north-facing rooms, with an east-facing window, into an oratory, carefully sprinkling fine sand over the terrace outside and erecting at one end a 'lodge' where the demons that are a by-product of the operation might be safely confined pending the advent of the Holy Guardian Angel. (Once he turns up, they become more biddable and far better behaved.) But Crowley had not yet mastered his trade and the spirits evoked, principally the four regents of the netherworld, together with a retinue of servants, escaped from the lodge and — literally — caused pandemonium. Worse, their malign influence persisted long after their departure, causing the Boleskine coachman, hitherto teetotal, to take to the bottle, while a lady guest of impeccable morals departed for London and took to the streets. Still more unfortunate was the local butcher who inadvertently cut his arm on a cleaver and bled to death on the floor of his shop,

"Take it with a pinch of salt," cautioned Mr James. "In any case Crowley got to meet his Guardian Angel in the end."

More necromantic in purpose was the conjuration undertaken in 1854 by the French magus Eliphas Lévi whose chief interest was the Kabbalah, a Jewish mystical system I'd get to know well only later, its principles, according to Lévi, as exact as mathematics and more profound than all other systems of philosophy put together. Not only did it offer the serious student privileged insight into the cryptic teachings of Abraham, Enoch, Hermes and King Solomon, but also invested in him the power to control unseen forces in what Lévi called the Astral Light.

Cryptic teachings I could do without and the comparison to mathematics, my least favourite subject at school, might have put me off,

---

32 Boleskine House, built in the eighteenth century, allegedly on the site of a church that burnt down with its congregation still inside, was acquired by Crowley in 1899. (He subsequently took to calling himself Lord Boleskine). The property is reported to have brought misfortune to several of its subsequent occupants and was itself severely damaged in a fire in December 2015. A report in The Scotsman (15 May, 2019) announced that disciples of Crowley had purchased the property and were planning to restore it. Some months later what remained of the house had fallen victim to another fire, assumed to be arson.

had the rest not sounded like fun. Moreover, given my residual attach-
ment to spiritualism — it would barely survive the summer — I was
drawn to Lévi's description of how, years before Mrs Duncan and the
Trianon Band, he had summoned up the shade of Apollonius of Tyana,
philosopher, wonder-worker and contemporary of Jesus: his biography by Flavius Philostratus was the cause of much bickering between
pagans and Christians, the latter uneasy about the similarity between
the events it described and the narrative found in the Gospels.

At the time Lévi was staying in London, possibly at the invitation
of the novelist Edward Bulwer Lytton, and he tells how, on returning
one night to his hotel, he found waiting for him the torn-off half of
a visiting card, with the Seal of Solomon on one side and a note on
the other explaining that the missing portion would be handed to
him outside Westminster Abbey at a certain hour the next day. His
curiosity aroused, Lévi kept the appointment and duly found himself
invited to step into a waiting carriage where a well-spoken woman,
her face concealed behind a veil, handed him the rest of the card.
She then proceeded to offer him all he needed — temple, ceremonial
robes and specialist equipment — should he consent to perform a
magical operation on her behalf, its purpose to conjure up the shade
of Apollonius and put to it a question of special importance to her. It
would, she pointed out, be an opportunity for him to ask a question
of his own, should he wish.

For the next three weeks Lévi reflected on the life of Apollonius,
even holding imaginary conversations with him, while for the final
seven days he observed a strict fast. When the big day arrived — it
was July 24th 1854 — the magus repaired to a room provided by
his benefactress, donned a white alb and crown of vervain leaves, then
stationed himself before a marble altar covered in lambskin on which
rested his magical textbooks, among them the *Nuctemeron*, a work traditionally attributed to Apollonius himself.

At the appointed hour, the necromancer, eyes tight shut, offered a
solemn invocation, while struggling to dispel the giddiness threaten-

ing to engulf him. When at last he found the courage to look over his shoulder, he glimpsed an apparition in one of the mirrors lining the walls but it took several more imprecations before it emerged and stood directly before him, a lean and melancholy figure, its beardless features as grey as the shroud it was wrapped in. At some point, the frightened conjuror managed to put to it two specific questions, the one requested by his patroness and the other of interest to himself, but no further conversation was possible for at some point the apparition reached out and touched the ritual sword Lévi was holding, causing his arm to go numb. With that, he fell to the ground in a faint. "Death" had been the answer to the lady's question, while his own involved the disclosure of certain secrets which, he boasted, "might change in a short space of time, the foundations and laws of society at large, if they came to be widely known."

What these secrets were, he never disclosed. Nor, to my knowledge, has there been much speculation about what they might be. It was Mr James who told me that before leaving London, Lévi called at an address in Soho where he divulged them to the man living there, a political theorist and occasional contributor to the *New York Herald Tribune*, who, like Lévi, had been influenced by the French Utopian socialist, Charles Fourier. (Lévi, who called his own beliefs '*le communisme néo-catholique*' had already been imprisoned following publication of his revolutionary pamphlet, *La Bible de la Liberté*.) The man he visited was none other than Karl Marx.

Do we owe the Communist manifesto, at least in part, to Eliphas Lévi? Or even Apollonius of Tyana? Probably not. In any case the former was never fully persuaded that the figure he saw and touched was really Apollonius, suspecting instead that the lengthy preparation and rigorous fasting had induced "a drunkenness of the imagination". At the same time, he confessed that while unable to explain "the physical laws" that allowed him to see and touch the apparition, see and touch it he indubitably did. "And this," he concludes, "is sufficient to establish the real efficacy of magical ceremonies."

As I was about to leave Tanrallt, Mr James went back inside the house, emerging a minute or two later with another gift, this one wrapped in newspaper.

"I know you're mad on circuses," he said gruffly as he handed it to me.

Only when I got to the main road did I unwrap the makeshift parcel. Inside was a piece of Staffordshire china that must have dwelt, unremarked by me, among the flat-faced dogs and other figurines, animal and human, on the dresser in Tanrallt. It depicted a bearded man, clad in a Roman tunic and meant to represent Isaac van Amburgh (1811-1865), an American lion-tamer and a favourite of Queen Victoria. He was depicted holding open the jaws of a lion with his bare hands. I still have it.

14

"Thomas Jefferson asked himself "In what country on earth would you rather live " He first answered "Certainly in my own where are all my friends my relations and the earliest and sweetest affections and recollections of my life." But he continued "which would be your second choice " His answer "France."
Thomas Jefferson

A t the beginning of my second year in college, I went to lodge with a respectable couple in Tooting, an arrangement similar to the one I'd abandoned twelve months earlier. The couple were in their fifties, and the husband worked for the London County Council, although I never discovered precisely what he did.

Until recently, the pair had enjoyed a modest notoriety, by proxy, so to speak, thanks to their uncanny resemblance to Laurence Olivier and his then wife Vivien Leigh. Their disappointment when the couple split up was still palpable, bringing an end, as it did, to the meals they'd been paid to eat in public view at posh West End restaurants, as well as appearances at suburban store openings and Masonic Ladies' Nights at the Café Royal, the latter the privilege they regretted most. "We've done all the Red Apron lodges," said the husband mysteriously one day "and we always got asked back." He later confided that he himself was 'on the square', although seeing him leave the house every third Tuesday wearing a suit and carrying a small leather case, I'd already guessed as much. I forbore to mention the shenanigans on Aberystwyth golf course.

Above all, I worked. Except for the odd film or night out with friends from my year, inside my room I stayed with my books. The faux-Oliviers, childless and glad to be parents by proxy, even to someone on the cusp of twenty, were quietly supportive, with the result that over the months that followed my French syntax improved by leaps and bounds, as did my acquaintance with every author of note from Antonin Artaud to Zola. And when not busy cramming, I set myself the challenge of ploughing through the two volumes, dauntingly titled 'Cosmogenesis' and 'Anthropogenesis', of Madame Blavatsky's *Secret Doctrine*. Even the long-winded Marcel Proust seemed a doddle after that.

In their third year, undergraduates could, if they wished, defer their finals and go off to teach English in France. This I now resolved to do and, after an interview, got a letter telling me I'd been assigned to a school in Brittany, not my first choice, had I been offered one, but not too disappointing either. While still trying to decide if I'd be happier in a city like Rennes or Nantes, or somewhere picturesque along the coast, the agency responsible for making the arrangements wrote to say I'd been assigned to Loudéac, a drab market town stuck in the middle of nowhere. It didn't even have a lycée, only a *cours complémentaire*, a place for country boys to get some kind of higher education, chiefly of a practical or technical sort, before going off to work at sixteen. That English was taught there at all, as well as in the girls' school next door, was due solely to its ambitious headmaster, Monsieur Le Bris, whose one aim in life was to have the school reclassified as a bona fide lycée. For him an English *assistant*, even if he happened to be Welsh, brought him one step nearer that goal.

His pride in the school was palpable on the Sunday I turned up there. After a dignified tea with him and his wife, he conducted me on a tour of the empty classrooms, uniformly drab and reminiscent of an old French film whose name I couldn't for the life of me remember. I stopped trying only when my guide ushered me into yet another room, no different from the rest, and I all but fell over a dead cow lying on its side beyond the door, '*Une vache tuberculeuse*' murmured Monsieur Le Bris, as if that were explanation enough, his only concern being my reaction to a strip of neon lighting fixed to the top of the blackboard. "Our Class 2 boys installed it," he announced, betraying no hint of disappointment when it failed to light up. For him the fact that it managed to stay in place seemed achievement enough. As we quit the room, with me doing my best to avoid the stricken cow, I remembered the film: *Zéro de Conduite*.

After a peep inside the dormitory upstairs — boys with too far to travel boarded from Monday to Friday — my guide led me through the playground to a low-walled brick enclosure next to the lavatories. Encouraged to peer over the edge I saw two pigs, one idly nudging a cabbage, the other seemingly lifeless but presumably asleep, though the *vache tuberculeuse* meant one couldn't be sure. 'For the winter,' murmured Monsieur Le Bris, loath perhaps to alert the victims to their fate. I was reminded of Tanrallt and of Mr James and briefly felt homesick.

And with that, my desultory tour came to an end, typifying what life in Loudéac would turn out to be like, although, happily, I was still unaware of it. As we parted, Monsieur Le Bris gave me a formal handshake, curling one finger, his middle one, inside my palm, something he'd also done when we met. The first time I'd assumed it was accidental, but now I felt less certain. Some days later, hearing him rage against a rival school on the far side of town, this one run by Jesuits ('*race de vipères*', he called them) I decided the handshake must be Masonic, although I couldn't remember the Olivier lookalike in Tooting doing anything similar when we were introduced.

Joan Moore, my equivalent in the girls' school, arrived a few days later and turned out to be no more English than I was, not only Scottish but, like many expatriates, fiercely determined to show and to sound it.

Clearly, whoever organised these things back in London had decided that Brittany and the other Celtic nations, with their uncouth ways and funny accents, deserved one another, while the rest of France was worthy of better. So the bona fide English were dispatched elsewhere, and few of them, I suspect, consigned to a *cours complémentaire*, let alone confronted by dead cows, bad electrics and doomed porkers when they got there.

By way of accommodation, I rented a room, accessible from the street, in the sub-basement of a house owned by a widow named Madame Le Pioufle. On one side of me was her garage, and on the other Madame's nonagenarian aunt, consigned below stairs but more fun by far than her niece. (I used to buy her a bottle of wine every now and then, as she insisted that a decent Beaujolais was the best thing for her anaemia, second best being fillet steak, preferably '*saignant*'.) According to my landlady's own account, privately challenged by her aunt, Madame Le Pioufle had been active in the Resistance during the war. "I 'ave slept with many Royal Air Force men in my attic," she assured me, keen to practise her English. Maybe she had.

Meanwhile my Scots colleague, Joan, found a room, just one street away, in a house that might well have been the model for the Bates family mansion in *Psycho*, all gables and lots of mock-gothic. On the day she moved in, her landlady, Madame Binginot, reminded her that water cost money, at which, as if on cue, her husband — the couple were well in their seventies — proffered the latest bill by way of evidence. With that Joan was told she might take a bath only once a week, must use the bidet sparingly and remember not to flush the lavatory, if all she'd had was a wee.

Meals we ate at an inn, L'Auberge de la Croix, not far from the school — in Loudéac back then one wasn't spoiled for choice — joining a bizarre assortment of regulars at a table in a private room behind the bar. Our number varied from four or five at weekends to twice as many during the week, mostly middle-aged men with jobs in or around the town, but also two women. Of these the older one, Solange, referred to always as Lozenge, ran the local telephone exchange, despite a lisp that made it hard to understand what she said, while the other, a mysterious creature called Monique, was reported to have been Brigitte Bardot's stand-in during the making of *And God Created Woman*. She wore black glasses at all times and owned the tiniest car I'd ever set eyes on, something called an Isetta. The male regulars liked to watch her climbing in and out of it. One day they got terribly excited after word spread that she drove it in her stockinged feet, even *sans* knickers, in hot weather.

It was in their company that I celebrated the eve of my twenty-first birthday. For the occasion the *patronne*, Madame Huby, produced a mammoth baked Alaska or *Omelette à la Norvégienne* as she called it, while the regulars helped me empty a bottle of Calvados, the result being that next day I kept to my bed until the evening when I cooked scrambled eggs for Joan and me, as well as two of her colleagues, the one, Thérèse, a woman so often crossed in love that the blame could only have been hers, the other our Bardot look-alike, Monique, by then engaged to an officer cadet at Saint-Cyr. "He's training to conquer," she confided in what I took to be a reference to their courtship until someone explained it was the Saint-Cyr motto. By then people were beginning to doubt her fiancé's existence, for although Saint-Cyr is barely fifty miles from Loudéac, not once had her officer cadet shown up in the flesh, let alone in the uniform — dark-blue tunic, red trousers and a shako with red and white plumes — Monique liked to boast about.

That night we indulged her, allowing her to prattle on about her Saint-Cyrien, real or invented, as she'd brought with her three bottles of vintage champagne, a gift from her father who owned a shop in Saint Brieuc. Shortly after midnight the four of us resolved to brave the cold and set off along one of the roads out of town but got no farther than the municipal cemetery, its tombstones an excuse for lots of maudlin speculation, fuelled by drink and far less profound than it seemed at the time, about life and the universe. I remember at one point I lay on a granite slab and looked up at the stars, determined to savour the terror Pascal had felt, on contemplating the 'eternal silence of those infinite spaces'. Our insignificance, like our mortality, is a sobering thought a few hours into twenty-one, even after too many glasses of Dom Pérignon.

By the end of February, the delights of rural Brittany, meagre from the outset, were all but extinguished, and so, with the consent of Monsieur Le Bris, I bundled my entire week's classes into three days, Wednesday to Friday, and took a room in Rennes, easily persuading Joan to follow my example. That way we could spend our weekends doing things not possible in Loudéac where the only highlights were a weekly film, years old but cheap to hire, at the town hall on Friday nights or a *soirée dansante* every other Sunday. In Rennes, we could study at the University library on Mondays and Tuesdays, as well as attend any lectures of interest. The only nuisance was that although Rennes was barely forty miles away, the bus from Loudéac took well over two hours to get there, meandering through the countryside as if to no purpose. Yet for reasons long ago forgotten, we never took the train. Perhaps it cost too much,

And it was from the bus one Friday, with Joan and me the only passengers on board, that I spotted a circus poster nailed to a telegraph pole on the outskirts of Rennes. Back at once came the old infatuation, its object less the attractions on offer — few ever lived up to their promise — than the notion of the circus itself, a feeling akin to nostalgia but with nothing in my past to feel nostalgic about.

By then the bus driver, it was usually the same one, had got to know us well so with no other passengers on board he let me disembark and examine the poster. Back on the bus I told Joan we'd be going to the circus next day. My treat. We even went there by taxi.

I must have been in funds for I also splashed out on the most expensive seats, a mistake as no one else had done the same, leaving Joan and me conspicuously alone at the ringside, while the other spectators crowded onto rows of tiered wooden seating farther back. They probably had a better view and for less than half the price.

The circus was small and, whatever its posters might boast, con-

spicuously down-at-heel, even shabby. As often the case, the wild animal act, in this case 'Luca Lambert and his forest-bred Lions', was the
final item at matinée performances and the opening one at night, an
arrangement that allowed the Big Cage, once erected, to be used twice
before being dismantled. As a result, the bars were directly in front of
us as we sat waiting for the show to start, so close that we could easily
have reached out and touched them, while an acrid scent of lion pee
wafted from the damp sawdust. I found the smell exciting. Joan said it
reminded her of Madame Binginot's.

At last a four-piece band played a few rousing chords, more noisy
than tuneful, after which an elderly man in sequined dinner jacket,
introduced on the tannoy as Monsieur Loyal, the French term for
Ringmaster, bade us welcome and, in a torrent of superlatives,
announced the first act. Scarcely had he finished speaking than the
forest-bred lions sauntered into the ring, each pausing to sniff the air
before jumping listlessly onto stools set at intervals around the cage.
Finally, into their midst, accompanied by another fanfare and lots of
flashing lights, strode their indomitable trainer, black-haired and handsome, bare-chested and studiously morose.

Squeezed into red tights, with black leather belt and golden boots,
he languidly commanded his charges to jump through hoops, as well
as over one another, roll on the floor, sit on their haunches, walk along
a plank and form a pyramid, before lying on his back and inviting the
animals to approach him one by one and flop down across his legs and
upper body. After some twelve seconds, at a signal from him, each in
turn got up and quit the cage, the last one borne aloft on their trainer's
impressively broad shoulders. The applause from the benches behind
us all but drowned out the four-piece band but the recipient of it, now
alone in the ring, seemed indifferent to the acclaim. A tilt of the head
and he'd gone.

It was then that Joan leaned towards me and whispered "Was he
staring at you or at me?"

I'd not noticed him staring at either. But then my eyes were focussed on the forest-bred lions. Well, on them and on the crimson tights. At that moment a dozen Arab youths, later to reappear as acrobats, set about dismantling the cage, the noise and bustle saving me the bother of a reply.

At the interval Monsieur Loyal, now in top hat and tails and looking more like a proper ringmaster, urged us to visit the zoo alongside the Big Top, in his words "a veritable Noah's Ark". Joan had no interest but I went, despite knowing I'd find only a few ramshackle wagons, the largest of them home to the lions, and the rest to a couple of monkeys, a doleful Himalayan bear, perhaps a leopard or two, a porcupine and one or two parrots. I was not disappointed. About to leave, I suddenly glimpsed beside the lions' travelling den the man who'd earlier put its occupants through their languorous paces, now clad in blue overalls but looking every bit as morose as he'd done in the ring. It came as a surprise, therefore, when, catching sight of me, he grinned broadly and strode over. Within minutes I was telling him about the animal trainers I'd seen in the course of my lifelong affair with the circus, painfully aware that I was showing off. His smile suggested he knew it too, but didn't mind.

Back inside the Big Top, I handed Joan the raspberry-flavoured candy floss I'd bought her.

"That chap with the lions. You asked who he was staring at."

"And?"

"Sorry, dear, *c'était moi.*"

By arrangement, the taxi that brought us was waiting when we emerged from the tent an hour later. The journey back lasted fifteen minutes, by which time I was beginning to wonder how much the evening had cost me: the front row seats were a genuine mistake but the taxi clearly an extravagance when there were plenty of buses, as were the candy floss, the zoo and a souvenir programme. Back in Rennes, our first port of call was a building near the Place St Michel, where Joan rented a small attic room. I cannot be certain but I think we agreed to meet up the following day. What I do remember is that once she was safely indoors, I told the driver to take me back to where we'd just come from.

And bugger the expense.

15

"Mais tout cela n'était qu'un fragile mirage
Et je reste tout seul avec mes lendemains."
Gilbert Bécaud

What followed was meant to last forever. First love always does. In reality, it lasted six months. Well, six months and a bit. I'm rather pleased about the bit because when I succumbed to one of my 'crazes', as my mother called them, be it collecting stamps or coins, learning to juggle, keeping tropical fish or trying to build muscles, she'd say "I give it six months." In view of my record she was right, although six months was usually too generous. The bodybuilding, involving chest expanders and a pair of Indian clubs found in the attic, hadn't even lasted a fortnight. Only my passion for the circus, this and the supernatural, never went away. That I spent not just six months with the owner of the forest-bred lions, but six months and a bit, has always struck me as confirmation that he was more than just another of my crazes.

Needless to say, the change meant some readjustment. Those weekends in Rennes went by the board for a start, as did the Mondays and Tuesdays that came after them. As luck would have it, Joan was by then more and more involved in a study project involving the castles and fortresses of Brittany, one that required her to visit as many of them as she could manage to fit in. As a result the four nights she spent each week in Rennes no longer made any sense.

And so, while I ran off with the circus, she hired a moped and set off to visit her châteaux, within hours ending up in a ditch, her *vélomoteur* beside her, while on her way to Tonquédec. After that, she travelled everywhere by bus.

That I'd run off with the circus would have alarmed my parents, had they learned of it, but not altogether surprised them. The warning signs were there all along. More than two years had passed since I'd left home but my bedroom wall was still festooned with posters I'd collected as a boy, the roll call still fresh in my mind even now: Kayes Bros. Circus (with 'Jubilee, the untameable lioness'), Ringland's Circus, Yelding's Premier Circus ('with a reputation second to none'), Cody's Continental Circus, Tom Fossett's Royal Hippodrome Circus, Lord John Sanger's Circus and Rosaire's Circus, the last with Captain Jim Parsons, not a patch on Luca, and three well-tempered lionesses.

On reflection I don't even think it would have surprised my parents to learn that not only had I joined the circus but moved in with its lion tamer — or trainer, as Luca preferred to be called. (In French the term is *dresseur* rather than *dompteur*.) For him the distinction mattered because no lion or tiger, whether born in the wild or in captivity, was ever fully tame, while the relationship between man and beast relied on mutual respect, even affection, not on fear and intimidation. Inside the big cage he was no more than first among equals, respected rather than feared.

By now public opinion is hostile to the notion of performing animals, a change on the whole to be welcomed. That said, circuses have become an easy target for those concerned about animal welfare yet reluctant to take on the vested interests: economic, social, and political, that sustain, for example, the intensive rearing of livestock, and sports like horse- and greyhound racing. Picketing the entrance to a small family circus that boasts a few Shetland ponies, perhaps a zebra or an elderly camel, is easier (and probably safer) than waving placards outside the Royal Enclosure at Ascot.

I remember sitting in the sun one morning, Loudéac by then well behind me, chatting to Luca's uncle. Though past seventy and unsteady on his feet, he served as ringmaster at every performance. "A glass of pastis keeps me going," he assured me, echoing Madame Le Pioufle's aunt and her faith in red wine. "It's the aniseed that does it." Known to everyone as Serge and, behind his back, as 'le Beau Serge', a reference to a film of that name, he'd been among the French soldiers evacuated from Dunkirk in 1940 and by opting to stay in London had acquired a fair command of English, certainly a better one than my landlady. That day he was reading a copy, several days old, of the *Daily Telegraph* I'd picked up in Pontivy, and must have got as far as the racing pages, for he looked up and asked if I knew where Goodwood was. I didn't. Before I could answer, however, he put down the paper and said "You know, if one of my horses dropped dead in the ring, let's say of a heart attack, there'd be a huge fuss. They might even force us to close. Yet a racehorse dies, say jumping over a fence, and things carry on as before." Several decades have passed since that conversation and few British circuses now own horses or ponies. Meanwhile at Aintree and elsewhere the horses still go over the sticks and, of those, some end up dead.

Every other morning the big cage was put up inside the Big Top and the lions, indolent by nature, were encouraged to play with old tyres or bits of tree trunk left about for that purpose. Often Luca would pick up a chair from the ringside and sit down among his charges, barely looking up from his newspaper when one of them approached and rubbed against his legs like a friendly pussycat. Once he confessed that his greatest fear at every performance was that the animals might enter the cage, curl up and doze off, made drowsy by the lights and all-pervading warmth inside the tent. The whip-cracking and the fortissimo efforts of the four-piece band were in part designed to forestall it. That said, the performance was not without danger. At any moment a fight risked breaking out among the animals, putting their trainer in peril, or an unexpected incident might unsettle them. A story told to me by Serge concerned a young man, Adolf Kossmayer (the name has stayed with me), who decided one hot August afternoon to give his polar bears a bath, only to slip on the soapy water and accidentally nudge one of them, his favourite and most docile of the lot, with his elbow. The bear felled him with a single blow.

"It 'appened in England. In 'Astings" he went on, "I knew the boy's father. He took over the act."

"And the bear?"

"Oh, it carried on performing. It wasn't to blame. On the contrary it was a good-natured beast."

As the weeks went by it should have dawned on me that I was as much in love with the circus as with Luca, possibly more. Helping to pull off sweaty red tights after every performance loses its appeal when what's inside them is reassuringly familiar. I knew, too, that in his affections I came second to the forest-bred lions and such would be the case no matter what. Meanwhile as time went by, the routine of stacking wooden seating onto lorries after the final performance in every town we visited, not to mention folding yards of wet canvas by the light of dipped headlamps, began to lose much of its charm. And although each place we stopped at was different, their names alone testified to that, there was about them a depressing sameness, perhaps because the circus functioned in a world of its own, apart and slightly aloof. Were that not the case, it might have lost a little of its magic.

Neither Joan nor my parents were aware of my secret life, although it took ingenuity, as well as careful planning, to keep it from them. Only once did I come close to discovery and that was quite early on. At the time, the show was still travelling through central Brittany, more or less haphazardly so far as I could tell, with the result that I seldom knew which town or village was next on our itinerary. Unaccustomed to so much hard work — I never properly got used to it — I had fallen into so profound a sleep one Sunday night that I didn't stir when our caravanserai set off at first light for the next town. We'd already arrived when I finally woke up.

I got dressed — Welsh modesty would be my salvation — and emerged into the sunshine, meaning to fetch water from a churn at the bottom of the steps and make coffee. Suddenly I heard excited cries of "It's Monsieur! It's Monsieur!" and beheld a row of small boys perched on a wall fewer than a dozen yards away. The wall, as well as the building behind it, seemed familiar, as indeed did the boys. We were parked right next to the *cours complémentaire* in Loudéac, its boarders out in force to watch the tent go up.

"What are you doing, Monsieur?"

"Monsieur, monsieur! That's where the lion tamer lives!" Paintings of lions, fangs and claws bared, adorned the sides of the wagon.

A barrage of questions followed before I thought of a response.

"What do you think I'm doing? I've been giving an English lesson."

That I was barefoot and holding a saucepan, I failed to notice. Happily, so did the boys.

In the months that followed I managed to persuade myself that my future lay with Luca and his Uncle Serge's down-at-heel circus. Here was my chance to live what up to then I'd only dreamt about from as far back as I could remember, so far back I'd sometimes wonder, only to dismiss the notion, whether I'd brought into this life the memory of a former one. Never, I kept telling myself, had I felt more content.

Only towards the end of August, following two weeks of rain and high winds, with several performances cancelled for fear the tent might come down mid-performance, did I face up to my doubts and, once acknowledged, these grew stronger by the day. A new academic year, with finals at the end of it, was due to start in three weeks and the college expected me back. So did my parents, by then aggrieved because my letters were infrequent, as well as puzzled because each bore a different postmark. (I told them I was helping Joan with her castles.) Their own letters to me they addressed, as instructed, to a farm near Le Mans where the circus spent part of the winter. Luca's grandmother lived there and dutifully sent them on.

"You're planning to leave us."

The words were unexpected yet no surprise. I was helping Serge count the previous day's takings, so meagre he scarcely needed my help. The way he spoke made it sound more like a statement than a question and that saved me from having to respond.

"You can always come back, you know," he continued gently.

"It wouldn't be the same."

"*Jeune homme*, you're far too young for things to stay the same."

He offered to break the news to Luca. Tempting though that was, I knew it was my place to do it, not his. For the first time since the cab dropped me off on the outskirts of Rennes, unsure where to go or what to say when I got there, I felt relieved that for Luca the lions always came first and me second. A close second, admittedly, and knowing how close made my job harder.

A week later, I was on the ferry to Portsmouth. That week, the circus was parked on the outskirts of Caen — it seldom ventured deep into the towns it visited, space being scarce and rents too high — so Luca insisted on driving me to Le Havre. Inside the car barely a word passed between us. Three days earlier the company had organised a whip-round and bought me a Caran d'Ache fountain pen, their plan to have my initials engraved on the stem unrealised, ostensibly because time was too short, though what was short, I suspect, was the money to pay for it. From Serge, I received Henri Thétard's two-volume *Histoire Merveilleuse du Cirque*, while at the very last minute he pressed me to accept a bottle of pastis. "It'll help you on the journey," he said with a wink, "*Ça fait remonter le moral.*"

From Luca there was nothing. And I gave him nothing either. To do so would have signalled a finality neither of us cared to acknowledge, even if, deep down, we were by then resigned to it. Fifty years on, I still ask myself, admittedly not often, if the whole thing would have happened, had it not been for my infatuation with the circus, the forest-bred lions, the boots, the belt, and the tights, and would things have worked out, had I stayed? Sometimes I'm able to persuade myself that they would.

16

**"He who has gone, but whose memory we cherish, abides with us,
more potent, indeed more present, than the living man."**
Antoine de Saint-Exupéry

It was one of the Miss Davieses that wrote to tell me Mr James had
died. By then, a full year had passed since my return from France
and, with finals behind me, I was feeling demob happy, the more
so after learning I'd done better in them than anyone expected,
myself most of all. (Who says magic doesn't work?) At the time, I was
living in Hammersmith, in yet another bed-sitter, and Miss Davies discovered my address on a letter I'd sent Mr James two weeks earlier. (I
had wondered why, being usually punctilious, he'd not written back.)
By then my parents had moved to Llandudno, my mother's birthplace,
after my father, now sixty, decided to sell the business and retire. The
following Saturday, I took an early train, the Cambrian Coast Express,
from London to Aberystwyth.

The Miss Davieses still lived in the small cottage they'd been born
and brought up in, about a mile-and-a-half from Tanrallt and a ten-min-
ute walk from the bus stop. Despite being alerted to my arrival — I'd
sent them a postcard — they affected surprise on seeing me but their

delight was unfeigned, as was the welcome they gave me. By then close to ninety, as one of them boasted, without revealing exactly how close, they seemed little changed since that Saturday, several Christmases ago, when we'd sat together plucking geese, our fingers blue with cold but all of us too busy to notice.

I was duly ushered into the front parlour, reserved for visitors, its stone floor freshly scrubbed for my benefit, while in the air there hung a smell of baking and of 'homeliness', to me one and the same, while a longcase clock ticked gravely away in the corner. Our tea we drank piping hot from Crown Derby cups normally confined to the oak dresser, a row of matching plates stacked behind them, their call to duty an honour that hadn't escaped me. Like Mr Howells, the minister, I was now a BA (Hons) and entitled to the best china. Mr Howells was a Bachelor of Divinity as well, so the privilege didn't go to my head.

I now learned that Mr James had not died in Tanrallt. Nor in Aberystwyth hospital. Like Uncle Davy, he'd suffered a stroke, so a relative in Birmingham, alerted by the Miss Davieses, arranged for him to go into a nursing home close to her. The old boy must have hated it, although the same relative, a cousin several times removed, assured the Miss Davieses that parts of Birmingham were 'very leafy', so he'd not miss Pumlumon one bit. Neither believed her. In the event he died just days later.

Tea over, and having been pressed to eat the very last scone, I had in mind to walk from there to Tanrallt, but changed my mind. Nothing would be the same anymore. And both Miss Davieses agreed. Goodbyes duly said and assured of a bus within twenty minutes, I'd just set off when the younger Miss Davies, normally content to let her sister do the talking, emerged from the house and summoned me back. Laying her hand on my arm, she said gently, "He thought the world of you, you know."

I wished she hadn't told me. I regretted not having written more often.

On the journey back to Aberystwyth — the route still familiar although the house with the nanny goats seemed now to be deserted — I thought of the last time I'd visited Tanrallt. It was after my return from France, so a full year must have passed since then. That morning, I'd arrived to find an unfamiliar car parked outside and the owner, clutching a brown paper bag, about to climb inside. Nearby stood Mr James, with a tartan scarf around his neck which I'd never seen before. Come to that, I'd never seen him wear a scarf before.

"This gentleman," the visitor now informed me, with a deferential nod to Mr James, "understands nature better than your cocky scientists. They think they understand it because they know a lot about it. But knowing and understanding aren't the same. Not the same at all."

He had a Scottish accent. The scarf must have been a gift from him.

I knew what he was trying to say. Scientists do know a lot about the world and it is to them we rightly turn to discover what it's made of and how it goes about its business. Whether that helps us understand it any better is less certain.

The objective approach scientists favour is commendable up to a point, even if the objectivity they profess is never as thoroughgoing as they like to pretend, not least because they themselves are part of the reality under investigation. Absent from it is any real empathy between observer and observed. Yet fully to understand something, the entire person, feelings included, needs to be engaged, just as when we meet someone for the first time, we draw on subjective impressions, derived from what we have in common, to assess what he or she is like. That way we learn more, far more, than we might from more objective criteria such as shoe size, fingerprints, blood group or DNA profile. Similarly, it is what we share with the world that equips us to understand it better.

For people like Mr James the constituents of that world, though subject to change and causality, are essentially integrated within an immutable, because timeless and transcendent, whole. And paradoxically it is from its very complexity that the world derives its unity, one already implicit in each of its parts. This was acknowledged in the *Bhagavad-Gita* where Brahman speaks of 'the countless gods that are my million faces', as well as by Neoplatonists, with Plotinus declaring that 'the whole is in all, as well as in each part,' a view echoed by German philosophers in the nineteenth century, notably Hegel who taught that the Absolute, the ultimate form of unity, is composed of parts that have no meaning save that unity, while the latter has no meaning other than its parts. All of which boils down to the simple truth that reality is both many in one and one in many.

Now, whereas most people regard themselves as one in many and, as such, in objective relation to everything else, Mr James discerned, at times exploited, the reciprocity implied by this relationship, neatly summed up by the hermetic principle 'as above, so below'. From this it follows that knowing oneself, the γνωθι σεαυτόν of Delphi, is also to know, at least intuitively, both the Whole and the parts that comprise it, as well as the relationships persisting between them, some closer and thus more significant than others. The knowledge of how this network of sympathies operates in the natural and supernatural worlds, often in things seemingly disparate, is what made Mr James a magician.

Whatever form it takes, from the formulaic rites of the kabbalist to the targeted abandon of contemporary pagans and witches, the intention of every magician is to reconcile these twin aspects of reality, the part and the whole, or, if you prefer, the conditional and the absolute. And it is done by transcending, so far as feasible, the limitations which our presence in the — fragmented — here-and-now brings with it.

Among the means available to us are what are commonly referred to by occultists as 'correspondences'. (The Welsh term *cyfatebiaethau* took me ages to get used to and, frankly, is no more helpful than the English.) These, according to our necromantic friend, Eliphas Lévi, constitute 'the last word of science and the first word of faith', for they are, he claims, the means of identifying, as well as exploiting, the subtle relationships that bind together 'the visible and the invisible... the finite and the infinite.' Herein lies the fundamental principle, the very raison d'être, of practical magic.

Whether these correspondences — like the gods and goddesses, angels and archangels of popular tradition — are real or contrived is irrelevant. It is the confidence we invest in them that counts. And because that confidence, nourished by experience, has endured for centuries, it not only validates such correspondences and the rituals they invigorate, but invests in them a power peculiar to themselves. In each there cohabit something of this world and something of the wider reality that contains and, *ipso facto*, transcends it. The former allows access to the latter and, as a focus of the magician's intention, empowers him or her to effect change 'in conformity', as Aleister Crowley put it, 'with [his or her] will'.

The paraphernalia and nomenclature favoured by those keen to work magic, irrespective of doctrine, tradition or taste, are the means to this end, most by now invested, through conviction and practice, with a quasi-sacramental function, being in the words of St Augustine 'a visible sign of invisible grace'. Or, as our friend Eliphas Lévi once put it, 'the last word of science and the first word of faith… the sole possible mediator between the visible and the invisible, between the finite and the infinite'.

All types of magical practice have thus a common purpose, whether they follow the informal approach preferred by Mr James, or something more structured and ritualistic, with an abundance of what Lévi called 'strange words and numbers, grotesque laws and ritual acts, personifications and mystifications', not to mention the robes, candles, and incense that frequently go with them. All is grist to the mill provided it helps strengthen the creative powers of the imagination so that, as Lévi again remarked, 'a practice, even though it be superstitious and foolish, may be efficacious because it is a realisation of the will.' For it is the will that fuels the changes magic aims to secure, whether directly as Crowley and others maintained or, as Dion Fortune suggested, through a shift in the practitioner's consciousness. Each is a particular manifestation of the universal will that both quickens and directs the universe and all it contains — the whole caboodle, as Madame Blavatsky used to call it.

Such were my thoughts on the journey back from Pumlumon. News of Mr James' death must have prompted them, giving me a chance to take stock of what, essentially, he tried to teach me on those Saturdays we spent together in Tanrallt. Not that he'd have cared for such specu-lation, not one tiny bit. "Too highfalutin," he'd have said. And of course he'd have been right. As usual. For that's how it sounds. But then the young BA (Hons) on the bus that late August afternoon was too newly fledged to notice. Reflecting on these topics helped him forget that, with Mr James gone, what he'd lost was a piece not just of his past but of himself as well.

17

"I do not think that what is called love at first sight is so great
an absurdity as it is sometimes imagined to be. We generally
make up our minds beforehand to the sort of person we should like,
grave or gay, black, brown, or fair; with golden tresses or raven locls;
and when we meet with a complete example of the qualities
we admire, the bargain is soon struck."
William Hazlitt

A month later, the university offered me a research scholar-
ship and, with no better idea of what to do with my life, or
at least the next three years, I decided to accept, reckoning
it would give me sufficient time to make up my mind.

Within a week of my return, I happened to find myself one afternoon in Great Queen Street, a short walk from college. Strolling past
the art deco eyesore that is Freemasons' Hall, I suddenly spotted the
Psychic News Bookshop on the other side of the road. I'd forgotten
it was there. By then seven, no eight, years had passed since Maurice
Barbanell, the paper's editor and mouthpiece of my erstwhile chum,

Silver Birch, had published my letter.[33] In his reply to my mother after being forwarded the request for my picture, he'd written that one day he hoped to meet me in person. And so on impulse I decided that, provided he was on the premises, this would be that day.

Inside the shop, I found shelf after shelf packed with biographies of prominent mediums, manuals on how to develop clairvoyance and competing accounts of the afterlife, many written by people already in it. Also on display were crystal balls (small, medium and large), Kilner goggles (for viewing the human aura), planchettes and hand-crafted ouija boards in a variety of woods and finishes. Like Uncle Davy, Mr Barbanell occupied a small office at the back. He even professed to remember me. Perhaps he did. Not many schoolboys write to *Psychic News*.

A dapper little man with thick glasses, he was born into a poor Jewish family in London's East End where his father earned his living as a barber and, when required, as neighbourhood dentist. So overcrowded was their home, he now told me, that as a boy he'd often had to sleep in the barber's chair, ready to be evicted, should anyone turn up after hours for a quick trim or to have a tooth pulled. Eager to get on in the world he'd tried his hand at various business ventures as a young man, at one point being offered sole distribution rights in Britain for the gadgets of an American engineer, Edwin Land, later to invent the Polaroid camera. By then, however, Barbie, as everyone called him, had committed himself fully to Spiritualism, having received what he regarded as irrefutable evidence in its favour. Had he stuck with Dr Land instead of Silver Birch he'd have been a wealthy man but, possibly, a less contented one.

When I arrived, he'd just finished going through his post and as we chatted, kept fidgeting with the sheaf of papers in front of him, as if unwilling to stay idle, triumphantly removing any paper clips he came

---

33 For the record I should mention that Maurice Barbanell, founding editor of *Psychic News*, quit that paper in order to launch a rival publication, *Two Worlds* in 1946, returning to his former post in 1962. That he replied to my mother's letter during this interim period, suggests he remained involved in both publications.

across and consigning them to a small earthenware pot, one of a pair, on his desk. "Waste not, want not," he said primly when he caught me looking. With the pot overflowing — its partner contained what looked like dressmaker's pins — he seemed unlikely to know want, not want of paper clips at least. I wondered what Silver Birch made of it, his weekly talks replete with loftier concerns. When that happened, Barbie, seemingly asleep, would slump on a sofa while the words of his spirit guide, allegedly described by Lord Beaverbrook as 'some of the most beautiful in the English language', issued unchecked from his mouth.

I asked about Mrs Duncan. "A wronged woman," replied Barbie, himself a witness for the defence at her trial, although I detected a certain reserve, as if he were not altogether persuaded of her honesty. Keen to press him, I mentioned the ectoplasmic parrot. "Mrs Duncan cut corners," he conceded, "although our pets do of course live on.[34] Helen materialised a pet rabbit once. It had belonged to one of the sitters." (On seeing it, the rabbit's owner shamefacedly confessed to having killed, cooked and eaten it.) More reliable, he assured me, were mediums like a woman named Estelle Roberts whose spirit guide, another Native American and a close chum of Silver Birch, was named Red Cloud. "A fine figure of a man," declared Barbie "with long hair and a feathered headdress". With that, he rummaged in a drawer and produced two postcard-sized pictures, one of Mrs Roberts, and another of Red Cloud, their features remarkably, nay suspiciously, similar.

"No one can fool me," he protested, as if reading my thoughts, "I've got a sharp eye. I can spot a fraud a mile away."

And with that he peered through his pebble glasses, nose all but touching the desk, and tried in vain to find an errant paperclip. Before I left, he presented me with that week's edition of *Psychic News* and urged me to call on him again, but I never did. He died in 1981.

It must have been a day or two later — I know it was a Saturday — that I arranged to meet a college friend outside Lyons Corner House,

---

34 In 1940 Barbie's wife wrote a book on the subject (see Barbanell, Sylvia, *When Your Animal Dies*, new ed., Spiritual Truth Press, Leatherhead, 2000).

the one which in those days stood next to Charing Cross Station. Oddly enough I'd never once been inside any of their branches, possibly because, no matter how cheap and cheerful they might be, my mother disapproved of them. (Mock-gypsy bands played while customers chewed on their mixed grills, a practice she found vaguely louche, while someone had assured her that food left on people's plates was later used to reinvigorate the minestrone soup.) On family trips to the capital we normally made do instead with plain, self-service lunches at any branch of the ABC which stood for the Aerated Bread Company, with dinner at somewhere grander like Scott's, not far from Piccadilly Circus. On my fifteenth birthday, she even treated me to *fruits de mer*, minus oysters, something else she disapproved of, at Madame Prunier's in St James' Street. If my father, more frugal, were with us, we had perforce to lower our sights, although he did have a fondness for Quo Vadis, an Italian restaurant in Soho, but not so far into Soho as to compromise respectable people like us. It wasn't cheap, but in its window was an endorsement by Evelyn Laye, an actress whose resilience — her husband deserted her for a soubrette named Jessie Matthews — he admired, so he usually paid without quibble. Wherever we were, we never, ever, drank wine.

All this demonstrates that, while naive when I first turned up in London, my only ambition being to find the Mousehole, I was not unsophisticated. No one confident enough at fifteen to tackle Madame Prunier's *fruits de mer* could be that. Having my mother's aunt living with us had helped: a former lady's companion, she boasted of having done the Grand Tour three times, as unaware as we were that this was traditionally undertaken by young gentlemen and then only once. Influential, too, had been Countess Barcynska, as well as her foes, the Armstrongs, at whose flat I smoked my first cigarette and, sublime decadence, sipped Green Chartreuse on a Sunday night when I should have been in chapel. Admittedly, since then little had been added to my sparkle but this might soon change as later that morning my friend and I were scheduled to view an attic flat in Jermyn Street, bang in the middle of the West End, the address more appealing than the two rooms on offer but the rent just about affordable. What happened on my way into town put paid to all that.

It began just before ten o'clock, when the District Line train I was in stopped at West Kensington station, a drab little place that always looked sorry for itself, being stuck between Earls Court and Barons Court stations, yet spurned by the Piccadilly line trains that run between both. Even clunky old District Line trains seem loath to stop here, groaning and shuddering as the brakes are applied, then unwilling to open their doors when they do. And, true to form, the doors stayed closed that morning. Well, to be fair, they did try to open but not hard enough, for after parting an inch or two, back shut they slammed seconds later. By then I'd looked up from the book I was reading so when they finally consented to open, I saw him — tall, broad-shouldered, with high cheekbones and tow coloured hair — the instant he stepped inside the carriage. And improbable though it sounds, I knew there and then that everything about me, everything that was the me that boarded the train minutes earlier, was obsolete. Not lost completely, being accessible at a moment's recall, but withdrawn, as it were, to make room for something new. It would be hypocritical to pretend the cheekbones and tow coloured hair played no part in all this, but it was still only part and a smaller part at that.

No sooner was I aware of it than the train had pulled into Earls Court station where its doors perversely opened without protest. As they did, the young man, endowed with everything the skinny, full-faced, mousy-haired me had coveted since old enough to fret about such things, prepared to get off. Thinking back, I'm reminded of a junk shop I spotted once in Brussels, just off the Rue Belliard, called 'All our Maybes'. Watching this stranger about to leave the train, I knew he'd take with him the most important 'maybe' I'd known up to then.

It was a sidelong glance that did it, so fleeting it was all but imperceptible. Knowing how shy I was, I must have dithered for a good twenty seconds before jumping to my feet and out of the carriage just as the doors were closing. The delay cost me dear, for nowhere on the platform was there a sign of my quarry. Seconds passed — I've never been a quick thinker — before it struck me that he'd not had time to reach the exit, a good hundred yards to my left, so must have taken the escalator to the Piccadilly line below. And by then I was doing the same, racing down it two steps at a time. At the bottom on my right was access to westbound trains, the direction we'd just come from, so I made for the opposite platform, only to find it deserted and a train just pulling out. As the final carriage disappeared into the tunnel, I turned to go back up the escalator and resume the journey I'd so recklessly cut short, only to see another yard or two of platform behind me. And there stood the biggest 'maybe' of my life up to then.

What followed was awkward and formal. He apologised for interrupting my journey, hoped I'd let him buy me coffee — he was, he said, travelling to Green Park — and, once aboard the next train, we began chatting about Paris. (He'd noticed the French novel I was holding.)

For coffee he took me to a small Italian place in a side street. Clearly a regular, he was served, without having to ask for it, a banana sandwich that he offered to share. "My weakness — *ma faible*," he confessed with a grin, getting the gender wrong, but so what? Would I, he enquired, like to come to his place the following afternoon? I could think of nothing I'd like more, but endeavoured not to show it.

With that, Ronnie Herbert took a visiting card from his wallet, the address was in West Kensington, and proceeded to draw on the back a map of how to get there from the station. Above an arrow pointing to his flat he wrote *chez moi*, but was no sooner finished than he looked up, crossed out the '*moi*' and replaced it with '*nous*'. We'd known each other for barely half an hour.

My friend was forgiving when I met him, unconscionably late, at the Corner House. It emerged he'd not been all that keen on Jermyn Street anyway. Within days I'd moved in with Ronnie, my maybe not a maybe after all.

18

"I think 'lunch' is one of the funniest words in the world."
Stephen Sondheim

After two weeks together, I was still unsure what Ronnie did for a living. Much of his day was spent in the betting shop next door to our flat where he seemed to win more money than he lost, refuting my father's claim that only bookies end up in pocket. After one lucrative triple, I arrived home from college one day to find 'Dinner on me' spelled out in five-pound notes inside the front door. We went to the Caprice.

A few Sundays later, he took me to meet the euphoniously named Christopher Christian, rector of St Peter's in Limehouse, a late Victorian edifice and poor sister of the official parish church, St Anne's, one of six London churches designed by Nicholas Hawksmoor. Father Christian, by then in his fifties, had previously served at another St Anne's, this one in Soho, but been exiled to Limehouse in the wake of a scandal, its nature never divulged but not too hard to guess. His was a late vocation and his fondness for liturgical extravagance — smells, bells and winsome altar boys — may in part have been compensation for all the time he'd wasted.

The organist at St Peter's, Michael Williamson, later to become

Master of the Queen's Music, had previously lived at the rectory and was still a frequent visitor, but his day job — at least from 3pm onwards — was pianist at the The Colony Room, a drinking club in Soho run by Muriel Belcher and a black lady said to be her lover, who'd berated me for some trivial breach of etiquette on my first visit. From then on, I dreaded walking past her, as she guarded the premises like Cerberus before the very gates of Hell. By contrast Miss Belcher, though notoriously tetchy, was always affable — 'friendly' would be an exaggeration — confiding to me once that she'd grown up in Birmingham and knew Aberystwyth as a child. By then I'd grown accustomed to being referred to as 'she', knowing Muriel did the same with everyone else, regardless of gender. It was the 'Blodwen' I disliked.

St Peter's stood in the middle of what had formerly been Chinatown. Next to it was the Customs House, today an upmarket eating place, one of several in an area which back then made do with a Chinese restaurant, two fish-and-chip shops and Charlie Brown's, officially The Railway Tavern, where they served warm pies, scotch eggs, and pork scratchings. There was also in those days a one-armed man, his empty sleeve neatly folded and held in place by a safety-pin, who sold whelks and jellied eels from a barrow on the corner of East India Dock Road but only, I think, at weekends.

The rectory was half a mile away in Stainsby Road. Rebuilt after the war — a German bomb had flattened its predecessor — it had a generous walled garden, most of it lawn, at the back. It was under its roof that a sixteen-year-old Ronnie found refuge after running away from home, as, probably, had several of the youths we discovered lounging about when we arrived. Not only was it somewhere for them to live, but a chance also to meet older men, many of them friends of the rector from his days at Cambridge, who by then had enough money, fame or influence, sometimes all three, to help their favourites get on in the world. Several had turned up that Sunday.

Oddly enough, there was nothing squalid about the arrangement. So fastidious, so 'Aberystwyth' was I back then that my first inclination would have been to disapprove but that didn't happen. Instead I found the company so congenial — a stiff gin-and-tonic may have helped — that I began to wish I, too, had run away from home and found a bed on the premises. True, each group took advantage of the other but the bargain was a fair one, entered into freely and of benefit to both, while Father Christian, to his credit, saw to it that neither side came to any harm. What struck me, listening to their banter but too timid to join in, was the absence of vulgarity. There was campery, yes, and lots of innuendo, but so good-humoured was it, with each side gently making fun of the other, that neither had cause to feel patronised, still less offended or demeaned.

Conscripted by our host to do something useful in the kitchen — "The boys have their talents," he murmured, leading me away by the arm, "but cooking isn't one of them," — I found myself next to a theatrical knight I'd last seen playing Uncle Vanya in Chichester, but who was now peering at the label on a bottle of port.

"Christopher will go berserk," he murmured. "I've used vintage for the sauce instead of plonk. We're having lamb by the way. No doubt you can smell it." (I learned later that he and our host were contemporaries at Magdalene.) On the other side of me, slumped on a chair, legs outstretched and in everyone's way, was a middle-aged man with a face that might have looked boyish, had it been less puffy and its features, the mouth especially, less inclined to droop. Staring fixedly ahead were tiny bloodshot eyes that seemed to take nothing in, as if their owner had temporarily made himself scarce, although the *saucier* beside me, noting my interest, pointed out that Francis was simply very, very drunk. "And that's from the night before last," he added, finally relinquishing the port (1927 was the year on the label). With that, he asked me to pass him the redcurrant jelly.

The table at which we sat was a long one. In accordance with established protocol, the younger men, myself among them, were at one end, while our seniors, some half a dozen, gathered at the other. (Absent was Francis Bacon, still in the kitchen, now with eyes tight shut and presumably asleep.) My contemporaries were a merry, talkative bunch, confident and fully at their ease yet, to my surprise, so scrupulously well-mannered that I wondered if the vicar had been giving them lessons. From the chap on my right, thick-set, with curly black hair and green eyes, I learned that he worked as a stevedore on the Isle of Dogs but earned more 'up West' on a Saturday night than he made in a week on the docks. Another, sitting opposite, told me he lived on the premises and was halfway through his first book, news that struck me as implausible but turned out to be true. (Father Christian used to lock him in a room until a prescribed number of pages emerged from under the door.) A well-respected novelist, he is today better known than the fully-fledged version he pointed out to me at the far end of the table, nephew (and later biographer) of Somerset Maugham[35] "He's a Duke," my neighbour confided, though it turned out he was merely a Viscount.

At some point during the meal, one of our seniors north of the salt began telling a convoluted joke, much of it in French, though none of those around me paid attention. What it was about, I've forgotten, but I recall that it involved a canary and that the punch line, when it arrived, was capable of improvement, sufficiently so for me, emboldened by drink, to provide it and show off my French in the process. No sooner had the merriment died down than I was summoned to move up the table forthwith. That was my place from then on.

Much of the conversation, I've forgotten. Still fresh in my mind, however, is the moment when, to my surprise, the name of Aleister Crowley came up.

"Unforgivable what he did to poor Nina," our host declared, in what the lodgers used to call his churchy voice. Only later did I learn that Nina Hamnett was a painter, though I should have known, as she came from Tenby in South Wales.

"What a girl!" said my neighbour. "She danced starkers on a café table in Paris. In Montparnasse."

---

35 Robin Maugham, pen name of Robert Cecil Romer Maugham, 2nd Viscount Maugham of Hartfield (1916 -1981), novelist and playwright.

"La Coupole," murmured Vivian Cox, a film director whose films were so forgettable they'd been forgotten even back then. He would later return to teach at his old school, Cranleigh, where, by coincidence, he himself had been taught by Michael Redgrave, the man who'd been so cavalier with the vicar's vintage port.

"La Rotonde, not the Coupole. And it was a private party. Modigliani was there. On his last legs and not yet thirty-five."

This came from Brian Desmond Hurst, seated on Father Christian's right, someone people seemed reluctant to offend, none more than Mr Cox. I discovered later that he, too, directed films, among them, *Scrooge*, a favourite of mine as a boy.

It was my neighbour from Norfolk who explained to me what Aleister Crowley 'did' to Nina Hamnett, with others contributing their pennyworth from time to time. The story went back to 1932 when the artist suggested in her autobiography, *Laughing Torso*, that Crowley practised black magic, describing with a touch of malice, what purportedly went on at his 'Abbey of Thelema', a run-down building he'd rented near Cefalù in Sicily. In London when the book came out, and himself short of funds, the Great Beast sued author, publisher and printer for libel. Proceedings commenced on 10 April in the High Court but despite a bravura performance, the plaintiff lost his case after the judge, shocked by material submitted by the defence ("Dreadful, horrible, blasphemous, abominable stuff,"), intervened in the proceedings. The jury, not surprisingly, found in favour of the defendants.

"Nina was never the same after that," observed our host. "She hit the bottle hard, and then things went from bad to worse. I'd see her cadging drinks at the Fitzroy. In the end she jumped from her kitchen window. Third floor up. Poor woman, impaled on the railings and dead within days."

"What's Crowley got to do with that?" I enquired.

"A curse, you silly boy," roared Brian Desmond Hurst, his brogue enfranchised by drink. "Crowley put a hex on her. The wiles of the devil, no less."

"Ephesians, Chapter Six."[36]

As Father Christian offered the precision Hurst solemnly crossed himself, knocking over his neighbour's wine glass with his elbow. And with that, they all went on to talk of something else.

---

36 "Put on the whole armour of God, that ye may be able to stand against the wiles of the devil." Ephesians, Chapter 6:11.

19

"Poverty is the discoverer of all the arts."
Apollonius *(De Magia)*

O ne day Ronnie disclosed that his brother Teddy was doing time in the 'Scrubs'. I've forgotten what for, petty theft possibly, or handling stolen goods. Ronnie and his older sister Joyce were going to visit Teddy that afternoon, although in the event they got no farther than the gate, having failed to register with the prison authorities far enough ahead.

Joyce was plump and jolly, and I'd taken to her at once. Afflicted with alopecia, she wore an auburn wig that neither suited her nor fitted the shape of her head, forever moving about as if endowed with a bizarre life of its own. On special occasions, she used denture fixative to keep it *in situ*, but the paste never did the job as well as she hoped, so in no time at all the wig would resume its aimless peregrinations.

From Monday to Saturday, Joyce worked behind the till at a posh greengrocer's, now long gone, at the bottom of Queensway, directly opposite Whiteleys department store, which is likewise no longer in business. On Saturday mornings, Ronnie would go there to buy enough fruit and veg to last us the week, including exotic fare like mangoes, kumquats, guavas and papayas, all hitherto untasted by me. One day, he returned with a bunch of edible pansies.

How he managed to pay for this cornucopia puzzled me, for its abundance never varied, undiminished even after a calamitous week with the gee-gees. It was only when I came across an itemised till receipt at the bottom of a carrier bag that my suspicions were aroused, for the items listed on it were nothing like those I'd just finished unpacking. No mention there, for instance, of courgettes and aubergines, yet the swede and turnips that did appear were nowhere to be seen. It took me two cups of coffee to work what was happening and Ronnie, when challenged, happily confirmed it.

The deception relied on a procedure followed by the shop. Customers would tell an assistant what they wanted and he or she would duly weigh, for example, a pound of carrots, put them in a bag and call out "pound of carrots" to Joyce in her glass-fronted booth at the back. She would register the purchase, and do the same for any others that followed. At the end of the transaction, all she needed to do was press the correct button and the till obligingly spat out the bill. Having paid her what was due, customers left with their shopping.

In Ronnie's case, the arrangement worked differently. When the assistant called out, say, three bunches of asparagus, Joyce would tap in three parsnips, while avocado pears, pineapples and artichokes, to name but a few, would metamorphose into something cheaper and more commonplace. The deception didn't stop there, for Ronnie was careful to hand the assistant enough money to cover the true cost of what he had actually purchased and this was duly passed on to Joyce. The difference between the true figure and the lesser one recorded by the till she'd then hand back to him the next time he saw her.

It was not the only criminal enterprise from which we profited, with me no longer able to plead ignorance, and thereby complicit in the offence. At around this time Ronnie's father, a builder by trade, was working on some council flats in Kensal Rise. One weekend, he managed somehow to smuggle out a complete bathroom suite — a vile green but the alternative was pink, which he and a mate installed for us in North End Road. Not to be outdone, his mother, cashier at a petrol station in Shepherd's Bush, procured and discreetly passed on so many sheets of trading stamps that we all but refurnished the flat at no cost to ourselves. Just sticking them into their albums, likewise provided, took the best part of a week.

Two days after his release from the Scrubs, Ronnie's brother turned up at our place with his girlfriend, as glamorous as people had told me to expect, although the effort she put into it somewhat diminished the impact. Most startling of all were the shiny black boots she had on, so long that they extended right up to the top of her thighs. Later that evening, when the four of us walked into the Chelsea Arts Club, a man I recognised — he read the news on television — took one glance and announced to the room "Puss in Boots". To which the lady serenely replied, "Not quite, dear, but almost."

There and then I knew that I liked her. She was, she told me, an erotic dancer, although she might have said 'exotic', the difference more semantic than real. Through her, I learned that a man from Aberystwyth, whose parents I knew, put on girlie shows at the Chiswick Empire, something no one at home, certainly not his mother and father, had ever got wind of. I learned, too, that sellotape had uses I'd never envisaged and that nothing kept nipples more perky than ice cubes. I felt sorry when Teddy dropped her and married someone else.

In the months that followed, I accompanied Ronnie to almost every gay club in the West End. Nearly everyone seemed to know him, and the few that didn't were eager to do so. Just off St Martin's Lane, up a narrow staircase, was the A and B, short for Arts and Battledress, its patrons more artistic than soldierly, and its walls bedecked with crimson flock. I think the lighting was also red but that might have been the Apollo, equally busy but seedier, two or three streets away. One of them — I can't remember which — also had a white piano which for some reason struck me as deliciously louche.

Behind Charing Cross Road were the Pink Elephant and, scruffiest of all, the Cross Keys, popular with crooks, and all the more appealing to some as a result. (The Kray brothers would drop in from time to time, sometimes with the boorish Lord Boothby in tow.) A favourite of mine, largely because its decorative young barman took a shine to me, was the Toros in Panton Street, formerly Le Boeuf sur le Toit, but forced to change its name after the original establishment in Paris threatened to sue. Next to it was a rival concern, prim but far from proper, called the Music Box but most prestigious — and pretentious — of them all was the Rockingham in Soho. It aspired to be a gentlemen's club, not as grand as its rivals in Pall Mall but tastefully done out all the same, with regency-stripe wallpaper, leather armchairs and a mahogany table bearing copies of *The Tatler*, *Country Life* and *The Field*, as well as that day's edition of *The Times* and *Daily Telegraph*. I remember also a lot of Black Watch tartan but forget if that was on the walls or the carpets, presumably indicative of a Scottish connection I knew nothing about. Unsurprisingly the establishment catered for an older, more affluent clientele, with a sprinkling of young men, enviably good-looking, who were happy to pay court to their better-off seniors, though their services, unlike *The Tatler*, *The Field* and *The Times*, were seldom free of charge. Ronnie had free membership for life, but I never found out why.

With homosexuality still proscribed by law in those days, places like these were forever at risk of being raided by the police. Stepping into them — usually through an anonymous doorway and up a flight of stairs (or down in the case of the Rockingham) — used to give me an agreeable twinge of excitement. In theory, admission was restricted to members and their guests, but in practice few got turned away, at least no one who was male, young and passably good-looking. All that was needed was a signature in the membership book kept by the entrance, it being tacitly understood that the name you provided would either be fictitious or indecipherable. To be safe, I made sure mine was both.

Eighteen months later, I'd submitted three copies of my thesis, neatly typed and professionally bound, to the University of London, and in due course was summoned to defend it before a panel of experts. Two stiff brandies beforehand meant I emerged with little recollection of what had taken place, but I believe there was talk at some point of Leibniz and his theory of monads. As neither Leibnitz nor his monads had featured in my dissertation, I probably imagined it.

Back in North End Road, money was suddenly tight. Yes, the gee-gees were going over the sticks without mishap, something Luca's uncle would have welcomed, but, sadly, no longer were they passing the post in the order Ronnie kept predicting. Day after nail-biting day his accumulators came to naught, while his each-ways and yankees fared little better. In addition to gambling he'd supplemented his income with modelling jobs, not without success, but now his face, for so long his fortune, suddenly went out of favour with the compilers of mail-order catalogues, while the sale of knitting patterns, hitherto a nice little earner, went into freefall, and with it went demand for his services. By then, too, advertisements for cigarettes, another lucrative sideline, were changing, with few showing people actually smoking. (The exception was Marlboro but no matter how rugged Ronnie could make himself look, he wasn't the cowboy type, happier betting on horses than sitting astride them.) As I said, money was tight.

"When one door closes, another door opens," declared Joyce, who was given to platitudes. She had slept overnight on our sofa, after an epic fight with her husband, walking all the way from Kensal Rise in her slippers. Contemplating the auburn wig, more skewiff than usual, I wondered if she slept with it still on.

But then all of a sudden, as Joyce had predicted, another door did open, or so it seemed at the time, revealing what looked like a sure-fire way of restoring our fortunes, even of making us rich. Our salvation, I perceived, lay in another of those crazes that enlivened my adolescence, this one after I'd purchased a book called *Astrology for All* in a second-hand bookshop, the work of someone called Alan Leo (a disciple it turned out of Mme Blavatsky). I still have it, the price — two shillings — neatly pencilled inside the front cover. And so, ten years on and mindful of the Harrieses of Pantcoy, not to mention Mr Lyndoe, I glimpsed a new career ahead of me, one that required nothing more than a set of ephemerides, essential for plotting where the planets were at any given hour, and a more up-to-date textbook. (Mr Leo died in 1917.) Thus equipped, I'd be open for business in no time.

It was in Limehouse the following Sunday that I made public my intention, expecting approval, possibly custom. Instead I was reminded by our host that divination was condemned by the Church Fathers, at which Brian Desmond Hearst, thought to be asleep, bellowed "Amen!" at the top of his voice, startling the man next to him, then nodded off again.

"I had my horoscope done by Aleister Crowley," boasted a neighbour somewhere on my right, "In Jermyn Street. France had just fallen."

"Don't believe him. Gerald's always telling porkies," murmured the man who owned half of Norfolk. By now he made a point of sitting next to me at table, his knee chastely pressed against mine.

Gerald Hamilton was the man who'd mentioned Crowley on my first visit to the rectory. Not one of the regulars and, when he did turn up, not all that welcome, he was inclined to grow sullen before the meal ended, surveying both the food and the company in a way that suggested neither met with his approval. By then in his seventies, he had been the inspiration for Arthur Norris, the eponymous wheeler-dealer in Christopher Isherwood's *Mr Norris Changes Trains*. On a previous occasion he'd declared that hearing me speak was like being restored to the company, sorely missed, of his friend, Dylan Thomas, though my Norfolk neighbour assured me he'd said it only to bolster the myth that he and the poet were once bosom pals. It was the sort of thing he did. In his favour was a willingness when tipsy to team up with Brian Desmond Hurst and sing Irish ballads, though once started, it was difficult to get them to stop. Still, the reference to Crowley was too good to overlook.

"What did you make of him?" I enquired.

"Crowley? Not much."

I thought that was the end of it but was wrong.

"The old goat spent a weekend buggering Victor Neuburg in Paris, then pretended it was magic."

"Perhaps he meant 'magical'," volunteered someone I knew only as Simon. In deference to him, pork and shellfish were omitted from our Sunday lunches.

"Magical? Not with Victor Neuburg," huffed Gerald, relapsing into his sulk.

"My uncle said Crowley leeched off everyone," drawled Robin Maugham, the novelist mistaken for a duke on my first visit. "He did it for a living. Later on, he sold quack medicines and worked spells to order."[37]

"A kind of occult practitioner," murmured Simon.

There and then I decided to be not just an astrologer but an occult practitioner as well. I rather liked the sound of it.

I spent what remained of the afternoon chatting to Simon, whose family name, he told me, was Lipschitz, although for reasons Mrs Abraham-Williams would have well understood, his father had changed it to Lister. For the first time since coming to London I found myself talking to someone about Mr James. We agreed to meet for lunch, the two of us, before the month was out.

Long before then, as if by magic but probably not, Ronnie's finances took a turn for the better, so much better that it enabled me to place an advertisement in two obscure magazines, both with an occult bias, telling readers that 'Prior to opening consulting rooms in Paris and New York' I was offering my services as 'Astrologer and Occult Practitioner' to a few discerning clients. By post only. (Seeing my address in North

---

37 Typical of the potions Crowley peddled was 'Amrita', a name derived from the Sanskrit for 'immortal' and etymological parent of the ambrosia that nourished the gods of Ancient Greece. Mindful of the relationship between microcosm and macrocosm, Crowley believed that each spermatozoon contained within itself something of God's creative impulse. It followed that the consumption of semen would lead to union with the divine through its role as vector of the Logos. The notion may be derived from Gnostic, in particular Manichaean sources, where creation is viewed as a fructifying effusion of supernal light, the Logos Spermatikos, which permeated the universe before withdrawing to its heavenly source. A week's supply of Amrita cost 25 guineas, a hefty sum even today, let alone 70 years ago when Beecham's Pills, a popular laxative and pick-me-up, advertised as 'worth a guinea a box' could be bought for under a shilling.

End Road, no one familiar with London would have expected much of the consulting rooms in Paris and New York.) Enquiries were welcome but should be accompanied by a stamped-addressed envelope.

Only three letters reached me. And of those, one bore no stamp, meaning I had to reimburse the postman before he'd consent to hand it over. Off by return went a list of the services on offer, priced in guineas for a touch of class, but with no mention of occult services, partly because I was still unsure what these were, but chiefly because the Crowley-Neuburg business put me off. When no response came, I began for the first time to understand how Countess Barcynska had felt when so few people came to visit her blue stone. So much for consulting rooms on Fifth Avenue and the Rue Royale in Paris.

Which is how I came, reluctantly, to sit the Civil Service examination for graduate recruits, in those days the only means of entry into what was called the Administrative Class, topmost echelon in a system that accommodated an Executive Class, a Clerical Class and various specialist groups, all fastidiously labelled. In the event not only was I successful but came second from the top, consoled by the fact that the difference between me and the chap in front was just one measly point. Told the news, my mother wrote approvingly to say I could expect a good pension at sixty. That made me feel worse.

From the outset, the Foreign Office sought to claim me, but I turned them down, unwilling to risk an overseas posting that meant abandoning Ronnie in London. The next offer came from the Admiralty, more tempting as it brought to mind *HMS Pinafore*, with Jack Tars in blue collars and bell-bottom trousers (the curious alignment of the buttons on their flies a challenge to novice seducers). In those days however the Admiralty was virulently homophobic after one of its staff, caught on camera misbehaving at an all-male party hosted by the KGB in Moscow, was blackmailed into spying for the Kremlin.[38] On that account, I said *niet* to the Navy as well. Meanwhile

---

38 This was John Vassall (1924-1996). Arrested in 1962, he served ten years of a twelve-year prison sentence. A television film of the affair was broadcast by the BBC in 1980, with Vassall played by

still to be completed was the security questionnaire I'd been sent as a matter of course.

Much of the document was plain sailing. What newspapers did I read? None to be honest, but an answer was expected so I put down *Daily Telegraph* and *Guardian*, indicative of broad, if conflicting, political sympathies. What addresses had I occupied over the previous five years? Easy, though I omitted my nomadic stint with the circus. Was anyone else living with me at my current address? Yes — and why not? Most people my age lived in shared accommodation. What was the occupation of the person or persons I shared with? Trickier, that one. Unemployed would have to do. Gambler was a no-no and 'model' definitely suspect.

Next question was whether I'd had any contact or involvement with Communists or Fascists. My Uncle Gwilym used to read the *Daily Worker*, but stopped in 1957 when the Soviets invaded Hungary, so presumably that didn't count, while the reference to Fascism suggested the form had not been updated since Mussolini got Italian trains to run on-time. (It crossed my mind that, like the old man I'd see on my way to Tanrallt, someone in Whitehall had not been told the war was over.) But then, halfway down Page Three, there it was, ironically after an enquiry about hobbies and pastimes, the one question I'd been dreading all along. Had I ever, it asked, engaged in 'homosexual activity'?

After reflecting long and hard on the question and on what subtleties of language might help me avoid giving a straight answer, I dispatched a letter objecting to such rigorous scrutiny of my private life, careful to make it sound like an issue of principle rather than anything specific. I finished by saying I was minded to seek alternative employment.

By return of post came an invitation to meet the civil service commissioners, a surprise but then I had, after all, come second — and a close one at that — in their bloody exam. A week later I was sitting in front of them at their offices in Curzon Street.

John Normington, once a stalwart of the Earl Armstrong Repertory Company in Aberystwyth, and a frequent visitor to our house during my school days.

"It's the intrusion into my private life I find unnerving."

The commissioners collectively made a reassuring noise.

"My dear chap," declared one, "you've no cause for concern. None at all. Things will be fine as long as you keep your nose clean."

"And don't sleep with your best friend's wife!" joked his neighbour.

Everyone guffawed, none suspecting the best friend might be the problem, not his wayward wife. At their invitation, I stayed behind for sherry.

Within days, the form still unfilled, there arrived the offer of a job with the Board of Inland Revenue in Somerset House, right next door, as it happens, to my old college in the Strand. Barely three months had passed since I'd left, so it felt less like going back than of never having been away. My first inclination was to turn down the offer — taxation policy requires a brain wired differently from mine — but needs must, and so I resolved to give it a try. In the meantime, I would look for something better.

"You'll have to buy a suit," volunteered Joyce, who then, by way of afterthought, asked me to check her tax bill.

20

"Bats in the Belfry"

If God, as Einstein reportedly said, is the engineer behind every coincidence, then He'd worked overtime prior to my lunch with my fellow Limehouse regular, Simon Lipton. For my host's choice of eating place was none other than the Belfry, erstwhile home of, successively, Lady Caillard and Mrs Penry Evans (née Firth and alias Dion Fortune) in Belgrave Square. By then a private members' club, its no-nonsense interior betrayed nothing of its more eccentric past, although Simon made up for that by talking throughout the meal about the Kabbalah or Qabbalah, the latter being the spelling favoured by Aleister Crowley and Eliphas Lévi, both men one and the same, if we accept Crowley's claim that he had been Lévi in a previous life. (Perhaps I was Madame Blavatsky.)

The word Kabbalah, said Simon, refers to a body of wisdom, supposedly imparted to Moses by God during the several hours the two spent together on Mount Sinai. Tradition has it that the prophet later revealed these truths to seventy elders, who in turn transmitted them by word of mouth to their successors until, finally, the earliest written text, probably the *Sefer Yetzirah* or Book of Formation, appeared between the second and sixth centuries of our era. That book describes how God used the letters of the Hebrew alphabet, called *sefirot* or numbers, to name all the things that exist, impregnating each with something of His divine essence. Subsequent authors would go on to describe the *sefirot* as emanations rather than numbers, collectively representing the Shekinah or divine presence in the world and, more specifically, in the people of Israel.

Another esteemed kabbalist, Isaac the Blind, described God as the *En Sof* or Infinite, with the *sefirot* depicted once more as successive emanations but now limited to ten, some bearing a name, italicised below, derived from the blessing King David bestowed on his people: 'Yours, God, are greatness (*Gedulah*), might (*Geburah*), splendour (*Tifareth*), triumph (*Netzach*) and majesty (*Hod*),' (i Chronicles 29:12). The *sefirot* are further arranged by the author in an order that anticipates what Isaac Luria would depict in the sixteenth century as the Tree of Life or *Etz Chaim*.

By the early Renaissance, occultists were plundering the Kabbalah for its magical potential — symbols, spiritual entities (both angelic and demonic), amuletic seals and abstruse permutations of letters and numbers — but most, one suspects, were untouched by its deeper metaphysical, let alone theological, significance. For them, its advantage was that, unlike Christianity which proclaimed the existence of powers and dominions but was coy about naming them, the Kabbalah provided enough information to keep the most ambitious sorcerer happy. Here was something Cornelius Agrippa von Nettesheim made much of when compiling his influential *De Occulta Philosophia* (1531), while it enabled his pupil Johannes Wierus (1516-88) to list no fewer than seventy demons, together with their offices and titles, in his own *Pseudomonarchia daemonum*, originally an appendix to his *De praestigiis daemonum* where advice was given on their successful conjuration. (Worth mentioning is that in a letter to the Viennese publisher Hugo Heller, Sigmund Freud described *De praestigiis* etc as one of the ten most significant books of all time.)[39]

Of special interest to me was what Simon went on to say, with lunch over and coffee served, about the occult, or more specifically, magical revival that began in the second half of the nineteenth century and would produce both Aleister Crowley and Dion Fortune, the only names, together with that of Lévi, familiar to me when I was growing up in Wales. (Contemporary students of magic are far better informed.)

Central to its revival was the Hermetic Order of the Golden Dawn, created by a group of Freemasons in search of something more exciting, female company included, than the staid rituals of the United Grand Lodge of England. According to some, its origins go back to 1884 when an Anglican clergyman, the Reverend A. F. A. Woodford, chanced upon a collection of documents in a second-hand bookshop near Seven Dials in central London. Written in a script he could not identify, still less understand, he purchased them nevertheless. Three years later, still none the wiser, he lent some pages to a Dr Woodman, like him, a leading light in the Societas Rosicruciana in Anglia, a quasi-masonic group founded in 1865, and the remainder to another Brother, Dr W. Wynn Westcott, deputy coroner of the London borough of Hoxton. Equally baffled, they in turn showed the documents to a more flamboyant character — Messrs Woodford, Woodman and Westcott were, one suspects, anything but — named Samuel Liddell Mathers who reportedly grasped at once that the manuscript was written in Enochian, the Angelic language that fascinated the Elizabethan magus, Dr John Dee. With occasional help from his future wife, by all accounts a gifted clairvoyant, Mathers determined that the text described magical practices based on the Kabbalah.

Not at all, say others. In their rival version they maintain that the original documents were passed to Woodford by Kenneth MacKenzie, a Masonic scholar, who in his younger days was received into a conti-

---

39 See Heller, Hugo, *Neue Blätter für Literatur und Kunst*, Vienna, 1906.

nental branch of the Rose Croix in Vienna. (He was also said to have met Eliphas Lévi while passing through Paris.) Where Mackenzie, compiler of the *Royal Masonic Cyclopaedia* (1870) came across them is uncertain, some claiming it was in the archives at Freemasons Hall, but what nobody disputes is that MacKenzie surrendered the bundle to Woodford who, unsure what to do with them, handed them over to Westcott in 1886.

According to this version, the material was not written in Dr Dee's Angelic Script at all but in a code which Westcott and Mathers deciphered with the aid of an alphabetical key invented in the late fifteenth century by Johannes Trithemius, Abbot of Sponheim in what today is Rhineland-Palatinate, and author of a popular thesis on demons. Once uncovered, the text allowed its translators to cobble together the rituals that were later used by the Hermetic Order of the Golden Dawn.

Meanwhile, in a letter purportedly included among the documents was a request that anyone who succeeded in breaking the code should contact a certain Anna Sprengel at an address in Nuremberg, something Westcott did with alacrity in 1887. Or so it is claimed. Others argue that the mysterious Frau Sprengel, alleged to be the illegitimate daughter of Ludwig 1 of Bavaria and the dancer Lola Montez, was not, as Westcott insisted, a high-ranking Rosicrucian but an invention of his own, designed to give the initiative a spurious historicity. It was additionally claimed that she bestowed on each of the founding fathers the grade of Adeptus Exemptus, saving them the bother of progressing through the ranks like everyone else.

The first five of these ranks constituted the 'Outer' Order, to which alone, strictly speaking, the name Golden Dawn applied, the second or 'Inner' Order, established in 1882, being the Order of the Ruby Rose and Gold Cross or *Ordo Rosae Rubeae et Aureae Crucis*. (All involved, one suspects, were no less keen than Mr James to show off their Latin.) Only in the Inner Order did members get down to the serious business of magic, their time in the outer Order spent learning the rudiments of astrology, the meaning of the tarot cards and bits of the Kabbalah.

Meanwhile above the second order came a third, its elite membership composed of discarnate entities known as the Secret Chiefs, who dispensed advice and encouragement to Mathers and Westcott when, following Woodman's death in 1892, they agreed to run the outfit jointly, the one as Imperator, the other as Praemonstrator, a partnership that would end five years later when confidential documents mislaid by Westcott were discovered in a hansom cab parked outside Charing Cross station. Told by his employers in Hoxton to choose between magic and his day job, Westcott prudently opted for the latter. (Rumours persist that Mathers, keen to govern alone, had himself left the documents inside the cab.) Happily, Westcott still had Freemasonry to keep him busy, and the consolation soon afterwards of being appointed Grand Sword Bearer of the United Grand Lodge of England. Even Lord Tredegar never managed that.

Only in 1887 did the world at large or, rather, that section of it that subscribed to Madame Blavatsky's magazine *Lucifer*, learn about the Golden Dawn, following a dispute between its founders and a rival group ('overrun by fraudulent astrologers and fortune tellers', according to the magazine's editorial) in the Yorkshire town of Keighley. That said, the enterprise did not properly get started until the inauguration of the Isis-Urania Temple in London on 1 March 1888, housed in rented premises which, like the Master Temple in Portsmouth, scene of Mrs Duncan's comeuppance, fell sadly short of its grandiose name. Among the early members was Mina Bergson, sister of the philosopher, Henri Bergson (1859-1941), who chose as her magical pseudonym — everyone was expected to have one — Vestigia Nulla Retrorsum or 'I leave behind no Traces'. She subsequently went further, changing her first name to the Celtic-sounding Moina and her second to Mathers, the latter following her marriage to the Imperator, later Adeptus Exemptus (or was it perhaps vice-versa?) in 1890.

Other recruits included a fellow student of Moina's at the Slade School of Fine Art, Annie Horniman, daughter of a wealthy tea-merchant and founder of the Horniman Museum in Dulwich, the

American esotericist A. E. Waite, translator of Eliphas Lévi's books but best remembered nowadays for the popular Waite-Rider tarot deck, the Welsh journalist and author Arthur Machen, and the actress Florence Farr, former mistress of George Bernard Shaw, and by all accounts something of a bossy boots. The poet W. B. Yeats joined in 1892, following a dalliance with Theosophy, some six years ahead of Aleister Crowley. It is estimated that between 1888 and 1898 as many as 300 individuals were received into the Order, although it is likely that fewer than 100 were ever members at any one time.

Soon Mathers became a problem. As hinted by his magical title Deo Duce, Comite Ferro ('God is my Guide, my companion a Sword') his other great passion was the art of warfare, which may explain his belligerence when dealing with others. Always restless, he had by the end of the century moved with his wife to Paris, their expenses met by the ever-obliging Miss Horniman, where he established a new temple (Ahathoor). and began issuing diktats to the faithful back home in England. Meanwhile having previously added a 'MacGregor' to his name, he sought now to impress the natives by awarding himself the title of Comte de Glenstrae.

One evening, the newly ennobled Mathers chanced to be strolling through the Bois de Boulogne, presumably more salubrious after dark than it is today, when he bumped into three of the Order's Secret Chiefs, temporarily made flesh, who persuaded him, not, one supposes, with undue difficulty, that he himself was the visible presence of their supreme head, the Ipsissimus. Few back in London shared his joy when informed of it. On the contrary, the members of Isis-Urania were growing increasingly restive. Things reached a climax when Aleister Crowley, backed by Mathers, upset everyone by trying to clamber up the hierarchical ladder too fast, the ensuing brouhaha such that one group of rebels set up a rival version of Isis-Urania, although members in Edinburgh stayed loyal, changing the name from Golden Dawn to Alpha et Omega. Meanwhile the Ipsissimus continued to keep himself busy in Paris until his death in 1918, brought about, his widow would claim, by years of tireless service to the Secret Chiefs. By Spanish flu according to Dion Fortune, a former associate of Mrs Mathers.

"It's easy to poke fun at them," remarked Simon, having come close to doing just that. The fancy dress, the incantations, the fumigations and endless conjurations, however daft they seem, were, he claimed, justified, if they alerted the participant to a reality beyond the threshold of his or her everyday awareness, a reality no less valid for being subjectively, rather than empirically, experienced. These practices, he reminded me, were what Eliphas Lévi had once called 'instruments for the education of the will', a way of stimulating the volitional, as well as creative, powers of the imagination.

At this point, I told him about my dream-like excursion to the top of Domen Bedwyr, the first time I'd spoken of it since the Freshers' Party six years earlier.

"The Golden Dawners would say you met your Higher Self," he remarked, "as would Dion Fortune."

Having uttered the name, he looked around the room as if expecting Mrs Penry Evans to turn up at the Belfry to confirm it. When she didn't, he proceeded to explain how previous acquaintance with the Kabbalah might have enabled me to understand better my experience, recognising what was being symbolically expressed in the course of it. Such, he argued, was one purpose of the pomp and ceremony favoured by magicians like Lévi and Mathers and Crowley, the pentacles, sigils, charms and fancy dress a means of enhancing their imagination and focussing their will. The Tree of Life, he reminded me, was held to represent both the original process of creation and the reality, seen and unseen, in which we subsist and to which we belong, the forces represented by the various *sefirot* active not only in the world about us but in ourselves as well, a reminder of the hermetic connection between the microcosm that is each of us and the macrocosm of which we, like all else, remain part. By understanding and experiencing these forces, we are better equipped to understand both ourselves and the workings of nature, becoming, some might say, attuned to the mind of God as revealed through creation. Above all it is a way of proceeding from the known to the unknown, the visible to the invisible or, if you like, the human to the divine.

From then on Simon and I met often, sometimes weekly and normally on a Wednesday, but now at the Royal Automobile Club in St James, often joined at table by another member, a friend and contemporary of his, named Gerald Gough. As well as being a member of Dion Fortune's Fraternity, later Society, of the Inner Light, Gough had worked for the Foreign Office, sometimes clandestinely, and in September 1938 attended the annual Nazi Party Rally in Nuremberg. I've since learned that he was among the 2,300 individuals listed in Hitler's so-called Black Book (*Sonderfahndungsliste GB*) and scheduled for immediate arrest following the planned invasion of the British Isles.[40]

Encouraged by Simon, though little encouragement was needed, the well-informed Gough would treat us to gossip about the movers and shakers of the occult scene. My only regret was that in those days the food at the RAC fell short, well short, of what we'd consumed at the Belfry.

---

40 Son of a senior Anglican clergyman, Fitzherbert Charles Gerald Gough (1899-1986) began his career as Private Secretary to Sir Herbert Stanley (1872-1955), then Governor of Northern Rhodesia, later serving in both the Foreign Office and Home Office in London, as well as undertaking intelligence work for MI5, notably in Nazi Germany, up to the outbreak of World War II. Dismissed from his post in 1940 for an unnamed misdemeanour, he thereupon joined the Royal Air Force. Owner of a house, Gorse Cliff, in Nefyn, North Wales, he once told me that a statue of Pan in his front garden had caused enormous offence to the locals. In Hitler's 'Black Book' his address is given as 'Nevin, North Wales, Gosse Chliff'.

21

**"I'm Burlington Bertie I rise at ten thirty
Then Buckingham Palace I view."**
Harry B. Norris

My arrival at Somerset House, declared the board member assigned to welcome me, coincided with the date on which the novelist Iris Murdoch joined the Revenue in the 1940s, her heart, by all accounts, every bit as heavy as my own. Like me, she began as an assistant principal, the bottom rung of the career ladder for entrants to the administrative class, although within four to five years assistant principals could expect to mutate into fully-fledged principals before going on to become assistant secretaries, then under-secretaries and, if among the brightest and best, deputy secretaries or even permanent secretaries, this final step bringing with it a knighthood by way of a bonus. In the Revenue, members of the administrative class took care of fiscal policy and dealt with government ministers, rather than the routine business of tax gathering, a chore delegated to inspectors and collectors of taxes, groups viewed by my colleagues with patrician disdain. In their day-to-day work the administrators were supported by members of the executive class and, under them a populous clerical class, lowly and thus permanently disgruntled. In addition, there were the ladies of the typing pool, mostly spinsters of a certain age with a shared fondness for twinsets and pearls, sensible shoes and lisle stockings.

The building seemed to function in a time and place of its own, blithely indifferent to what was happening in the world outside. By then the Swinging Sixties were drawing to a close but within Somerset House they'd largely passed unheeded so their demise went unremarked. One of our older colleagues, Geoffrey Hartog, even wore spats, possibly an affectation, and lived at his club, the Reform, in Pall Mall.

The room allocated to me overlooked the central courtyard and on one wall hung two engravings of a section of the building designed by Inigo Jones, who died before its completion. Nearby hung a portrait of Rabindranath Tagore, but what he was doing there I've no idea, any more than I can account for a pen-and-ink sketch, drawn from life, of Hermann Goering and a distracted-looking Rudolf Hess, the pair of them in the dock at Nuremberg in 1946.

Like me, Iris Murdoch would have been told what to expect by way of promotion and, music to my mother's ears, what pension would be due upon retirement at sixty. But whereas I was then handed some case files to study, she by all accounts was dispatched to catalogue the lavatories throughout the building, no mean undertaking given its size, with a New Wing, West Wing, and a third nameless wing where the legal department was housed. (She was told she could omit the Probate Registry which, though occupying several rooms overlooking the Strand,[41] was not officially part of the Revenue.) Rumour has it that she abandoned the task halfway through and by threatening to resign on the spot, forced the civil service commissioners to sanction her transfer to the Treasury, its lavatories presumably catalogued already.

For the first few months, my job was to draft replies for Treasury Ministers to send to Members of Parliament whose constituents had

---

41 Even in my time at Somerset House, they outgrew the premises and moved to the South Wing, overlooking the Thames. Today they are lodged in High Holborn.

sought help in connection with their tax affairs. For this, all one had to do was solicit a report from the tax office responsible, and draft a letter in the light of whatever information it contained, avoiding so far as possible any technical gobbledygook. I suppose one was meant to make sense of the explanation offered, but, as I seldom did, that clearly wasn't essential. From time to time, a mistake would be identified in, say, a tax code or an allowance wrongly withheld, but usually what was needed was a firm but soothingly worded reply. A little *sapo mollis*, I was told by one of my seniors, though it took me time to realise this was Latin for 'soft soap', not some abstruse aspect of taxation. Best of all was the discovery I could get by — just — despite my pathological aversion to figures.

It must have been a few months later I suggested to Ronnie that we leave North End Road — there was talk of demolishing our side of the street — and move to a mansion flat in Chiswick, a short walk from Turnham Green, childhood home of the poet, W. B. Yeats, sometime member of the Hermetic Order of the Golden Dawn and its successor organisations. The rent was just about affordable on the salary I was earning. And then no sooner were we newly installed than Ronnie got a job, a real job, finally.

Also around this time Father Christian suddenly quit Limehouse and joined a Franciscan Community in Dorset. As a result, we inherited as much of his furniture as we could accommodate, among the better pieces three William Morris chairs, a longcase clock and an upright piano, battered but still defiantly in tune. I began to miss those long and slightly louche Sunday lunches.

Over the next few months it became clear to me, if not yet to my superiors, that I'd never make a success of the job. True, I'd no difficulty drafting letters for ministers, my efforts free from the technical jargon my colleagues seemed unwilling or unable to forego, but I knew I avoided it only because the technicalities it described were far beyond me. At the sight of them my brain ceased to function, yet it was all too plain that without mastering them, I'd no chance of a career in

Somerset House. Unless I got out soon, I'd be oldest assistant principal in history by the time my pension fell due.

Nor did my problems end there. For some time, I'd been trying to persuade myself that a shift in the relationship between Ronnie and me, so subtle that it took a little time to notice, was only to be expected when two people live together, their passion, if not spent, then certainly diminished by routine. Things evolved, that was all. The sensible course was to get used to it, confident that where love was present all would turn out well. As Mrs Winkler liked to say in my schooldays, *omnia vincit amor*, the poet Virgil second only to Lloyd George in her esteem.

As for Ronnie, he seemed unaware of what was happening, possibly more content at 31 than he'd ever been before, content and settled. The pipe he'd taken to smoking, the cardigan and the velvet slippers, even *The Times* crossword, were proof of it, outward and visible signs of a newfound serenity. Other changes, this time within myself, I failed to notice or chose to overlook, and this time there was no Serge on hand to force me to confront them. Nor was there any pastis to console me when, finally, I did.

Every end has a beginning, and this end began on a Friday, the last Friday in May, outside Dunn's, a gentleman's outfitters in the Strand, its wares too fuddy-duddy for people of my age, even those employed by the Inland Revenue. Already late, I was rushing back to work after lunch with an old friend from college — a bottle of wine and shared beef sandwich — when I remembered that in my pocket was my weekly letter home. After a quick dash to the post office in Southampton Street I was no sooner back on course than I saw him walking towards me. What I remember are his eyes. They were blue. Not spectacularly so, yet something about them seemed to grab my attention, abetted no doubt by too much wine and not enough beef sandwich. Once he'd passed, I turned to look over my shoulder and, as I hoped but only half expected, he did the same. It was by no means a heart-stopping moment, yet enough to persuade me to walk back to a point midway between us but, I vowed, not a step farther. If he did the same, fine, if not, I would turn around and head straight for the office. In the event he walked the required distance.

"And what part of Wales are you from?" he asked, on hearing me speak. As he did, my ear detected a faint, barely discernible, lilt.

"Aberystwyth," I replied, "and what part of Anglesey are you from?" Gotcha.

After admitting he came from Holyhead, he suggested we meet the following Sunday outside the Ritz in Piccadilly. Would four o'clock suit me? The prospect of tea and cream cakes may have clinched it. I told Ronnie I was meeting friends of my parents, in London for the weekend. I even said we were going to the Welsh chapel in Harrow, my tendency, then and now, being to over-embellish my falsehoods, as if the more detail they contain, the more credible they sound.

When we met two days later, Edward Jones was wearing a Brigade of Guards tie and a brown trilby hat. I remember we formally shook hands but to my disappointment it was not through the doors of the Ritz we proceeded but along Piccadilly and into Green Park. On our way we passed a row of amateur painters like those in Bayswater Road, possibly the same ones, their canvases propped up against the park wall or suspended from the railings above it. From time to time my companion paused to survey their efforts, valiant at best, but said nothing until we reached an elderly man whose work betrayed a fondness, verging on the obsessive, for classical ballet. On every canvas were depicted ballerinas, all identical, all emaciated and all either studiously *en pointe* or fiddling with the ribbons of their shoes.

"What do you make of them?" enquired Edward. Not much was the answer, but I felt more was called for.

"A bit Dégas-esque," I quipped. I always tend to show off when I'm nervous.

Halfway across Green Park any residual awkwardness vanished when we switched from English to Welsh. There was still a hint of arrogance about him, but by now a manageable one. No longer did I feel inhibited by it. Before we drew close to Buckingham Palace, I'd decided that despite the brown trilby, the Guards' tie and Crombie coat with its ridiculous velvet collar, the chances were that he lived in a bedsitter off Vauxhall Bridge Road. He probably worked in the Army and Navy Stores around the corner. Selling ties perhaps. Just my luck: instead of the Ritz's Palm Court, with all its Louis XV kitsch, I was being led to some dingy room in Victoria, a washbasin in one corner and a gas ring beside it. Already I could see the laminated wardrobe, the rented television, the two-bar electric fire, and of course the narrow bed pushed up against a wall, probably with a candlewick bedspread on top.

The more then was my surprise, though I contrived not to show it, when suddenly he grabbed my elbow as we walked alongside the Palace, and steered me through an iron gate, across a small courtyard and into the building itself. I half noticed the plain-clothes policeman in a cubby-hole behind the door, although I do remember that he nodded amiably as we went by. (In time I'd get to know him well.) Once inside we proceeded in silence down a long, windowless corridor, past empty kitchens and pantries, until finally we turned right and came upon an antiquated lift. So powerful was the fragrance it emitted when its doors opened that I remarked on it, even though I'd resolved minutes earlier to feign indifference to my surroundings.

"It's the cut flowers," volunteered Edward, sounding as if he'd said it many times before. "They arrive twice a week. From Windsor." I wished I'd kept my mouth shut.

Three floors up we emerged into another corridor, grander than the first, with a series of caricatures, many of William IV, hanging the length of one wall. (I was tempted to show I recognised the artist, James Gillray, but thought Dégas was more than enough for one afternoon.) Eventually we came to a panelled door, slightly recessed, on which was a card bearing the name E. C. Jones in fine copperplate, and beyond it a comfortable sitting room, its furnishings, a mixture of antique and anodyne, reminiscent somehow of the furniture department at Peter Jones in nearby Sloane Square.

The room overlooked the gardens at the front of the palace — cognoscenti know that the bit facing the Mall is the back — and later that afternoon, as we sat talking, my host glanced through a window and murmured "Ah, there's Mother taking the corgis for a walk." Guessing that this remark had induced previous visitors to leap up and take a peek, I made a point of staying put. For good measure I went on to announce that I was a committed republican, its impact diminished by my failure to remember the Welsh for 'republican'. (It's *gweriniaethwr* – I looked it up when I got home.) By then we'd finished our tea, brought to us by a man in navy-blue uniform, with EIIR embroidered in red on a breast pocket. It consisted of dainty cupcakes and minuscule sandwiches, doubtless pilfered from the kitchens we'd passed earlier, and intended for mouths more patrician than mine. There was no candlewick bedspread.

22

"There are two Paths to the Innermost: the Way of the Mystic, which is the way of devotion and meditation, a solitary and subjective path; and the way of the occultist, which is the way of the intellect, of concentration, and of trained will; "
Dion Fortune

Within weeks of our lunch at the Belfry I told Simon of my excursion, real or imagined, to the top of Clogwyn Bedwyr, and the vervain I might (or might not) have brought back with me. By then he'd begun talking about what he called the Higher Self, mine in particular, suggesting it was this that I'd encountered on the mountain top that night.

The term 'Higher Self' was one favoured by the Hermetic Order of the Golden Dawn although W. B. Yeats preferred the word 'daimon', an idiosyncratic spelling of 'daemon', a concept dear to Socrates and one which the Neoplatonists would later adopt. For them it often meant the elemental ruler assigned to each of us the moment we draw our first breath, a part of ourselves that functions beyond the three-dimensional world, enabling us, if we let it, to become aware of things inaccessible to the senses and reason alike. By coincidence, it was MacGregor Mathers' brother-in-law, the philosopher and Nobel laureate, Henri Bergson, who rendered the notion easier to grasp by suggesting that knowledge of what is real and absolute, rather than what is derived, transitory and dependent, becomes available only when we acknowledge the limits of reason and consciously surrender to our intuition. By doing so, we reconcile our outer and inner — or, in occult terms, our lower and higher — selves. Achieving this state of wholeness is comparable to the 'individuation' which Jung identified as being the key to personal fulfilment and the means of better understanding the world.

In Buddhism, such an undifferentiated state of consciousness, one where subject and object are experienced as one and the same, goes by the Sanskrit term *samadhi,* a precursor to ultimate enlightenment and hence to *moksha* or final liberation. Here, the higher (or 'real') self is comparable to *atman,* not only the potential to attain buddhahood but also the agent that permits us to experience the true meaning of things rather than the meaning we unconsciously impose on them, something similar to, but not quite the same as, Kant's *Ding an sich* or its Classical precursor the noumenon. From us, little more is required than to suspend for a moment the 'I' that is our conscious personality, a construct shaped and nourished by our experience of the world around us and, as such, reactive rather than original. Once we achieve this reconciliation of our two selves or, rather, the twin elements of our one self, we perceive things for the first time as they really are, not as our consciousness presents them to us. It becomes less a manner of experiencing a reality separate from us, than of experiencing a reality of which, even as observers, we are an integral part.

All of which may well describe what the Higher Self does but not what the Higher Self is. Here it helps to be reminded of the esoteric belief that the personality that is ours in our lifetime, fashioned to some extent by what we experience as it unfolds, is the manifestation within space and time of a 'self' independent of both. Each lifetime, whether unique or successive, is thus an educational process, governed by what Hindus and Buddhists call the law of karma. The same tradition also maintains that a residual portion of the self never incarnates. Instead it remains detached from the self that undergoes successive incarnations, a tactful reminder of our supra-natural origin. It is our 'Higher', because discarnate and eternal, Self.

Some people, Simon among them, mindful of the relationship between microcosm and macrocosm, have drawn on the Kabbalah to help them understand this better, likening the process of incarnation to how God, whether concept or phenomenon, experiences the world through his presence in each sefirah on the Tree of Life. That, too, is why the Gnostics frequently spoke of the Higher Self as the Logos or divinity within us, and why Aleister Crowley bestowed on it the title Adonai or Lord.

Unsurprisingly, this concept of a Higher Self, simultaneously part of us and yet separate, becomes easier to grasp if we treat it as something independent of ourselves. Aleister Crowley suggested that the relationship between such an entity and its client 'is that of friendship, of community, of brotherhood, of fatherhood.' He then adds sternly, 'He is not, let me say with emphasis, a mere abstraction from yourself and that is why I have insisted rather heavily that the term "Higher Self" implies a damnable heresy and dangerous delusion'.

A delusion? The point Crowley makes is that the Higher Self is not some nobler or more elevated version of the you or me that goes about his or her business in this world but, as we saw earlier, is a reality subsisting outside it. As long as this is borne in mind, we can, *pace* Crowley, stick with the term, even agree when he states that the Higher Self, properly understood, is 'something more than a man, possibly a being that has passed through the stage of humanity'. Here he has in mind the occult belief that our enduring self, the one that submits, in part at least, to a series of incarnations, is not the discrete entity we like to imagine, but a composite being made up of several identities, each with its own history, both pre- and post-human. Such a notion, reflected in suggestions made by Rudolf Steiner, is unpalatable because it undermines the comforting belief in our personal uniqueness. Yet it is undeniable that even if differentiated or at least perceived to be so, we are, each of us, components of a single whole, both many in one and one in many.

And my own Higher Self? Encouraged by Simon, I had in previous weeks revisited the kabbalistic symbolism I'd discovered in books on magic but never put to the test. To begin with, he recommended a technique favoured by the Golden Dawn and known as the Lesser Banishing Ritual of the Pentagram, regarded as so important that only after mastering it were members permitted to advance from the Outer to the Inner Order and assume the grade of Adept. Its purpose was to create a protective barrier that rendered the practitioner impervious to baleful influences that might issue forth once the gate between the outer and inner worlds was opened. Basically, it involves tracing a pentagram, pictured in terms of shimmering light, at the four cardinal points — East, West, North and South — and investing each in turn with one of the divine names. When this has been done, the elemental rulers traditionally assigned to each are summoned and visualised appropriately, in this case the four Archangels, with Raphael (Air) pictured on a purple hilltop, his yellow garments billowing in the breeze, Gabriel (Water) in blue and surrounded by cascading torrents, Michael (Fire) clad in scarlet and bearing aloft a sword, and finally Uriel (Earth), standing before a fertile landscape, its browns and greens matching the colours of his cloak.

But that's not the end of it. There has next to be visualised a five-pointed star overhead, its interlaced triangles anticipating the fusion of the celebrant's temporal self with the higher one soon to be encountered. Only with a second formulation of the kabbalistic cross is the exercise completed.

The procedure is deemed a prudent way to commence any 'magical' exercise, although the specifics, particularly the words and images, may be adapted to match individual, religious or cultural preferences. Anyone uncomfortable with the judaeo-kabbalistic references might for example replace them with others taken from, say, Hinduism, using the seven chakras or psychic centres linked to various parts of the body.

Often depicted as lotus flowers, each with its distinctive colour, they have an affinity with certain letters of the Sanskrit alphabet, one that enables the matching Hebrew terms to be dispensed with.

The opportunity to put these techniques into practice came to me one day when Simon asked me to house-sit for him while he was away on business. On the premises and in need of company were two elderly cats and a border terrier, even older but blind and diabetic as well. (When I called to collect the house keys, I was shown how to grab the scruff of its neck and administer the insulin jab it needed first thing each morning.) All that was required would, he assured me, be on the kitchen table when I got there, all, that is, except the insulin which was stored in the fridge.

And true enough, a bag of dog food and two tins of Whiskas were waiting for me when I let myself in, together with a wine glass and bottle of Gevrey-Chambertin (premier cru, no less but with no sign of a corkscrew). Also there, in the room I was to sleep in, were a small incense burner, a matchbox next to it, and a note from Simon suggesting that if there was nothing to watch on television, I might care to spend an hour reflecting on the Tree of Life and see if the 'stuff' — his word — we'd talked about had kindled my imagination. By way of aide-memoire he left a picture of the Tree, its sefiroth named, numbered and appropriately coloured. The incense, he assured me, would not be unfamiliar, with two exclamation marks, their significance lost on me, at the end of the sentence. 'Light a candle or several if you like' he added as if by way of afterthought, with an arrow pointing to a shelf where, sure enough, I found a box of squat pillar candles.

And of course, he was right. The incense was not unfamiliar. It was the scent that filled Tanrallt on the night when part of me, unsubstantial but real, had ended up on Clogwyn Bedwyr. That evening at Simon's, as I dutifully went about the business of delineating pentacles and visualizing archangels, feeling less foolish and self-conscious as I progressed, but glad to be alone and unwatched all the same, I began suddenly to experience, not without disquiet, a feeling of detachment from the physical me, a feeling similar to what I'd known more than ten years before in Tanrallt. With it came the prospect of an adventure similar to last time, although my destination turned out to be different....

.... It was the shabbier end of a fairground, a tawdry fringe of booths, with show fronts that might once have been jaunty, even garish, but now were scruffy and in desperate need of fresh paint. One depicted a rainforest, the greens and yellows of its foliage badly faded, with ethereal fauna just about discernible among the pallid leaves. 'Giant Rat' announced a sign above the entrance, while two more on either side offered the chance to see a mangabey ape, a mongoose, a porcupine and — 'Born Alive' — a two headed pig. (The 'Born Alive', while perhaps true, disguised the fact that the creature was pickled in alcohol.) Next door was the 'Headless Woman' ('Must be Seen to be Believed') and beyond her, 'Selene, Mistress of Allure' who, according to the man drumming up custom, was the only female fakir in the world. The Mistress of Allure, looking nothing like her name, stood impassively on a podium behind him, her bare midriff and a chiffon yashmak vaguely suggestive of the mystic east.

But it was not towards these I found myself drifting as I crossed the muddy patch between this sad crepuscular world and the raucous bustle of the fair, its lights and cheerful music, shouts and laughter, by then well behind me. Here the illuminations were less bright, the panatropes muffled, and reality, if no less real, was ever so slightly askew. This was a place where pigs were born with two heads, while close by dwelt a lady with no head at all. Even the Mistress of Allure, according to the man listlessly touting her virtues, swallowed razor blades and slept on a bed of nails. Nothing was quite as it should be.

Just as Dorothy, once over the rainbow, knew she'd quit her native Kansas, I now realised I was a long, long way from Simon's house in Chelsea. At the same time, I realised there was not much I could do about it. I felt equally unable to resist stepping up to the small pay box in front of a booth even more dilapidated than its run-down neighbours. On my left a frail, solemn child, with shiny epaulettes pinned to his sweater, half-heartedly banged a drum, pausing from time to time to rattle a tambourine, encouraged by an elderly woman dressed in black, her hair the same brassy yellow as the epaulettes, who wordlessly accepted the shilling I placed in her hand. Only as the little drummer boy drew back a purple curtain across the entrance did I notice he was in fact a wizened old man. That discovery shocked me less, however, than hearing him greet me by my name.

Inside, on a trestle table along the middle of the tent stood an assortment of mesh cages, as well as several large jars containing prodigies that might or might not have been 'born alive' but were now very much dead, among them a three-legged duck, a snake (its deformity unclear as the label on the bottle had faded), a toad with five feet and, finally, a parsnip-shaped object said to be a genuine mermaid but immersed in such murky liquid that it might well have been a parsnip after all. Inside the cages were two squirrel monkeys, huddled together for warmth, and various other small mammals, all of them, from what I could tell, endowed with the correct number of heads, limbs and appendages. It was a squalid exhibition, and the plight of the exhibits, at least those of them with breath in their bodies, made me sad.

Close to the exit was a final attraction, two large distorting mirrors propped up against the iron struts that kept the tent upright. Designed to make the viewer look grotesquely misshapen, either squat and fat or tall and skinny, sometimes both, it was impossible to miss them. Yet when I looked into their curved surfaces, the reflection I saw was none other than my everyday self, with no hint of distortion or as much as a detail out of place. That would have been enough to persuade me I was dreaming, even had a languorous voice behind me not confirmed it.

"Nothing here's what it fucking seems," it drawled, "if you'll pardon my French."

I turned to find a magpie watching me from a cramped little cage. Now even if magpies, like budgies and parrots, can talk, the sentence it uttered struck me as remarkable, the more so as it reflected perfectly what was going through my mind.

"Oh come on, you daft bugger, stop gawping and open this bloody door."

Before answering, I checked there was no one within earshot.

"You want to come out?"

"No, dearie, I want you to fucking come in."

A magpie not only gifted with speech but sarcastic as well. Camp, too, by the sound of it.

I opened the door to its cage.

While my attention was distracted, the canvas walls, even the fairground beyond, must have melted away for on looking up I found myself in open countryside, alone and with no sign of the newly liberated bird. Not before time I set about trying to gain control over what was happening or at least make sense of it.

To do so, as Simon had presciently explained, I needed to refer to the symbolism embodied in the Tree of Life. Into my head came a statement by that intrepid necromancer — well, not so intrepid, given that he passed out halfway through the operation — Eliphas Levi who described the Kabbalah as 'a philosophy as simple as the alphabet and infinite as the Word; a theology which may be summed up on the fingers; an infinite which can be held in the hollow of an infant's hand.' Fine words but just then the philosophy, not to mention the theology, would have to wait. (The theorems were beyond me anyhow.) No, what I needed to do and do urgently was refer to the symbolism of the *Etz Chayim* or Tree of Life, at least as much of it as I could remember, in the hope of finding out where I was and, as the magpie would put it, what the fuck was happening.

From a magical perspective the Tree of Life is a diagrammatic representation of forces active within us and in the macrocosm of which we are part. It supposes that the universe coincided with God's awareness of himself, a cosmogenic event that involved four kinds of manifestation — the initial emanation, its creative dynamism, the subsequent appearance of form and, finally, the material universe. Because it portrays all that exists, the Tree is held to offer a convenient guide to varieties of manifestation beyond sense experience which enable us to venture from our native Malkuth, the bottom sefirah, and discover the rest of them in turn. Such an expedition is no less valid and will appear no less real for being undertaken in the imagination, with symbols representing what itself is inconceivable.

Those symbols and their meaning became clear to me once I calmed down and reflected on my unexpected trip to the fairground. The muddy ground for instance was indicative of Malkuth, traditionally represented by earth and water, as were the pale greens and yellows, twin colours of that sefirah, dominating the jungle vista at the front of one of the sideshows. Even the double-headed pig and the Headless Woman next door hinted at the illusory quality and subtle distortions associated with Malkuth, just as nearby, Selene, Mistress of Allure, emphasised its lunar connections. Indeed, nothing could be more suggestive of the Sphinx, imputed to that sefirah by, among others, Aleister Crowley in his *Liber 777*, than the ghost of a smile, just about visible through the chiffon, that now and then crossed her otherwise expressionless face. As for Crowley's preference for salamander black, speckled with gold, as the colours congenial to Malkuth, these were conspicuous in the dress and hair of the crone to whom I paid a shilling to enter the booth. Only later would I discover that Crowley made a point of linking this particular sefirah to the discovery of one's Higher Self or, as he put it, one's Holy Guardian Angel.

Other commentators link this momentous occurrence to the neighbouring sefirah, Yesod. There is much to be said for it since Yesod, home to archetypal paradigms, is regarded as the sphere most sympathetic to the subliminal reaches of our mind. The Hebrew word means 'foundation' (יסוד) and is not inappropriate, given that here we find the prototype of everything awaiting concrete expression in the natural kingdom (Malkuth). It is also the vehicle through which the life of the universe, reminiscent of Bergson's élan vital writ large, is channelled. That I must have moved by then from the realm of Malkuth was further suggested by the purple curtain at the entrance to the sideshow, this being one of the colours attributed to the sefirah, as also is the reddish-white, more pale russet than pink, of the five-footed toad, again a creature proper to Yesod. As for the snake displayed next to it, that, too, was significant, though it struck me only later, given the phallic associations of this particular sefirah, indicative of its life-imparting function. Finally, the rainbow that greeted me when I found myself out in open countryside is again a symbol of Yesod, a luminous bridge between the visible and invisible worlds.

And the magpie? Ah well, thanks to Mr James, I already knew this was one of the symbols of Mercury or, rather, of the planetary spirit identified as its custodian, the others being a king on the back of a bear, a handsome youth and a fleet-footed dog. With Mercury the rising planet in my natal horoscope and thus, astrologers maintain, the ruler of my innermost self, the little magpie, chutzpah and bad language notwithstanding, was the ideal bird to encounter that evening.

Time must have passed, although I failed to notice it, for I saw now that the rainbow had vanished and a lambent moon had risen in its place, softening the greys, greens and browns of a landscape already misted with fine rain but now, as in a painting by Corot, endowed with an illusory, almost dream-like quality. Yet as I wandered over brooding stretches of moorland like some disembodied Heathcliff, cold, damp and with no idea of where I was heading, all around me seemed perfectly real. I tried not to think of how to get back to where I'd started from, by which I mean not the enigmatic fairground but Simon's house in Tite Street. I could only hope that would take care of itself.

At some point the scenery struck me as oddly familiar. Moreover in a vague, slightly ambiguous way, it began to feel less hostile, even well-disposed towards me, although it wasn't until I spotted a patch of vervain at my feet that I realised where I was. The bleak slopes of Pumlumon were a long way from Chelsea, but in some way they felt a lot closer to home. As I knelt to touch the tiny mauve flowers, I knew before looking up that in front of me stood the man who'd called on Mr James all those years ago. This time his features — and the discovery surprised me less than it might have done — were undeniably my own.

I remember thinking there and then that the bored-looking woman at the Freshers' Party had been right after all. That first trip to Domen Bedwyr, just like this one, had been a matter of the self, in this case mine, looking in upon itself. But only partly right for what it went on to find was not a reflection of itself but itself magnified, as in one of those fairground mirrors I'd noticed earlier. Facing the seventeen-year-old me and now facing me seven years later was my Higher Self, a part of me I'd lost touch with as a boy but met up with again as a man. Together, even if temporarily apart, the two of us were connected in a way that Yeats described in relation to himself and his daimon:

'What marks upon the yielding clay? Two marks
Made by my feet, two by my daimon's feet
But all confused because my marks and his
Are on the selfsame spot. His fell
Where my heel fell, as he and I
Pausing a moment in our headlong flight
Face opposite ways, my future being his past.'

That night my Higher Self and I were one.

"We've met before," I muttered stupidly.
"Silly bugger, of course you've sodding well met before!"
Perched on a nearby rock was the magpie. And do you know what? He sounded just like Mr James.

23

"Do what thou wilt shall be the whole of the Law."
Aleister Crowley

In my second year at college, I came across an eighteenth-century writer called Nicolas Chamfort, little known outside his native France, who died in 1794, months after a botched suicide attempt. (The pistol he was using malfunctioned and blew off half his face.) Among the aphorisms for which he was famous is one that describes love as 'the exchange of two fantasies and the contact of two sets of skin'. (It sounds far better in French: '*L'amour... n'est que l'échange de deux fantaisies et le contact de deux épidermes.*') I remember being relieved he'd put the fantasies first, having never been too fussed about the other.

Whereas at the outset Ronnie seemed a different but complementary version of myself, a reflection of what I'd like to be but, sadly, was not, by now he'd not only ceased to be that but in some perverse way allowed himself to become more like me than I even was myself. The slippers and cardigan he took to wearing at home, *The Times* crossword and a sudden liking for chess were symptomatic of a gradual mutation, conscious or not, into what he perceived to be me, something he may have expected to consolidate our relationship, whereas in truth it did the opposite. Once he stopped being his edgy, slightly louche self, there were no fantasies left to exchange.

And so it ended in tears, mine more perhaps than his, when, inevitably, he found out about Edward Jones, my excuses for staying out late or being absent at weekends by then more and more implausible. Yet even at that point, had he reverted to being the person I'd met four years earlier, I'd not have hesitated to patch things up and carry on. The truth was that despite being Welsh and indisputably good-looking, Edward lacked the visceral appeal of Ronnie. He was handsome, certainly, as well as charming, but for me charm never warranted the bother of taking off my clothes. Yet for him, take them off I did. The earth didn't move but then, again, for me it rarely does.

Six weeks into our relationship, if it could yet be called that, he went off to Balmoral Castle with the royal household once Ascot ended, but suggested I join him there for a week's holiday. Accommodation would be available in one of the estate cottages, with permission to move about freely and visit his rooms at any time. I agreed but opted to stay at a hotel in nearby Ballater.

The plan was for me to hire a bicycle and ride to and from the castle each day and so on my first morning Edward arranged to show me how to get there. As I waited for him in the street, a young man approached me on an old-fashioned bike and muttered something that didn't sound at all like English. Remembering that I was in the Cairngorms, I explained that I didn't speak Gaelic, the words no sooner out of my mouth than I realised the man was Edward and the language had been Welsh. That I'd not known him disconcerted him every bit as much as it did me. Ronnie I'd have spotted half a mile away.

In those days, security at Balmoral was less rigorous than it is now. Even so, being allowed to cycle through the gate and up to the castle without challenge puzzled me until I learned there were armed sentries concealed not only behind the trees along my route but inside several dummy trees as well. Edward's room was located in the tower, accessible by a stone staircase with a tartan carpet not dissimilar to the

207

version favoured by the Rockingham. By then he'd instructed me to greet the Queen, were I to encounter her but not to engage in conversation unless she instigated it. Fair enough.

"And say Your Majesty the first time, then Ma'am afterwards," he continued, "I know you're a bloody republican but you can leave all that behind at the gate."

It must have been on my third or fourth visit that I unexpectedly came upon a small, slightly built woman vigorously chopping logs, a sight so unexpected that I'd observed her for a good thirty seconds before it dawned on me that here was the sovereign herself. All of a sudden, she glanced up but soon resumed chopping. She may not have noticed me or perhaps discerned in me the republican I was.

"It's something she enjoys," remarked Edward when I told him. "Odd thing is, the Kaiser, Great-Uncle Willi they still call him here, liked nothing better than chopping wood. It runs in the family."

"But she looked, I don't know, so frail."

"Don't you believe it. In any case, it makes no difference. The Kaiser had a withered arm, but he could still swing an axe."

I was wrong in thinking the Queen hadn't noticed me. Next day she suggested to Edward that his 'cousin' — either she was poorly briefed or wished to be tactful — might care to join the family and their guests to watch a film after dinner that evening. The film was *The Night of the Generals,* ancient even back then, and before it started, liveried footmen offered cigars to all the men, while the ladies got chocolates, with two pages on hand with rugs, should they start to feel chilly. A warm rug and some Godiva soft-centres would have suited me nicely.

From the start the landscape on Deeside reminded me of Pumlumon — to Victoria and Albert it resembled his native Thuringia — so it was not inappropriate that Mr James should re-enter my life while I was there. This happened after Edward put me in touch with a Thelemite, the first of the breed I'd encountered.

By then the term had already been appropriated by devotees of Aleister Crowley, less numerous than they are now but every bit as keen on the man and his message. I remember that some, rumoured to include Jimmy Page, guitarist and founder member of the rock band Led Zeppelin and future owner of Boleskine House, ran a shop selling books by Crowley off Kensington High Street. It was still there, though seldom open, when Edward and I moved to Notting Hill Gate after buying the London home of Camilla Parker-Bowles and her then husband. Now the Duchess of Cornwall, she is herself no stranger to Buckingham Palace or, for that matter, Balmoral.

With me that afternoon, making short shrift of the shortbread, was a redoubtable woman Edward had arranged for me to meet. He'd come across her after Stephen Barry, then valet to Prince Charles, found himself chatting with her at a reception in, of all places, the Papal Nuncio's residence in Wimbledon. Owner of a house near Abergeldie, not far from Ballater, she'd pressed Stephen to call on her when next in the area, adding for no special reason that unlike others in the room that evening, she was not a Roman Catholic but a Thelemite. The word meant nothing to Stephen and after consulting Edward, his confusion only grew when, thinking he meant catamite, Edward read out the dictionary definition of 'a boy kept for unnatural purposes'. She must have said 'socialite' both had decided by the time they turned up on her doorstep some weeks later, Stephen reluctant to venture there alone.

It was Edward who told her of the misunderstanding. Only then did she put the record straight by telling them she was neither a socialite nor a catamite but a Thelemite, although her explanation of what that implied left them little the wiser.

"It's something to do with magic," he told me, "so I've suggested you'd like to meet her while you're here. She'll be at the hotel around three. And your tea's paid for by the way."

A feisty old girl, she greeted me in a loud voice. I felt glad we had the lounge to ourselves. Later I found out she was deaf.

"Phyllis[42] told me once about your Welsh farmer friend." she

---

42 Phyllis Playter (1893-1982), an American, had lived with Powys, her senior by 22 years, from 1922 until his death 41 years later in Blaenau Ffestiniog, North Wales (see page 276).

declared without preamble. "John Cowper went to see him a couple of times about his stomach. An ulcer probably. I can't remember. Did he teach you about the importance of the will?"

"As in Nietzsche?"

I was showing off.

"Not at all. Nietzsche believed in the will to power. And even that he pinched from Schopenhauer."

All I knew about Schopenhauer was that he'd owned a poodle named Atman, a detail too trivial to mention. By all accounts, he doted on the dog.

"Nietzsche died insane," she continued. "In Weimar. That gifted but rather silly man, Rudolf Steiner, paid him a visit. He got no sense out of him, but was deeply impressed by his profile."

The word Thelemite is popularly thought to be derived from, the fictional Abbey of Thelema described by François Rabelais in his *Gargantua and Pantagruel* (1534), its motto 'Do what thou wilt' (*Fais ce que voudras*) cribbed from St Augustine of Hippo and adopted by both Sir Francis Dashwood's Hellfire Club and by Crowley who declared in his *Book of the Law* (1904) that 'Do what thou wilt shall be the whole of the Law.'

"Thelema means more than ordinary people think," declared my new acquaintance once our tea arrived.

"Universal Will?"

I still hoped to sound clever.

"Inasmuch as Universal Will reconciles cause and effect," she conceded, "given that both are contained within it. Thelema is plenitude, the pleroma of the Gnostics. It comprises all that is and, from our perspective, all that as yet is not."

Access to it, she explained between mouthfuls of shortbread, was gained by exercising our 'true' will, the key that releases us from the grip of causality, and empowers us to function in a new, more sovereign, way, independent of others but, provided they, too, obeyed their 'true' will, in harmony with them.

"We are all," she announced, looking slightly pleased with herself, "stars of the same galaxy."

And with that I was dispatched to fetch more shortbread.

"And some hot water wouldn't go amiss," she bellowed as I went off in search of the kitchen.

She was still picking crumbs off her plate when I returned.

"Volition — the act of willing — lies at the heart of everything."

Mr James had once said something along those lines, assuring me that 'will' was not peculiar to us, but the primary agent of all that happens. Without it, life would not have emerged from inert matter, while every sort of action is ultimately a manifestation of it, the act of willing and the event willed existentially one and the same, each manifesting itself in and through the other. This, I took to mean that, for instance, each time my companion helped herself to more shortbread, the action would not have happened, had it not been willed, just as the act of willing would not have objectively existed without the concomitant action, cause and effect not just co-dependent but essentially one and the same.

Although my companion professed to being a Thelemite, I was reluctant to mention Aleister Crowley too often. Apart from her appetite for shortcake, all about her — tweed suit, sensible brogues and deerstalker hat — suggested moderation and that provincial respectability I remembered so well from my childhood.

"Whether they know it or not, everyone who dabbles in magic is a Thelemite," she boomed, as if reading my thoughts, "although the Crowley lot might disagree. For them, theirs is the one true church. The rest of us are heretics. 'Savages' was the term the old boy favoured."

By the 'Crowley lot' she had in mind the Ordo Templi Orientis (O.T.O.), a quasi-Masonic organisation set up by Karl Kellner, an Austrian industrialist, and Franz Hartmann, sometime disciple of Madame Blavatsky and a resident at Adyar. It was Kellner's successor, Theodor Reuss, who recruited Crowley in 1910, putting him in charge of the British branch, known as Mysteria Mystica Maxima (M.M.M.), and allowing him to devise new rituals that reflected his views on

Thelema, as well as a Gnostic Mass to meet the devotional needs of the faithful. By 1921, Crowley had effectively taken over from Reuss, by then unwell, and two years later, with Reuss conveniently dead, he proclaimed himself his successor.

Now, even before joining forces with Crowley, the founding fathers of the O.T.O., Kellner, Hartmann and Reuss, had been exploring how sexual techniques, among them certain tantric practices, might induce in practitioners a state of heightened awareness, even mystical enlightenment. They would have known that such elevated states were likened by the Gnostics to sexual union between the human and the divine, a conjunction symbolised by Ouroboros, the serpent that swallows its tail. One technique favoured by Reuss involved reciprocal touching of the phallus, a pastime confined of necessity to male participants and one that led to the accusation that that he and his supporters indulged in homo-erotic practices. (The Nazis made much of it to justify their wholesale ban on esoteric organisations throughout Germany.) Defenders of Reuss have sought to justify such behaviour by pointing to a verse in Genesis (24:9) where a manservant 'put his hand under the thigh of Abraham, his master, and swore to him concerning that matter', an act of intimacy which, they maintain, traditionally accompanied pledges of loyalty. They further propose that this is what Casanova had in mind when he referred to 'the oath of the Rosicrucians'.

Not that a bit of furtive groping by consenting adults would have done much, magically or erotically, for Aleister Crowley. Sex, he maintained, was an important constituent of magic because every orgasm imitated in microcosmic terms the creative impetus that brought the universe into being, an event comparable to the impregnation of Nuit, the Egyptian sky goddess, by her consort Haduit, traditionally compared to a circle whose centre is everywhere and outer ridge nowhere. Nuit thereby ensured that the void within her became filled with plenty and the unmanifest was made manifest in Time.

It was Crowley's belief that each spermatozoon contained within itself something of God's creative impulse, a notion derived from Gnostic, particularly Manichean, sources, where creation was viewed as a fructifying effusion of supernal light, the Logos Spermatikos, which permeated the universe before returning to its heavenly source. Left behind were the sparks it emitted as it penetrated and vivified matter, their trace present still in the intimate fluids of men and women. Presumably it was this eccentric notion that accounted for the dubious medicines Crowley peddled towards the end of his life (see page 176, footnote).

One cannot help thinking that Crowley's preoccupation with intimate fluids, as well as with blood, tells us more about him than about magic, as does his pathological urge to be humiliated, preferably by the Scarlet Women he tirelessly recruited, although few provided those extremes of degradation that he, by his own reckoning 'the sublimest mystic of all history… the self-crowned God', so relentlessly craved. That said, it would be foolhardy to dismiss outright his thoughts on magic, even his theological speculation, simply because his sexual predilections are not to everyone's taste. In any case the concept of Thelema or Universal Will is valid regardless of whatever bizarre recreations its chief advocate happened to enjoy.

That the redoubtable woman sitting opposite me that afternoon in Ballater knew, let alone condoned, what Crowley got up to, seemed so improbable that I hesitated to make even an oblique reference to it. As tactfully as I could, I alluded to Crowley's reputation for sexual excess.

"Dirty," was the stentorian response. "Dirty and depraved. And I cannae forgive him for what he did to that poor wee cat."

(On Crowley's orders, the cat in question, Mischette, was to have been killed, as part of a magical operation conducted at the so-called Abbey of Thelema in Sicily. In the event the sacrificial victim wriggled free, its throat half-cut, and ran about the room splattering blood on the horrified participants before finally being recaptured and successfully despatched. Any blood left over was then drunk by those present.)

"Mr Grant would never do such a thing," she continued.

I'd no idea who Mr Grant was but, with other people by then in the room, some within earshot, I forbore to enquire.[43]

"Do as thou wilt," trumpeted my companion when, with tea (or, rather two teas) over, I helped her climb into her car outside the hotel. She invited Edward and me to lunch some days later, an event that turned out to be more formal than expected. I'd been warned about the butler and the maid, but not the redoubtable hat our hostess wore for the occasion, a tweedy affair with pheasant plumage secured by a large amber brooch, partner of an even bigger one, thistle shaped, on her lapel. Ladies always wore hats for lunch, the ever-helpful Edward later informed me, which may be true, but I still found it odd that someone would do so in her own home. For the record, the mulligatawny soup was lukewarm and the salmon criminally under-poached.

"I need to fill myself up," our hostess declared, seemingly to herself, as she smashed her way through the crust of — what else? — a second *crème brûlée* (like Steak Diane and duck à l'orange, *crème brûlée* was hugely popular back then). The colour of its crust matched the amber of the brooches.

"I'm dining at Birkhall tonight. Lots to drink but never enough to eat. Never."

"The Queen Mother's house," Edward explained later. "You pass it on the top road to Balmoral."

The next day, out of curiosity, I took the top road, longer and more scenic than my usual route and again reminiscent of Pumlumon. For all that, I saw no sign of the house. I must, however, have passed the estate, for as I pushed my bike up a modest incline, reflecting on how less fit I'd become than the teenage me that cycled each week to Tanrallt, a car overtook me, its engine so quiet I'd not even realised it was there. Deep

---

43 Kenneth Grant (1924-2011), a pretender to the throne left vacant when Crowley, the Great Beast and Outer Head of the O.T.O., succumbed to bronchitis in 1947. As a young man, Grant became Crowley's assistant and, though not formally appointed his successor as Outer Head of the O.T.O. — that honour went to a German-American named Karl Germer — Grant was given a free hand to run the O.T.O.'s affairs in England, doing so with flair, and introducing novel ideas and practices. He later set up his own Thelemic organisation, the New Isis Lodge, its aim being to exploit what its manifesto termed the Sirius-Seth current. His wife Steffi, a talented artist, died in 2019.

lilac in colour and a Rolls Royce, it stopped a few yards ahead. From one of its windows there emerged what I took to be a bouquet of flowers.

"You're making for the castle, aren't you? Would you care for a lift?"

Drawing closer, I saw that the bouquet was a hat and its wearer Queen Elizabeth, the Queen Mother. Uncertain whether the bicycle would fit into the boot, as she now suggested, but reluctant to abandon it, having paid an exorbitant deposit for its hire, I declined the offer, adding a few gratuitous 'Ma'ams' but not enough to compromise my republican convictions.

"I know who you are and I know all about you. Everything."

The Thelemite, no doubt.

With that the pastel coloured flowers withdrew inside the car. I half expected a cry of 'Do as thou wilt' but, no, the purr of the engine was all I heard as the vehicle resumed its decorous ascent.

Two days later, I flew from Aberdeen back to London, with Ronnie there to meet me at Heathrow. His face, I noticed for the first time in ages, hadn't changed much since that first Saturday when I'd watched him board the train at West Kensington station. Had he consented there and then to make a fresh start, I'd have abandoned Edward Jones and all his royal connections but, no, off he went to work for Shell in South Africa, while Edward quit the grandeur of the Palace, and moved in with the rectory piano, the longcase clock, the William Morris chairs and me.

Oddly enough, it was at Heathrow that I saw Ronnie for the last time. Ten years had elapsed by then. Due to catch a plane to Paris, I was making a quick dash to duty free before my flight was called, when suddenly there he was, walking across the departure lounge towards me. Apart from the suit and the air of respectability it conferred on him, he seemed little changed since our first serendipitous encounter.

"Hey," I said, genuinely pleased to see him. "Surprise, surprise!"

He told me to fuck off.

24

"**Books choose their authors; the act of creation is
not entirely a rational and conscious one.**"
Salman Rushdie

ris Murdoch managed to escape from Somerset House before she
got around to writing books. I did not. Instead the book I wrote
became the instrument of my escape. Our destination, the Treasury,
was the same.

For me, it began when a group of us went to the first night of *Hair*
at the Shaftesbury Theatre on, my diary reminds me, 27 September
1968, a date chosen by the show's creators because, though less pro-
pitious than that of the Broadway opening five months earlier (when,
for the record, Jupiter, Uranus and Pluto occupied the 10th House,
Neptune graced the Ascendant, and the Moon was favourably disposed)
the auspices were encouraging nevertheless. On a night so well-starred,
it was inevitable perhaps that on my way home I announced to Edward
that I planned to write a book on magic, real magic, not the smoke
and mirrors kind, my aim being to persuade my contemporaries, the
Hair generation, that magic could be fun, wholesome and, a challenge

seldom faced, intellectually plausible as well. I can't remember his reaction, which suggests it was lukewarm at best.

For Mr James, magic — although I'm not sure he'd have used the word — was in part a way of investigating our environment so as to understand it better, an ambition similar to that of orthodox science. Similar, but not the same, because by 'environment' he had in mind *all* existence, perceived and imperceptible alike, the challenge being to transcend the limitations of our sense experience in order to engage with a totality to which everything, ourselves included, necessarily belongs. Mindful, however, of the need to persuade people to buy the book, I would later declare — and that on the very first page — that my aim was also 'to enable the adventurous reader to discover whether magic actually works', promising that 'precise instructions will be given later so that anyone so inclined can try a little magic for himself.'

Such was the challenge I set myself while travelling home after *Hair*, the chorus of 'Aquarius' still ringing in my ears. The following Monday, I got down to work. From then on, reports submitted by tax inspectors up and down the land were treated more cavalierly than ever, while the *sapo mollis* was dispensed in such hefty dollops it's a wonder government ministers, members of parliament and taxpayers alike weren't overwhelmed by the scent. Perhaps they were, for a number of complainants felt sufficiently grateful to send letters of thanks even when their grievances had not been addressed, let alone upheld. In no time at all, I'd even cleared a backlog of cases left by my predecessor, a conscientious soul who'd striven to understand the issues in dispute, even redone the calculations, sometimes more than once.

"You've cleaned the Augean stables," exclaimed a member of the board I encountered in the corridor one Friday afternoon. I was the Hercules of Somerset House.

What neither he nor anyone else realised was that this accelerated dispatch of parliamentary correspondence left me free to press on with my book. Behind a barricade of files, I was able to write about magic for hours on end, using official paper, a pale-blue crown at the top of each foolscap page, and ballpoint pens provided free of charge. Meanwhile, concealed from view in the top right-hand drawer of my desk, the clandestine manuscript grew thicker by the day. Even my lunch hours were productive, spent either at the public library in Charing Cross Road or in the depths of Watkins' bookshop, specialists in esoteric literature, in nearby Cecil Court. (It is said that one day, in a fit of pique, Aleister Crowley caused the entire stock to vanish from its shelves, though the books reappeared once the Great Beast had stormed off the premises.) I had no money to purchase the volumes I consulted, so had to memorise whatever information I needed — lists of planetary spirits, angelic beings and other curiosities Mr James was never over-fussed about — then jot all of it down on scraps of paper once outside on the street.

The book was finished by the end of April. The unwieldy manuscript, its pages littered with changes, some barely legible even to me, and overlaid with strips of paper bearing new bits of text, had now to be typed. By happy coincidence (or, if you're into such things, thanks to Saturn in Aries on the night the opus was conceived, a portent of triumph over adversity) the woman who did the chairman's typing, Miss Margaret Williams, came from North Wales and, thanks to that connection, I persuaded her to undertake the job for £40, twenty upfront and twenty on completion. It was not a huge amount, even in those days, but as I pointed out, by doing it in her working hours, she was in effect being paid twice over.

The snag was that when, as often happened, there was nothing to fill those working hours Miss Williams, turned fifty but not yet resigned to spinsterhood, liked nothing better than to promenade around the building in what people called her party frocks, homemade confections reminiscent of Dior's New Look. (Full-skirted and in the brightest of colours, they accompanied her also to the tea dances she attended every Saturday afternoon with portly Mrs Kingham from the typing pool.) On these leisurely perambulations Miss Williams would pause to gossip with any other women she encountered, their time likewise heavy on their hands, foremost among them a Scots lady, Chrissie McKay, who did the filing for the board's medical officer and was thus a valued source of information on people's ailments and infirmities. (Miss McKay's great-nephew was later arrested for murdering several rich widows in Knightsbridge, though that piece of information she was careful to keep to herself.) With my typed pages arriving in dribs and drabs, and some weeks neither, I got into the habit of searching for Miss Williams whenever I found her absent from her desk, scouring the corridors, the board's library (where she went to read the early edition of the *Evening Standard*) and, my final port of call, Miss McKay's little cubbyhole near the covered footbridge between the New and West Wings. In the end, fed up with being harassed, Miss Williams consented to stay late each evening to work on the book, an arrangement that kept her safe from rival distractions but turned out not to be the sacrifice she made it sound after it emerged she'd claimed overtime from the Revenue for the extra hours 'worked'.

With the typescript finally in my possession, the next step was to find a publisher. A friend from college, an editor with Penguin Books, recommended Jonathan Cape in Bedford Square so I squeezed Miss Williams' neatly typed pages — hers was the only electric typewriter in Somerset House — into a large brown envelope marked 'On Her Majesty's Service' and enclosed a covering letter. That lunch hour, off I set for the company's headquarters and twenty minutes later was handing my package to an unsympathetic receptionist, aloof to the point of rudeness and smelling of *Shalimar*.

"At least you finished it," I told myself over a celebratory beer at The Globe in Covent Garden before returning to the files and yet more *sapo mollis*.

Within Somerset House it had long been the custom every afternoon at four o'clock sharp for people to close their files and troop solemnly off for tea and sweet biscuits. Each month, for the sake of change, they'd gather in a different colleague's room, segregated by rank but bound by a common understanding that for the allotted fifteen minutes nobody was permitted to talk about work. There was the principals' tea club, to which we assistant principals were admitted, the assistant secretaries' tea club and an elite group consisting of under-secretaries, mostly members of the board, as well as its two deputy chairmen and the chairman himself. Tea, brewed in a cubby-hole at the end of the corridor by a squad of elderly messengers, was the same for everyone but members of the board drank it from bone-china cups around a mahogany table on which Lord Nelson was rumoured to have ravished Lady Hamilton when the Admiralty had its home in Somerset House. (The identical claim was made of another table in the eponymous Nelson Room elsewhere in the building so either one was an imposter or the First Sea Lord availed himself of both.) Next to the table stood a Thomas Tompion longcase clock, a repeater that struck every quarter of an hour, discreetly alerting those present when their fifteen minutes were up. Farther down the corridor our approach to timekeeping was more cavalier, with breaks of forty minutes not at all uncommon.

One afternoon, when it was my turn to host the principals' tea club, watched by Messrs Goering and Tagore (poor Rudolf Hess too befuddled to notice), the telephone rang. As a rule, such calls went unanswered, given that most related to work and any discussion of official business during the tea break was a grave breach of etiquette. Personal calls, too, were best ignored, the trouble being that if one picked up the receiver, the room immediately fell silent as those in it stopped talking, even mid-sentence, or halted whatever else they were doing, leaving teacups midway to lips or cigarettes, still unlit, dangling between them. In part, it was done out of courtesy but in part, too, from good old-fashioned nosiness.

It must have been inadvertence therefore, or perhaps force of habit, that induced me to pick up the phone that afternoon, only to find myself listening to an unfamiliar voice, American by the sound of it, which clearly had no interest in discussing income tax, corporation tax or any other kind of fiscal impost.

"I've read your manuscript,", it drawled, "and must ask you something. Are you saying that if I do as you say, I'll conjure up lots of sexy she-demons?"

While working out how best to answer, knowing a straightforward 'Yes' might lead to further embarrassing questions, while a 'No' would discredit the book's magical pretensions, I could hear a colleague beside me trying to munch a custard cream as soundlessly as possible without visibly moving his mouth.

I believe in the end I said 'Yes', if only to shut the caller up. I know I agreed to drop in at his office after work that same evening. His name was Ed Victor, then on the board of Jonathan Cape and subsequently a well-known literary agent. Within a week, I'd signed a contract and received the first instalment of my advance.

Ten months later, the book was published under a pseudonym dreamt up at the last minute and intended to forestall problems at work. By coincidence its publication coincided with my birthday at the end of January, one day after the *Sunday Times* published an article about me by Philip Oakes, written after several hours spent together over a boozy lunch at L'Escargot Bienvenu in Soho. Later, and by then the worse for drink, I allowed myself to be photographed outside Somerset House, with the result that readers of the paper were treated to a picture of me on the steps of the building, with Inland Revenue clearly visible above my right shoulder.

And in case anyone should miss it, the piece was headed 'A Magician from Somerset House'.

At work the next day nothing was said. The tea club convened as usual and though tempted to stay away, I forced myself to put in an appearance, reckoning that the longer I left it, the harder it would be to show up. But again, none of those present made any reference to what had been in the paper the previous day, enough to encourage me to hope they might all be readers of *The Sunday Telegraph* or *The Observer.*

Over the next fortnight, there were more interviews but no more photographs, while from the publishers came the first batch of readers' letters, some from people more famous than I would ever be.[44] But one letter gave me more pleasure than any of the rest, more certainly than the sender could have foreseen. Over two pages in violet ink, in a script so tiny it was barely legible, the writer described how pleased he'd been to see Aberystwyth mentioned in *The Sunday Times* article. Had I, he enquired, come across his late mother who'd formerly lived there? The writer was Nicholas Sandys, son of Countess Barcynska. Nicholas was the jeune premier who had left town in 1939 with a valedictory swish of silk scarf, vowing never to return.

But return he did, for the next time he got in touch, it was from an address in Powell Street, Aberystwyth. In a rambling narrative, he wrote at length and with conspicuous affection of his mother before disclosing that he planned to buy a caravan and see out his days near New Cross ("Y Gors" in Welsh) the hamlet where she and Caradoc had lived and where both by then lay buried. Sadly, it was the last I heard from him.

The weeks passed. I did radio interviews and was even the subject of a half-hour television programme, part of a series called 'Six Remarkable People'. (My father commented that I was the only one nobody had heard of.) By then I was beginning to enjoy my newfound celebrity, until out of the blue there came a summons from the chairman of the board.

'Treasury ministers have read the piece in the *Sunday Times*. So has the Chancellor of the Exchequer. I'm told the Prime Minister has seen it as well.'

The speaker looked as grave as he sounded. Sitting opposite him in a red leather chair which, like others in the room, had recently been re-covered — the tea club grumbled for a week about the extravagance — I was uncertain how to respond.

---

44 Among the correspondents who have since died, were David Bowie (see 'The Resurrections of David Bowie': James Parker, *The Atlantic* magazine, April 2016) and William Burroughs. The latter would refer to the book several times and, together with Dion Fortune's *Psychic Self-Defence*, it was among the items listed as being in his room when he died. (See also Matthew Levi Stevens, *The Magical Universe of William Burroughs*, Mandrake, Oxford, 2014). He also wrote to me several times, often neglecting to put a stamp on the envelope.

If apologies were called for, the *Sunday Times* should proffer them. After all, it was they that blew the gaff by getting me (by then, tipsy) to pose in front of the building. Next door in the Board Room the Tompion repeater primly struck the hour. Then, as if on cue, the chairman gave a grin.

"Well," he declared, "You've got more in you than most people here, even if they do keep out of mischief and know more about taxation than you ever will. You've learned an important lesson: never trust the press. Journalists are in it only for themselves. Plus, they're forever dodging tax, either that or fiddling their expenses."

I neither spoke nor shifted in my chair, the first because I'd not yet worked out what to say, the second because the chair's new leather made whoopee cushion noises whenever I moved.

"We've a proposal to make. Now that we're set to join Europe, there's a job going in Brussels. With the U.K. delegation. You'd be helping to keep an eye on the commission's budget, monitoring expenditure, that sort of thing. Do you want it? At least you'd be out of the spotlight."

And the *sapo mollis*.

I was minded to ask for more time. It never paid to seem too eager. Plus, I'd begun to like the spotlight.

"Full diplomatic status. You'll be seconded to the Treasury, and they in turn will lend you to the Foreign Office. With all the perks, you'll come close to tripling your salary. And on top there's an allowance for this, an allowance for that and your rent is paid for. You'll be better off than all of us!" That clinched it.

25

"Magic's just science that we don't understand yet."
Arthur C. Clarke

Up to now, I've bandied the word magic about without doing much to defend its reputation, let alone explain how its practice is compatible with what we know about the world and our place in it. I need to put right that omission, or at least have a try.

The subject is one I touched upon in the opening chapter of my book, but stopped short of exploring, chiefly because readers in those days were more interested in results than the mechanics behind them. In any case, as its title made plain, the book was a primer, not a treatise.

'Magic makes the impossible happen' is how several well-respected dictionaries define the term, overlooking the fact that if something 'happens', it ceases to be impossible. What they mean is that magic makes things happen that would be impossible without it.

How it does so is never explained. Not surprising, given that magic — true magic, that is, not the smoke and mirrors kind — involves engaging with a reality beyond the here-and-now, yet one to which the here-and-now necessarily belongs. Contrary to what people, even magicians, may suggest, there is nothing 'other-worldly' about such a reality, for it accommodates, as well as transcends, the world our senses equip us to perceive. And it is no less real for being imperceptible.

Few nowadays would deny that such a reality exists. It is implicit in the behaviour of elementary particles, the very building blocks of matter, behaviour that is puzzling but by no means 'supernatural', being subject to our observation of it and to laws no less 'natural' for not being fully understood. What it does suggest is that matter, functioning as wave, is exempt from the spatio-temporal constraints to which, as particle, it is constitutionally bound. Instead, there prevails at the subatomic level a state of probability, ostensibly erratic, even capricious, that hints at realities beyond the one we take for granted, each of them part of a single, possibly infinite, whole.

An inkling of such realities or at least the possibility of them may have started when our ancestors first became aware, not of themselves and the world about them, a privilege not uniquely human, but *aware of themselves being aware*. Such a detachment from, as it were, the process of thinking, represents a kind of self-emancipation. It is what makes us more than our biological selves, allowing us to function both inside and outside the world perceptible to us. One might say that in a functional, as well as constitutional, sense we are ourselves both particle and wave.

As a result of this development, the earliest human beings were intuitively aware of a reality beyond sense-derived experience, as well as persuaded that their awareness of it might somehow determine its behaviour. As a result, they sought on occasion to adapt that behaviour to match a preferred outcome. Such was the fundamental purpose of magic, summed up, you may remember, by Aleister Crowley, as 'the science and art of causing change to occur in conformity with Will'. (The same tendency accounts also of course for the prevalence of superstition.)

We can discern here something akin to the so-called observer effect mentioned earlier, although scientists currently insist that when this occurs, it does so involuntarily and then only on the subatomic level, a localised curiosity which does not impinge on the 'real' world. Such may well be true — indeed one rather hopes it is — yet if, as seems likely, the behaviour of waves and particles is determined by our observation of them, then we must agree with the physicist Sir James Jeans that each individual consciousness is comparable to a brain-cell within a universal mind. In short, we dwell within a participatory universe and, knowingly or not, each of us collaborates in its behaviour.

That said, most contemporary researchers remain hostile to the notion that consciousness permeates — and may well have preceded — the manifested universe. They label such notions 'woo-woo' science, especially when peddled by occultists like me. Yet the truth is that any attempt to make sense of reality, given what we know about the subliminal connivance between observer and observed, is as much a metaphysical as a scientific challenge. One person's speculation is another person's woo-woo.

Of course, there are limits to the comparison between the changes magic purports to engineer and those at a subatomic level, willed or not, that derive from our observation. Neither 'proves' the other. That may be, however, because both are essentially one and the same.

A further challenge when trying to explain how magic works is that we lack the words to describe it. Language relates to, indeed derives from, our experience of the world about us so only by reference to the here-and-now can we speak meaningfully of anything beyond it. Even then it is often by describing what this something is *not*, that we manage to convey (or at least suggest) what it is. Thus infinity, as the word implies, is 'end*less*', ghosts are '*in*corporeal', telepathy is '*extra*sensory', while the '*super*natural' depends on the 'natural' in order to mean anything at all.

A fundamental premise of quantum physics, one alluded to earlier, is that the objects around us are not so much discrete entities (what classical physics called *res extensa*) but are comprehensible only in terms of fluid or mathematical structures. Magic shares, indeed exploits, the same premise, implicit acknowledgement that ideas constitute the reality behind all observable phenomena.

The claim is made nevertheless that magic is irrational. Whatever its shortcomings, it is not. Something is not irrational just because it defies explanation. If a princess kisses a toad that turns into a prince, the effect is not irrational just because it cannot be explained. It may escape our understanding, yes, but the event itself is no less real on that account. What is irrational would be to deny it ever happened. Unexpected it might be, however welcome, but the fact remains that it happened.

Of course, reason is constantly nourished and shaped by experience. It might be said, therefore, that kissing toads in the hope they turn into princes is not rational behaviour. Yet no less irrational would be to deny the metamorphosis if, kiss over, one were confronted by a handsome prince, six-foot-three in his socks and as untoadlike as humanly possible.

The example is of course frivolous, but it permits me to show that magic does not require a suspension of disbelief. On the contrary, scepticism is every bit as important as belief. What it does require is a suspension of prejudice. It invites us to keep an open mind, judging it by the results secured, not by the procedures we follow in order to secure them. Scientific enquiry, too, demands nothing less.

That said, before labelling something 'magical', we need to be sure it doesn't appear so just because we cannot determine what caused it. A rational explanation has always to take precedence over any other sort. As a small boy I loved watching 'Professor' Humo pull rabbits from top hats or snatch playing cards out of thin air on Aberystwyth bandstand every afternoon from July to September, weather permitting and Sundays excepted. (Halfway through the performance his daughter Pearl, my age and all smiles, would pirouette to a scratched record of The Skater's Waltz while, off stage, her father sorted out the rabbits and the airborne cards.) I never ceased to marvel at the performance, but even at five or six I never doubted that it was the Professor who engineered the tricks, not some supernatural agency he'd recruited to help him. Everyone with an interest in occultism should do as much when presented with an effect that lacks an identifiable cause. Even the handsome prince might turn out to be a sex pest dressed up as a toad.

Anybody wishing to explore the supernatural can resort to no better tool than Brother Occam's celebrated 'razor'. The fourteenth-century friar was at pains to insist that the correct explanation for any event is likely to be the simplest, one which, as Sir Isaac Newton put it, 'is both true and sufficient to explain' it. In other words, we must 'shave off' superfluous explanations, the more outlandish the less probable, when a simple one does the job perfectly well. In short, look around for a discarded toad-suit before running off with the prince.

Our tendency to favour a supernatural explanation when a straight-forward one is at hand, reflects a craving for the numinous — from the Latin *numen*, meaning a divine or spiritual, presence — that is part of the human condition, a product of the self-transcendence, intellectual and emotional, that makes us aware of being aware. This has sometimes been described as a longing for the spiritual both in and beyond the material world, evidence of a dissatisfaction with our humdrum sur-roundings which the German novelist Jean Paul dubbed *Weltschmerz*. The notion owes much to Schopenhauer, who maintained that our senses register an objective reality which our intellect then adapts to match our capacity to perceive it. It thus follows that the everyday world we perceive is not the 'real' thing (*das Ding an Sich*, as Kant would say) but a phenomenal representation tailored to match our limited percep-tion. Schopenhauer went on to argue that this underlying reality is the expression of an all-pervasive Will, a notion that made him sympathetic to the practice of magic. Anticipating Aleister Crowley, he saw magical practice as a collaborative attempt by the magician's will and its univer-sal parent to produce a desired result. For him the ritual trappings that went with it, were a device to hone the practitioner's will but of little intrinsic merit, a point made also by Eliphas Lévi, although that never hindered him, still less Crowley, from indulging in ceremonial and, in the latter's case, a bit of hanky panky as well.

What is undeniable is that magic, with its emphasis on the duality inherent in matter is not unrelated to the animistic beliefs of primitive societies. Theirs was the conviction, once regarded as naive, that objects, animate and inanimate alike, possess a spiritual element peculiar to each yet in essence common to all, being a particular manifestation of the wider, possibly infinite, reality to which they belong. This affinity between part and whole is nowhere stronger than in human beings, the awareness of ourselves-being-aware creating an ontological connection between the individual and the whole. Such is the basic premise of what is called hermeticism.

The name derives from the mythical Hermes Trismegistus or Thrice-Greatest Hermes,[45] whose purported writings, the *Corpus Hermeticum*, were much admired by early Christian writers, including St Augustine, and by the Neo-Platonists, then largely forgotten until the Renaissance when they enjoyed something of a resurgence, one that would be renewed in the nineteenth century thanks to the occult revival, notably by the eponymously named Hermetic Order of the Golden Dawn.

Of special appeal to magicians was the Second Book of Hermes, the so-called Emerald Tablet, found in an Arabic text, the *Kitah Ustuqus al-Uss al-Thani* ('Second Book of the Elements of Foundation') and containing the maxim 'That which is Below corresponds to that which is Above, and that which is Above corresponds to that which is Below, to accomplish the miracle of the One Thing.'[46] What these words seem at first to imply is that anything happening on one level of existence can have repercussions on another, as, for example, in the case of psychoso-

---

45 The name is proper to the Greek Hermes and the Egyptian god Thoth, both of them associated with magic and with writing. Given the Hellenistic influence — indeed presence — in Ancient Egypt, Hermes Trismegistos may be less an amalgam of two deities than the same deity under different names. The Wisdom god, Thoth (known as Tehuti) was chiefly worshipped at Khemenu, known also as Hermopolis, and was the mediator between opposites, a role alchemists would attribute to Celestial Mercury, (C. G. Jung would describe the archetypal Hermes as a conciliatory and transformative force.) Readers curious to know more about the mythical Hermes and the tradition bearing his name, cannot do better than read the works of Frances A. Yates, notably her *Giordano Bruno and the Hermetic Tradition* (1964).

46 A version rendered by him into English was among Sir Isaac Newton's papers at the time of his death.

matic illness where mental states may produce physical symptoms. The deeper, more traditional meaning, is that the microcosm that is each of us, fuelled by our awareness of ourselves being aware, creates an interactive relationship between the universe and us.

Magic is a technique that exploits this relationship. What the observer of quantum-scale particles causes to happen, voluntarily or not, at their micro-level, the magician strives to accomplish in the everyday world, although both worlds are of course essentially one. How to go about it is what I'd tried to explain while scribbling away in Somerset House, my efforts concealed behind the files stacked up on the desk. And it is there you must look, if you want to learn more. What I remember is that by the time I reached the final chapter, I could have sworn that inside his picture frame Rudolf Hess, no stranger to occultism, was looking less bemused than when I'd first arrived in the building. Even Reichsmarschall Goering seemed to be giving a conspiratorial wink. On the other hand, perhaps both were pleased I was finally quitting Somerset House, my ambition from the first day there. Ahead of me lay the prospect of a sybaritic life in Brussels.

I told you: magic works.

26

**"Even if the aliens are short, dour, and sexually obsessed—
if they're here, I want to know about them."**
Carl Sagan

Uccle is one of the more genteel suburbs of the Belgian capital. And my flat lived up to its pretensions, a heady mix of brocades, tapestries, oriental rugs and generous dollops of gilt, with each room, even the bathroom, illuminated by chandeliers of varying pomposity. (Called *lustres* in French, there was a shop, aptly named Le Palais des Lustres, selling nothing else slap in the city centre). The furniture was a mixture of Louis XV and Empire, all of it reproduction but 'quality reproduction', as the letting agent pointed out, having first tried to persuade me it was the real thing. Even my inexpert eye could see it was not.

"But you know, *cher Monsieur*," he assured me after I pointed it out, "the fake stuff is often superior, far superior, to the original. More realistic for a start."

The work was undemanding. Every Thursday I attended a weekly meeting of the budget and finance committee, comprised of civil servants from all nine member states, the six founding members and three newcomers, Denmark, Ireland and ourselves. The committee's mandate was to scrutinise the commission's budget proposals before they were submitted to our bosses, the permanent representatives, and finally to government ministers for eventual adoption. Most of the discussion was in French, although my Belgian neighbour, staunchly Flemish, switched occasionally to Dutch, catching everyone out. Two things I remember from my first meeting are that I learned a new term, *cheptel bovin,* meaning 'cattle', something the French were forever banging on about, and, secondly, that I made eye contact with an Italian interpreter, darkly handsome behind the smoked glass of the booth where he sat. His name, he told me later, was Massimo. It suited him. He was a very big boy.

For the rest of the week, my job involved little more than discovering what the commission was up to, or securing answers to questions raised by civil servants back in Whitehall, an exercise best undertaken over a hearty lunch and a bottle of wine, something my new colleagues were quick to recommend.

Within a month, I'd tracked down several gay bars, cosier than their brasher counterparts in London. I'd also made friends with a man of my age called Hubert, whom I seemed to bump into whenever each of us was out on his own and glad of someone to talk to. (Few things are worse than standing in a gay bar looking abandoned and forlorn.) Not long afterwards, Hubert got into the habit of coming over for supper once, sometimes twice, a week or I'd go over to his place in a less salubrious part of town, a way of escaping from the faux Louis XV and those unforgiving *lustres.*

A landscape architect by profession, he occupied the top floor of a small building in the rue Cornet de Grez. On one side were a partitioned-off bedroom and a tiny kitchen, made even tinier by the shower cabinet squeezed between the fridge and the end wall, while the remaining area functioned both as studio and living space, the latter as untidy as it was snug. Within months of meeting we'd become close — he took me several times to see his parents in Charleroi — yet the more I got to know him, the more persuaded I became that there was more to him than I was equipped, perhaps entitled, to discover.

And that brings me to the hard bit, made harder because much of what I've written previously, will already seem far-fetched. Still, what I'm about to narrate, however improbable, does at least belong to the reality we live in, not to some hypothetical alternative, let alone involve ghostly old ladies or phantom trips to Clogwyn Bedwyr in the dead of night. To that extent it is not other-worldly, even if in another sense it is precisely that. Supernatural it certainly is not.

I said that Hubert was a landscape architect. Few jobs are more down-to-earth. Tall, enviably well-built (he went to the gym twice a week), with long hair and a lumbering gait, he sometimes reminded me of our caveman ancestors, having the kind of broad, flattish face attributed to them. Only his eyes hinted at more, seeming at times to emit a peculiar radiance, so subtle it was barely perceptible, yet no less real on that account. To blame, I decided, was short-sightedness, yet knowing the cause did little to diminish the impact and while I continued to enjoy his company, I became persuaded that something about him was not what it seemed. By this I don't mean that anything was wrong, just that part of him seemed hidden from me, a part I was ill equipped to understand. It never bothered me unduly.

Until, that is, one Sunday night when he came by to collect something he'd asked me to order for him duty-free, another perk of the job. This time it wasn't the usual cigarettes or bottle of Southern Comfort, his favourite tipple, but a litre of plain alcohol. (His plan was to empty it into a jar, leaving room enough to suspend a pear above it, his hope being that the liquid would eventually turn into Poire Williams.) By the time he arrived at my place I'd already drunk several glasses of wine but now, with all this talk of hooch, we got stuck into the brandy. Was I drunk? No. When I'm about to get drunk, I first become queasy, a signal to stop, then I swallow hard and, if that doesn't work, end up being sick. That Sunday I was close to drunk but no more.

Close enough, however, to start interrogating Hubert for the first time. I can see us now, him squeezed into an armchair and me reclining, feet up, on a Directoire sofa, not unlike Madame Récamier in the well-known painting by Jacques-Louis David. Whether because of the brandy or the *lustres*, the strangeness of Hubert's eyes seemed more pronounced than ever.

"Tell me," I heard myself say, "about your secret."

"What secret?"

Had I known, I'd not have asked. I tried again.

"There *is* a secret, isn't there?"

I'd put the question to him half a dozen times before I got an answer.

"Yes."

It left me none the wiser but seemed to be progress of sorts.

"Are you going to tell me what it is?"

Again he took his time to respond.

"No."

And that was it. He stood up, picked up his car keys and left.

Despite being annoyed by his refusal to enlighten me, I never questioned his right not to do so. And yet here was I, normally the most pacific of creatures, furious that I'd come close to an explanation, only for him to get up and scarper.

Not until I heard him trying in vain to start his elderly Citroën DS did I begin to calm down. "You'll be sick, if you don't," warned an inner voice, the one that sounds like my mother.

Finally, the car consented to start. Moving shakily into the bedroom I lay on the bed and yelled at the ceiling "If there's anything out there, please, please tell me what this is about."

The answer came in a flash, so sudden but above all so unexpected that I sobered up at once. What strikes me today is the total, almost imperative, conviction it brought with it, the more remarkable because it was not at all an answer I expected, still less wanted, to hear. Yet I had no choice but to believe it. And that certainty has stayed undiminished — and no more welcome — ever since.

Now, there's one type of literature that has never appealed to me and that's science fiction. In the cinema, too, films like *Star Wars* and the *Star Trek* series leave me unmoved. (Having fallen asleep through the original *Alien,* I still don't know how it ends.) Neither have I been all that interested in flying saucers or tales of abduction, my view being that sightings of the former, when not an optical illusion, are probably imagined, while the latter hint at some kind of psychosis.[47] I remember, too, that C.G. Jung suggested flying saucers were projections of the Collective Unconscious — he tended to blame everything on the Collective Unconscious — although he did finally concede there might also be something more to them. Which is why I felt so let down when the answer I got that night was that Hubert was from another world. I mean — really! — the last thing I wanted to hear was that an extra-terrestrial had been sitting at my faux Louis-Philippe table ('splayed legs and decorated with brass ormolu mounts' gushed the inventory) yet, like it or not, that was the answer I got.

---

47 Often overlooked but of interest is a sighting at Peibio, near Holyhead, in 1743. One morning a farmer, William Lewis, and his servant were out ploughing when they saw a ship in full sail travelling across the sky from the direction of Snowdonia. Lewis promptly fetched his wife, who arrived in time to see the vessel retreat to where it came from, sails now furled and pennant lowered to the deck. Within days, word of it reached Lewis Morris, writer, antiquarian and, by profession, a marine surveyor, who turned up to investigate the case, prudently interrogating each witness separately. In the event it was Mrs Lewis, though unfamiliar with nautical terms, who gave so detailed an account that Morris was persuaded she had indeed seen the vessel she painstakingly described. Her husband, interviewed in a Holyhead tavern, was described by Morris as honest, sober and without a trace of that 'melancholic' disposition that leads people to imagine things or tell untruths. He was adamant that what he'd seen was a genuine ship, not some trick of the light, confounding those who suggested it might have been the reflection on clouds of a packet boat moored in Holyhead harbour, by insisting he'd observed the keel from underneath. He also described how he'd noticed the sails billow in the wind, counted the ropes of rigging and watched a flock of curious seagulls circle the vessel until it began to move backwards, at which point the birds flew off as one in the opposite direction. What also impressed Morris, judging by the report he penned that night at (appropriately) the Ship Inn at Dolgellau, was the farmer's assurance that he'd witnessed a similar phenomenon ten years earlier. It seems plausible that Lewis and his wife (whose main concern was what the neighbours might think, if word of their experience got out) did indeed perceive 'something' in the sky above Peibio but then pictured it in terms familiar to them. The same might be true also of the pilot Kenneth Arnold, who on 24 June 1947 reported seeing what looked like nine shining discs passing Mount Rainier in Washington State, moving, as he put it, as a saucer might do 'if you skipped it across water'. From then on what other people reported seeing were not ninety-ton ketches in full sail, with pennants proudly flying, but saucer-shaped objects every bit as shiny and fast-moving as the Mount Rainier originals. It suggests that witnesses may well perceive 'something' but it is their expectation or their imagination that lends it form and detail.

Next morning came and I woke up with no trace of a hangover. What I did have and could well have done without was the conviction that I'd been in the company of someone from another world. On the other hand, I still couldn't bring myself to think of Hubert as essentially other than himself: the extra-terrestrial element might be part of him, perhaps the defining part, but in all else he was no different from the person I'd by then got to know well.

I needed to tell someone. Near the office was a self-service restaurant, too humble for my colleagues to patronise and so, confident we'd not be disturbed, I invited the ambassador's secretary, Fiona Comber, to come there with me for lunch. She'd met Hubert a couple of times and I was keen to discover if she'd noticed anything odd about him. Best of all, Fiona was fastidiously discreet.

"I saw Hubert last night," I said, as we walked along the Avenue des Arts.

"And when are they going to invade us?"

The words were no sooner out of her mouth than she stopped in her tracks. I can see her now, Loden coat, Hermes scarf and auburn hair, sensibly cut.

"Good Heavens," she said, "What made me say that?"

Until recently, the two of us would sometimes talk about what happened, the last time just days before she died. And she remembered every detail. The only thing we disagreed about was the coat. I insisted it was green, she said navy blue.

I mentioned that Jung had linked flying saucers and alien encounters to the Collective Unconscious. An incident from my childhood suggests he may have been right. At the time, like many other seven-year-olds, I belonged to a gang. In truth I was the boss of it, the only gang of interest to me being one I was in charge of. Typically, we had our cryptic signs and passwords, as well as the names I'd bestowed on each member, five in all, which I'd also incorporated in a rather tuneless ditty that we'd chant on our way home from school. It began with Magonia, which was the name I'd given myself, then Magousta, that of my friend, Colin

Samuel, followed by others. What inspired these bits of nonsense, I no longer recollect, any more than I remember why I used to tell the others that Magonia was a civilization somewhere out in space.

Not until forty years later, long after I'd quit Brussels, did I read that in the ninth century, the then Archbishop of Lyons, had written a treatise on the weather in which he, too, spoke of a planet beyond ours called Magonia. He reported that local peasants believed its inhabitants travelled in 'cloud ships' which might sometimes be observed zig-zagging across the sky, with storms often coming in their wake. Shortly afterwards, I encountered the name again, this time in a reference to a book named *Passport to Magonia: from folklore to flying saucers* by Jacques Vallée, scientist, ufologist and supposedly the model for the character played by François Truffaut in Spielberg's *Close Encounters of the Third Kind*, a film dear to sceptics and believers alike. While not questioning the sincerity of those claiming to have witnessed UFOs or consorted with aliens, the author rejects the literal interpretation normally favoured. Instead he proposes that such events are part of a multi-dimensional reality which may occasionally impinge on the three-dimensional one we inhabit. All of which sounds plausible enough but Hubert, for now at least, was undeniably part of our world and tangibly real.

The following Thursday, I was due at his place for supper and in the absence of any word from him, took his silence to mean he still expected me. This would be my first opportunity to confront him with what I'd discovered. The trouble was that I'd no idea how to go about it. I was still undecided when I turned up at the Rue Cornet de Grez. All I knew was that I'd never manage to bring myself to ask outright where he came from. And judging by his reaction the previous Sunday he'd probably throw me out, if I did.

Also invited that night were Nicole, the daughter of Hubert's landlord, and her best friend Jacqueline. Both were at the kitchen table when I got there, with a jar containing alcohol and a rather sweaty pear in front of them. They were trying to persuade Hubert that the pear should be immersed in the alcohol, not suspended over it by a piece of string. Its correct position was still in dispute when the meal ended.

Next morning both girls had to begin work early so they left soon afterwards. To get out of our host's way while he stacked plates and glasses in the sink, I went off to the next room and perched on the stool in front of his drawing board. With no door to the kitchen we were able to carry on chatting while inside my head I tried to work out how to question him about his 'secret'. Simply to blurt out "Are you an extra-terrestrial?" seemed crass, rather like quizzing someone about his bowel movements or sexual preferences. Worse, it sounded comic, even bonkers. He might laugh it off.

At some point, I glanced around the room and in the corner where he kept his LPs, spotted the music from Stanley Kubrick's film *2001: A Space Odyssey*. Over I went to fetch it and was no sooner back on the stool than Hubert came into the room.

"By the way," I began, trying to sound casual, the album flat pressed flat against my chest, "I think I know your secret."

The hope was that on seeing the record sleeve, he'd put two and two together and own up.

"What secret?"

It seemed more like a challenge than a question. Having got this far, I was not about to stop.

"Tell me, are your origins the same as mine?"

"What are my origins?"

A hard one, that.

"I think your origins lie beyond the sun."

It sounded a bit precious but got things out in the open. I even thought it clever.

"I'd like you to leave."

"But is it true?"

"Out. I want you out. Now."

I stayed put. I had the upper hand. His eyes had briefly lost a little of their mystery.

"I'll go when I've had an answer. I'm entitled to one."

Of course, I had no such entitlement but then I'd given him my friendship, fed him umpteen times and virtually kept him in cigarettes, not to mention Southern Comfort. If Hubert was typical, Southern Comfort have an untapped market somewhere out in space.

"I'll go when you tell me what it's all about."

"How do I know what it's about?" he shouted. And suddenly I felt sorry for him.

We returned to the kitchen. There was wine left over so he removed two glasses from the sink, rinsed them under the tap, and we sat down again at the table. With that he proceeded to tell me how he'd known for as long as he could remember that his home, his true home, was not in our world but in another so fundamentally different that he himself had no words to describe it. And that despite fleeting memories of it every now and then. Since he'd grown older, the knowledge was easier to live with but as a child he'd yearned to return to wherever he'd come from or at least remember what he'd left behind.

"I was born, I'll fall ill and I'll die. Just like everyone else. But then," and finally his eyes grew luminous again, "the real me will go back to where it belongs."

"Are there other people like you?" I enquired.

"Yes, but I don't know them. We're here to understand what it feels like to be you. Where I come from, nothing's the same. That's why we must lead fully human lives. To get to know things first-hand. When I go back, I'll take the experience with me."

I asked if anyone else had uncovered his secret. Only one, he replied, an artist from South America, from Argentina, who took LSD and had 'seen' what I'd intuitively grasped. The man had gone on to paint strange, psychedelic landscapes that were meant to be an approximation of what things were like wherever Hubert came from. Apparently, he'd done a brisk trade selling his work in places like Amsterdam, London and Berlin. According to Hubert, the money would by then have more than paid his fare home.

"I've told you enough, too much," he concluded. "In any case it's not safe, not for you and not for me either."

I was about to say something when he rose and pointed to the door.

"You must leave. Now. And you've got to understand I can't see you again. I'm sorry. This has come between us."

"It's the truth that's come between us."

Even back then it struck me as melodramatic. I still wish I hadn't said it.

"The truth can harm as well as do good," replied Hubert.

But by then I was halfway down the stairs.

If I'd hoped his admission would make me feel better, I was soon disappointed. Worse, over the next few days I began to feel that what-ever world Hubert belonged to, it was beginning to impinge on my own, Well, not so much impinge as render the here and the now less important and, in a subtle way, less relevant. Not only was there some-thing else 'out there' but the something, now that I'd got close to it, left me restless and dissatisfied. There seemed only one remedy and that was to head off home, to revisit the past I'd grown up with, even speak Welsh again, and so reaffirm who I was and where I'd come from. I telephoned Edward in London — he'd stayed behind but frequently came over to Brussels — and suggested he pick me up at Heathrow so that we might drive straight from there to my parents in Llandudno.

In the event we interrupted our journey to call on his sister in Northampton. While there, she drew our attention to a record player she'd recently bought, an elaborate affair in a walnut cabinet that looked old-fashioned even back then. Sensing our lack of enthusiasm, she praised the quality of the sound, playing us some music to prove it. Her choice was the theme from Kubrick's film, Richard Strauss' *Also Sprach Zarathustra*, the album cover identical to the one I'd held in Hubert's garret only days before.

We were close to the Welsh border when I told Edward what had happened. He was sceptical. In his place I'd have been the same. And then no sooner was I finished than ahead of us were the mountains of Snowdonia — *Eryri* or Home of Eagles in Welsh — but for the first time ever the prospect failed to move me. Something was different. Something had changed. Not the mountains, certainly. They'd not changed for centuries, but something inside me.

Next day we travelled to Anglesey to visit Edward's mother. Again, we stopped on the way, this time for coffee with my cousin in Llanfairpwllgwyngyll, the village with '-gogerychwyrndrobwllllantysiliogogogoch' tagged on to entertain the tourists. As we sat talking, her eldest son, Rhodri, then six or seven, walked in from the garden, marched straight up to the record player and put on the Zarathustra piece before going out again without a word.

On Sunday we were back in London. Before driving to Heathrow, Edward took me to a street market somewhere between Kennington and Waterloo Station. By then he'd left the Palace and opened a small antique shop in Chelsea, so he was always on the look-out for new stock. Wandering among the stalls on my own, I came upon one selling candles, aromatic oils, joss sticks and the small patches we used in those post-hippy days to stick on jeans and denim jackets, often with messages of love and peace embroidered on them. One that attracted my attention bore the legend 'Come Share my Star'.

"Why don't you buy that for your extra-terrestrial?"

Edward was standing behind me. I asked the price, but thought it way too much for a scrap of machine-embroidered cloth. Within three hours, I was back home in Uccle.

There was no further word from Hubert. Later that week, however, there came a reminder of him, no more than coincidence certainly, when I went with Lady Palliser, the ambassador's wife, with whom I got on well, to the opening of an art exhibition. (Her son's paintings were among those on display.) Sitting on the floor in one corner of the room was a young couple, half-stoned and wearing more scarves and beads than even Countess Barcynska, not averse to ornamentation, would have deemed tasteful. They got up and ambled unsteadily towards us.

"Hi, you're extra-terrestrial?" said the boy, his face too close to mine.

I told him I was not.

"Well, if you aren't, you've been with someone who is."

"Recently," the girlfriend chipped in.

And with that they meandered back to the patch of floor they'd made their own.

Days later I saw Hubert again. He was among a group of people invited to supper by one of the embassy secretaries, a woman named Barbara Jeffries, who'd met him through me. (Over two years she would appropriate several of my gay friends, her hopes of redeeming them indifferent to failure.) I remember he and I exchanged nods, nothing more, neither of us disappointed to be seated at opposite ends of the table.

At some point during the meal, our hostess enquired about my recent trip home.

"And did you enjoy our music?" enquired Hubert before I had time to reply. Instead of answering I muttered something about having nearly brought him something back from London.

"I know," he murmured wistfully, "but you didn't want to share my star."

That was the last time we spoke. I went on to make new friends and somehow or other we no longer seemed to be in the same place at the same time. Not even at the Bélier. A few years ago, I learned that he'd died of Aids at the end of the 1980s.

He may have already been dead when at some point I made a business trip to Amsterdam; the European Patent Office for which by then I was working, had a branch in The Hague, so I flew there often. This particular occasion chanced to coincide with the appearance in Dutch of a new book I'd written, my third, called *Secret Wisdom*. Too impatient to wait for the complementary copies publishers send to authors, I bought one in a bookshop near the Leidseplein and went into the bar of the American Hotel to examine it more closely. A man seated at the counter — we were the only customers in there — must have seen what I was reading for he suddenly asked in English if I were interested in the supernatural, nodding towards the book in my hand.

"Sort of," I said, before vanity got the better of me, and I confessed to having written it. I told him it had just come out in The Netherlands.

"Then we must drink to it. A Bols. Pick any colour."

From the row of bottles behind the bar I chose blood-orange. My companion opted for something green, probably kiwi fruit or lime.

"I know nothing about secret wisdom," he confessed, after gulping down his drink, "though I did meet an extra-terrestrial once. In Brussels of all places."

"Hubert Wattiaux."

It was not a question, and he never took it to be one.

"I guessed you'd met him. From the moment you walked in. That business with the book, it was just an excuse to start talking. Another Bols? Let's try the blue curaçao. It matches his eyes, don't you think?"

Here was the South American Hubert had mentioned. He'd not gone home to Argentina after all.

"Have they got you doubting the whole thing yet? It's what they do, you know. First you're 100% certain, then you start to question this or that. In the end, you're half persuaded you made the whole thing up. All of it. With me it didn't work."

"Nor me."

He paid the barman, stood up and shook my hand.

"Don't talk about it. You never know. People will think you're crazy — *Más loco que una cabra con pollitos!*"

And with that he was gone.

What did not go, and remains to this day, was the conviction that in or perhaps through Hubert I encountered something not of this world, though precisely what or where it came from, I've never worked out. Over the years I've toyed with a variety of possible explanations, things like meaningful coincidence, telepathy and mutual self-deception but am unpersuaded, not least because — and it's happening as I write these words — I have only to think of what happened that Sunday night in Uccle for whatever overwhelmed me then to return and do the same again. The Force, as *Star Wars* might put it, is still out there.

27

"Witchcraft was hung, in History,
But History and I
Find all the Witchcraft that we need
Around us, every Day"
Emily Dickinson

"I'm off to see the Witch of St Giles" announced Simon Lipton one Saturday afternoon, shortly after my return from Brussels, "I've got a book of hers I keep forgetting to return. Come with me. We needn't stay long."

I knew it was an attempt to cheer me up. Gone now from my life were the perks I'd taken for granted, the entertainment allowance, the diplomatic immunity, the long boozy lunches and the CD plates on the little Austin Mini I'd come home in. I'd even begun to miss the fake Louis Quinze and those coruscating *lustres*. True, I'd been promoted, a consolation of sorts, to assistant secretary, not bad at thirty-two, although my mother did point out that my former rank — principal — sounded better, as did first secretary, my official title in Brussels. Assistant secretary sounded too much like a junior in the typing pool.

Widely referred to as the Witch of St Giles, but not in her presence,[48] Madeline Montalban occupied a mansion flat off New Oxford Street, more stage set than home, with a decor that mixed the darkly gothic with a festive, almost frivolous, baroque, a bit like the lady herself. 'Madeline Montalban' was her adopted name, more euphonious than Dolores North, as she became following her marriage in 1939. As Madeline Montalban she'd been familiar to me since my school days, chiefly from articles she contributed to a magazine called *Prediction*, her monthly reflections, often on the Tarot, by far the best thing in it.

"Don't let on you're gay," warned Simon as we arrived at the front door. "She's got a thing about it, though the poor dear's camper than a row of tents." I took this to mean I should avoid sitting with my legs crossed and not smile too often.

Camp she certainly was, with flowing garments reminiscent of Countess Barcynska but in her case, at least on that day, uniformly black. Resting on her head was what I took to be a wig, too luxuriant to be true but far superior to Joyce's. From time to time she patted it, as if to check it was there.

Her 'thing' about gay men may have stemmed from the views she held about the respective and, in her opinion, disproportionate contribution men and women make to magical operations. For her women were far better equipped to generate, possibly channel, those currents of energy needed to produce a desired effect, while men were constitutionally deficient in this regard.

"Angels are more sympathetic to women," she declared, waving her hand as if to an invisible, possibly angelic, audience. "Our sensitivity is more attuned to theirs. You men should accept that joyfully."

My suspicion was that she regarded gay men as a challenge to this female hegemony.

---

48 The name refers to the part of London, now within the Borough of Camden, where she lived, its parish church being St Giles in the Fields.

Soon she and Simon were immersed in a discussion about the authorship of a work attributed to the sixteenth-century writer Cornelius Agrippa. Purportedly the fourth volume of his *De occulta philosophia* and filled with detailed instructions on exorcisms and the conjuration of spirits, it lacks the profundity of the three earlier volumes, in which Agrippa explains how magic is the key to understanding God and his manifestation in nature. Our hostess was suggesting that Dr Dee had a hand in the forgery, possibly while living in Prague. (He and his accomplice, Edward Kelley, had gone there to manufacture alchemical gold for Rudolf II, an experiment that ended in failure, with Kelley finishing up in jail and later dying in a botched attempt to get out.) Simon was trying to persuade her that the disputed book had been in circulation by the 1560s, long before Dee paired up with Kelley, but she robustly contested the dates he proposed. As the two locked horns, I found myself studying a portrait on the wall of another monarch, Richard III, presumably a favourite of hers, as we'd passed several others in the hallway. What intrigued me were the semi-precious stones the owner had painstakingly glued onto every piece of jewellery depicted in the pictures. Years later, I learned that her maiden name was Royals but whether that had any relevance, I have no way of telling.

"And what are you reading nowadays, young man?" she broke off to ask, perhaps sensing I felt out of my depth. Before answering, I remembered to uncross my legs.

Now, as it happens, I'd just rediscovered an old paperback edition, acquired on a school trip to Edinburgh, of Gerald Gardner's *Witchcraft Today*, and so expecting it to meet with her approval, I told her. That was a mistake.

"Vile creature! Don't believe a word" she cried, not so much at me as at the world at large. "With him it was beg, borrow and steal. Plus of course the *bondage*."

Following this outburst and the fit of coughing it brought on — she was a heavy smoker — we didn't stay long. Mention of Gardner had clearly put her in a bad mood — her temper was legendary — although the Dr Dee business can't have helped either. But why Gardner? Surely not his penchant for ritual scourging, a practice alluded to in his writings and a mere peccadillo compared with Crowley's more ambitious debauches. Yet she'd alluded to Crowley with no hint of disapproval. Was it really because, as Simon claimed, the old boy once invited her to tie him up and tickle his privates with a feather?

Certainly, Montalban and Gardner had once been close. He'd even attended a magical operation in her home, possibly in the company of Kenneth Grant, Aleister Crowley's sometime secretary: conducted with scrupulous decorum, it involved neither feathers nor fetters, although the arrival of an unexpected caller brought proceedings to a premature end. At the time Madeline, recently demobbed from the Wrens, was encouraging people to think she'd served as Lord Mountbatten's personal seer while he'd been Chief of Combined Operations. If true, her clairvoyance was not up to much, for it was during this period that the ill-conceived Dieppe raid took place, resulting in the death of a thousand soldiers, most of them Canadian volunteers.

Gerald Gardner also claimed to have done his bit to help the Allied cause, participating in an effort by the witches of England to frustrate Hitler's invasion plans in 1940. This took place on the feast of Lammas, when several covens gathered in the New Forest to create a 'cone of power', using, in Gardner's words, 'mighty forces . . . of which I dare not speak', subsequently dispatched to Germany to weaken the Führer's resolve. The 'mighty forces' were helped on this occasion by the willingness of two participants to sacrifice their lives as part of the exercise: frail and elderly and, like everyone else, stark naked or, as witches put it, 'sky-clad', they declined to smear grease on their bodies to ward off the cold and died as a result. All of which seems a bit far-fetched as Lammas fell on 1 August and weather conditions in Hampshire that night are recorded as having been mild, with only one or two light showers.

Another unsung hero of World War II was Aleister Crowley, provided, that is, we accept his claim that MI5 invited him to organise some woodland magic of his own, codenamed Operation Mistletoe, this time in Ashdown Forest in Surrey. Rumoured to have also been involved are Ian Fleming, creator of James Bond, and Dennis Wheatley, whose novels about magic and witchcraft were immensely popular when I was a boy. While undeniable that both men worked for the security services during the war, there is no evidence that they participated in any such exercise, reportedly the brainchild of their boss, Maxwell Knight, who was in my day an occasional visitor to the rectory in Limehouse. (His sometime MI5 colleague, the predatory Tom Driberg MP, was less welcome: a former chum of Crowley's, he was famously described by Winston Churchill as 'the sort of man who gives sodomy a bad name'.)

With them in Ashdown Forest that night were forty soldiers, yet more unfortunate Canadians, who wrapped themselves in army blankets bearing occult symbols and promenaded around a dummy figure intended to represent Hitler. Crowley would maintain that as a result of these high jinks the Führer's party deputy flew to Scotland some days later. A triumph of sorts perhaps, even if the arrival of Rudolf Hess did nothing whatever to change the course of the war.

It is quite possible of course that after hearing of this episode Gardner fabricated his story of the New Forest escapade and those powerful, but unmentionable, forces. What is indisputable is that by 1938 he and his wife had moved to Highcliffe, near Christchurch on the South Coast, where he was introduced to people involved in witchcraft by a fellow Liverpudlian — Gardner hailed from the genteel suburb of Blundellsands — named George Sullivan or Frater Aureolis, head of a quasi-Rosicrucian order he'd established in 1911, called the Order of Twelve (later the Crotona Fellowship). Sullivan, whose admirers included the daughter of Annie Besant (at whose home Madame Blavatsky spent her final years), and Peter Caddy (a founder of the Findhorn Community in Scotland), was also running the Christchurch Garden Theatre, with several practising witches among its patrons and supporters. Their coven, according to Louis Wilkinson, the friend of Crowley and John Cowper Powys, was a mixture of 'middle class intellectuals and local peasantry'. It was the middle-class intellectuals, one imagines, who spotted that Gardner was one of their own.

Especially keen to introduce him to witchcraft was a local elocution teacher, Mrs Edith Woodford-Grimes, nicknamed Dafo, who purportedly arranged for his initiation at the home of 'Old Dorothy', since identified as the fifty-eight-year-old Mrs Ellen Clutterbuck, although official records suggest she was by then no longer Clutterbuck but a Mrs Fordham, following a second marriage three years earlier. Little in Highcliffe, one suspects, could be taken at face value.

Whatever the New Forest witches got up to, it seems not to have satisfied Gardner. The majority of them, one suspects, were back-to-nature enthusiasts, willing at most to strip off and invoke pagan deities, even chew magic mushrooms when they felt daring.[49] At any rate before the war ended, he'd moved to Bricket Wood near St Alban's, close to a chum from his early days in the Far East, John Sebastian Marlow Ward, former priest of, wait for it, the Orthodox Catholic Church of the British Empire and by then its Archbishop-Metropolitan, as well as owner of an open-air museum of rural arts and crafts in nearby Barnet. From him, Gardner acquired a small wooden edifice, supposedly Elizabethan and known as the Witch's House, which he erected on a patch of land close to the Five Acres Naturist Club, an establishment of which he was part-owner. (I'm told that even today there are several such clubs around Bricket Wood, famous also for its Morris Dancing.) With the building in place, Gardner established a coven of his own, with Mrs Woodford-Grimes travelling up from Hampshire, to serve as High Priestess. Absent, however, was the Archbishop-Metropolitan, forced to quit England in 1946, following a scandal involving a minor. He found refuge on a plot of land that Gardner owned in Cyprus.

By his own account, Gardner was already trying to bring some order to the jumble of beliefs and practices he'd come across within the

---

49 Eleanor 'Ray' Bone (1911-2001), one of Gardner's High Priestesses and a friend of Mrs Woodford-Grimes, would maintain that the New Forest coven could trace its origins to the twelfth century. Few, apart from the faithful, believe it.

New Forest coven. (Not everyone is persuaded of its existence.) As part of the exercise, he did not hesitate to draw on a variety of sources to create a more coherent system, among them the Key of Solomon and Agrippa's *De occulta philosophia*, as well as such Golden Dawn material as was then available. He also lifted bits from *Aradia or the Gospel of the Witches*, a book on Italian witchcraft by the American folklorist Charles Leland, published in 1899, as well as from the Masonic rituals familiar to him as a member of the Craft. Likewise useful, not least because they appeared to give academic legitimacy to his claim that witchcraft was the remnant of a pagan religion formerly prevalent in pre-Christian Europe, were two books by the anthropologist, Margaret Murray, *The Witch Cult in Western Europe* (1921) and *The God of the Witches* (1931). Best of all, in May 1947 he made several visits to Aleister Crowley, by then languishing in his boarding house in Hastings, and paid £300, a hefty sum in those days, for authority to set up a chapter of the O.T.O. By way of bonus, Crowley elevated him there and then to the Order's fourth degree, giving him access to the rites and practices of the organisation. Some of this material would find its way into Gardner's novel, *High Magic's Aid,* privately financed by the author and published in 1949 by the Atlantis Bookshop in Bloomsbury, a stone's throw from the then home of Dolores North, aka Madeline Montalban. Indeed hers were the willing fingers that typed the manuscript prior to publication.

Whatever might have led her to denounce Gardner years later, it was unlikely to be resentment at not being paid for her typing. Or indeed that business with a feather. A more likely explanation is that she recognised the sources he'd drawn on when manufacturing his rituals, hence her reference to 'beg, borrow and steal' when we met. Equally dismayed was a young woman named Doreen Valiente, perhaps the brightest of Gardner's recruits, who, intrigued by an article in a popular magazine, wrote to Cecil Williamson, owner of the Folklore Museum of Superstition and Witchcraft on the Isle of Man and mentioned in the article, who then passed her letter on to Gardner. Towards the end of 1952, Mrs Valiente was duly invited to tea at the home of Mrs Woodford-Grimes, with Gardner present, and initiated on Midsummer's Eve the following year.

Only then did Mrs Valiente, no stranger to the sources exploited by Gardner, discover the full extent of his plagiarism, although her dismay was due mainly to his reliance on Crowley whose notoriety, she feared, risked damaging the reputation of witchcraft. With Gardner's consent, she set about re-writing the Book of Shadows, known as the Witches' Bible, removing much of Crowley's input and replacing it with her own, some original and some, yet again, pinched from elsewhere. By then, too, she was Gardner's High Priestess.

In 1954 came Gardner's first non-fictional treatment of the subject, *Witchcraft Today*, prompting a spate of enquiries from people interested in joining the Craft, as well as more attention, most of it disapproving, from the press. Soon the papers were hinting at devil worship and sexual excess, with Gardner portrayed as a grave danger to the nation's moral health. With the support of the ever-dependable Mrs Valiente, he did his best to refute the more salacious allegations in a second book, *The Meaning of Witchcraft* (1959), prompting more enquiries, more negative reporting and, finally, the interest of the police. Yet Gardner continued to give interviews to all and sundry, even letting himself be photographed in his birthday suit, by then the worse for wear, alongside the man who helped him run the nudist club and his girlfriend, both similarly naked. The picture appeared alongside an article that referred to witchcraft as 'a repulsive pagan sect'.

Fearful for the future of the Craft, Valiente renewed her pleas for caution, but these fell on deaf ears. Finally, to end her carping, Gardner unexpectedly produced a set of wiccan rules nobody knew existed, one of which required every High Priestess to 'recognise that youth is necessary to be representative of the Goddess. So she will gracefully retire in favour of a younger woman, should the coven so decide.' Thirty-five-year-old Doreen saw in this a bid to replace her with a more youthful but, above all, more compliant successor, so resigned on the spot. Rumour has it she had in any case never been too keen on that business with the feather, her preferences being somewhat more robust.

In 1964, Gardner died of a heart attack while on a Mediterranean cruise, and was buried in Tunis. Foremost among those willing to acknowledge their indebtedness to him was Doreen Valiente. As she admitted, it was undeniable that in his lifetime he almost single-handedly invented, possibly reinvented, witchcraft, enriching it with a variety of foreign, but seldom alien, elements that were more or less compatible with the meagre source material at his disposal. The end result has been a system that comfortably accommodates the historical fantasy on which it depends and, in a sense, legitimises it. More importantly, witchcraft, like paganism generally, continues to offer religious and spiritual consolation to thousands of people all over the world.

The credit, however, is not Gardner's alone. Neither is it due to the pioneering work of his more articulate disciples, foremost among them Doreen Valiente, now commemorated by a blue plaque outside her former home in Brighton. Some of the credit goes to Alex Sanders, regarded as an upstart by the Gardnerians, partly because, according to them, he lacked the 'lineage' (i.e. the initiatory credentials) by which they set store, but also because he contrived to make witchcraft less solemn, ridding it of the fuddy-duddy image — nudity and ritual flagellation notwithstanding — which the septuagenarian Gardner and his successors never quite shed, even when baring their all to the cameras. With his natural chutzpah, even sense of fun, Sanders and his wife, Maxine, equally committed to the cause, made witchcraft attractive to young people seeking new ways to indulge their spirituality. That the new ways, edgy and defiant, might be rooted in a pagan past, even if largely invented, added to their appeal.

Alex Sanders died in 1988. Since then, like the East-West divide of the Christian church in 1054, witchcraft is rent by schism, split between those who call themselves Gardnerian and those who profess to be Alexandrians, with smaller factions somewhere on the edge or in between. And the difference? Well, apart from the dispute over Sanders' initiation — 'lineage' is considered important by all the rival factions — the difference is more one of style than of substance. True, some observers detect a greater emphasis on the masculine, represented by the Horned God, among the Gardnerians, with the Alexandrians favouring the female element (the Goddess) but this distinction is arguable at best. What is undeniable is that Sanders, as his enemies gleefully point out, was not averse to incorporating an eclectic mix of elements in his rituals, displaying the pick and mix approach favoured by Mathers when setting up the Golden Dawn. But then Gardner had himself done exactly that, as Doreen Valiente discovered — before, that is, she got around to helping him do still more of the same.

"In the end," declared Simon, "there's more that unites them than divides them. Ultimately both seek access to the divine in and through the natural world."

I thought of Mr James. Few people were more connected to the natural world than he'd been. If witches found that secret rites and pagan gods helped them better experience the unconditioned reality to which the natural world bears witness, that was fine by me. Most religions use ritual, some more than others, to help their members have access to the numinous. I just didn't think that secret rites and pagan gods, not to mention ritual scourging, were ever my thing. And, as I said earlier, it takes a lot to get me to undress other than at bedtime.

Before we parted Simon scribbled an address on the back of a card.

"Here," he said, "if you want to know more about witchcraft, go and see Alex and Maxine. You'll feel at ease with them. Just say I sent you. At least they keep their clothes on. Most of the time anyhow. It's the basement flat."

A few days later, curiosity prompted me to take the 52 bus to Notting Hill Gate where I peered down the steps leading to the basement of 15 Clanricarde Gardens. That was the closest I got to becoming a witch, although Maxine Sanders and I are by now old friends.

28

"The besetting sin of civil servants is to mix too much with each other"
William Beveridge

N o longer part of my life in Somerset House were Rabindranath Tagore or the two Nazi bigwigs in the dock at Nuremberg. I'd grown rather fond of Hermann Goering, positively jovial in comparison with Tagore and the frowning, bushy-browed Hess. Now I occupied a room in a different part of the building, lighter and bigger and overlooking Waterloo Bridge. The extra space made me feel important. The downside was the job.

I'd been put in charge of something called the economics division, its remit to advise the government on the impact of fiscal policy, so clearly more was expected than the *sapo mollis* I'd liberally doled out in the past. Luckily, in my absence the Revenue had recruited several bright young graduates and two of them were members of my team. Better still, each was set on outshining the other so their rivalry, discreetly encouraged, allowed me to survive the first twelve months without anyone suspecting I'd no idea of what I was up to. By then, too, I'd managed to get on nodding terms, nothing more intimate, with stalwarts like Adam Smith, John Stuart Mill and John Maynard Keynes so could name-drop whenever it felt safe to do so. Keynes, I was pleased to discover, would have felt perfectly at home at those long Sunday lunches in Limehouse.

My fiefdom extended also, though I never understood why, to the valuation office in nearby Carey Street, its staff charged with assessing the worth of private and commercial properties up and down the land. Head of the outfit was a chief valuer who, it turned out, was as relieved to discover I had no wish to get involved in his affairs as I was to let him manage them without me. What I cherished most was his hospitality for here was a man who never overlooked an excuse for a party: a successful court case, a staff transfer or a promotion, a new recruit, a retirement or a landmark birthday, for him each was cause for celebration and, best of all, there was usually something to celebrate each week.

Responsible for organising these events was a man named Jack Hewit, faux-posh, foul-mouthed and camper than a row of tents. In his late fifties, he was, he told me, intending to retire within a year, having secured the lease on a flat in Uxbridge Road. ("That's Shepherd's Bush, darling, not that god-awful place on the Piccadilly Line.") Though nominally employed as a clerk, his principal function — and the job he cherished most — was arranging the chief valuer's parties, something he did with spectacular panache. If in a good mood (by no means guaranteed) he'd go about filling people's glasses or hand around the canapés, but usually would behave like any other guest, muttering to me from time to time about the shortcomings, aesthetic and sartorial, of the people around us. After I'd got to know him better, he'd mutter "Vada the omi with the bona cartes," whenever a new recruit's trousers had contours deserving of my notice. Ronnie and my time with the circus had taught me enough polari to get by.

Jack had been sixteen when he quit his native Gateshead to work as a chorus boy in London. Within months he became the lover of Ivor Novello, film star, actor, and prolific composer of West End musicals, although by 1938 he'd moved on to Christopher Isherwood, sharing his favours with W. H. Auden, who mentions him in one of his poems. One afternoon, more subdued than usual, he described how he'd waved the pair off when they sailed for America in 1939, in his ears Isherwood's promise, never kept, to send for him once he'd settled in what would become his new home. Shortly afterwards, Jack went to live with the art historian Anthony Blunt and, through him, got to know Guy Burgess, undoubtedly the love of his life. From then on, he and Burgess — handsome, feckless and, according to Jack, the owner of a 'bonissima cartes' — were together until the day Burgess, with fellow spy and Foreign Office colleague Donald Maclean, did a bunk and defected to Russia. That I'd been born in Aberystwyth like their friend, Goronwy Rees, worked in my favour.

With the departure of Burgess and Maclean, things turned nasty for Jack, harassed by security officers uncertain of his involvement in the couple's treachery and resentful at having been outsmarted. During this time, he lived on the fringes of Mayfair and, according to him, the only people to show him kindness were the prostitutes in Shepherd's Market. Everyone else stayed well clear. In the end the authorities concluded he'd not been privy to the spying and to make amends found him a job in the Civil Service, sequestering him in the valuation office where, as I said, office parties were his forte, as was the home-made liver pâté, well-laced with brandy, he brought along to them. "That's the story of my life," he sighed one afternoon, nodding towards what was left of the pâté, "all the bijoux were just paste." It was, he confided, 25 years to the day since Burgess had hotfooted it to Moscow.

Notoriously prickly, he'd taken to me on discovering that I knew Ava Gardner, not well but well enough to secure him the signed picture he'd long coveted. Better still, it came with a message addressed to him personally. In those days, the actress was living in Knightsbridge, and we'd met through someone named Gil Karnig, rumoured to have been the youngest ever general in the US Army, although that honour, I've since learned, belongs to the splendidly named Galusha Pennypacker, made a general at twenty in 1864, so I may have got the rank wrong. By this time Karnig and an associate were peddling an investment scheme involving an animal called a beefalo, a cross between a cow and a buffalo, which allegedly thrived on the meanest of pasture. Whereas ordinary cattle need 15 to 20 lbs of food to produce 1 pound of meat, the beefalo made do with a mere 5 or 6, scarcely more than the 4 lbs required by turkeys. Both men were smooth talkers and had just persuaded several Arab rulers that beefaloes grew fat on desert scrub, possibly even on sand, when an exposé in a Sunday newspaper put paid to their deception. Like Burgess and Maclean, they packed their bags and did a runner.

My chance to do the same would arrive when there came out of the blue that October the offer of a senior appointment in Munich, this time with an international organisation due to open in a few months' time. Here, finally, was my chance to escape for good from Somerset House and the Revenue, as well as finally make use of the German Mrs Winkler had taught me all those years ago, a prospect that delighted her no end when she came to learn of it. We'd always kept in touch and now, at her suggestion, the letters we exchanged were in German, my grammatical lapses corrected more tactfully than they had been twenty years before. Sadly, she died within weeks of my departure.

It was also in October, in this case 70 years before, that my grandfather had set sail for New York on board the R.M.S. Lusitania. It was not his first Atlantic crossing. That had been on the maiden voyage of her sister ship, the Mauretania, seven years earlier. Family legend has it that only a plate of dodgy shellfish, consumed on the eve of his departure for Southampton, kept him off the Titanic, when she set sail on 14 April 1912. By then he was running a small construction company, mainly employing workmen from North Wales, which, even if they did not 'build Jersey City', as my mother liked to claim, may have accounted for one or two modest buildings on the west bank of the Hudson.

Also on board that October, three months into the war and a mere seven before the Lusitania was sunk off the Irish coast by a German submarine, was none other than Aleister Crowley.[50] Indeed, it was shortly before his return to England five years later that he published the blue-covered book Mr James had given me when I saw him for the last time, part of a series called *The Equinox*. In it, I discovered, were two portraits Crowley had painted, one of himself as the sage Kwakw, alias Kwaw Li Ya, a Chinese poet he sometimes pretended to be,[51] and another of an entity named Lam[52] whose features anticipate what today passes for an extra-terrestrial, notably the eponymous E.T. In the picture Lam is depicted without ears so it's ironic, but perhaps not entirely accidental, that the image is placed above a reprint of Madame Blavatsky's meditative essay *The Voice of the Silence*.

Whether Crowley regarded Lam as extra-terrestrial is difficult to tell. In his lifetime, he applied the notion to non-human beings which, he claimed, were exempt from the laws of space and time, not because they dwelt on other planets but because those laws were inoperative in the alternative reality they occupied. Of course, the same may also be the case on planets other than our own, just as different laws have necessarily to apply in that part of the universe — 99 percent of it, no less — said to be composed of dark matter or, as physicists call it, non-baryonic matter. (Baryonic matter is what you, me and everything else are made of.)

The term 'dark' matter is appropriate. For it is matter that cannot be seen because there is no light by which to see it. The black holes at the core of every galaxy are so jam-packed with the stuff, that each long ago collapsed under its own prodigious gravity, squeezing out the last faint glimmer of light. What goes on inside a black hole is anybody's guess, but it has been suggested that were we able to pass through one

---

50 For the record, I should add that also among the passengers was the seven-year-old Joan Grant, travelling to New York with her parents. She would later make a name for herself as author of *The Winged Pharaoh* (1937). In it she describes — aided by a faculty she dubs 'far memory' — how in a previous incarnation she had been Sekeeta, priestess and daughter of a pharaoh. Similar books would follow. Lots of them.

51 See *Vanity Fair*, August, 1915, Vol. 4 No. 6, p 46.

52 'Figure 14. The word Lam is the Tibetan for Way or Path, and Lam is He who Goeth, the specific title of the Gods of Egypt, the Treader of the Path, in Buddhistic phraseology. Its numerical value is 71, the number of this book.'

we might emerge into a universe that is one of multiple variants of our own, a place in which choices not made here have been realised, precipitating an alternative version of history. One may wonder if the 'real' Hubert dwelt in such a universe, or the two old ladies who made my bedtimes so wretched, or even, come to that, Mrs Duncan's genial phantoms (apart, that is, from the all-singing/all-dancing lady's vest).[53]

And so there I was, barely two years after returning with a heavy heart from Brussels, poised now to quit the black hole that was Somerset House for a second time, this time for good, and heading off for Munich, sometime *Hauptstadt der Bewegung* or 'Capital of the [National-Socialist] Movement'. Perhaps Messrs Hess and Goering, whose pen-and-ink portrait had greeted as well as puzzled me on my first day in the building, were a portent of what would happen fifteen years later, a hint that those black holes may at times be closer than we think. Further proof would not be long in coming.

---

53 Someone who claimed to know the answer was Kenneth Grant (1924-2011), who in 1955 proclaimed himself Head of the OTO, or at least its 'Typhonian' variant (see pp 214, 247). Grant received the original portrait of Lam from Crowley in 1947; a conduit, according to him, for 'trans-platonic' energies. Such was Grant's high regard for its subject that he even set up a Cult of Lam, its members required to meditate on the egg-shaped head depicted in the text, allegedly 'an astral vehicle for travelling to Lam's domain, or for exploring the extra-terrestrial spaces in which OTO Tantric Time travellers travel through the Tunnels of Set in cosmic and chthothian capsules.' One can see why one of Grant's admirers, the comic book writer, Alan Moore, described his work as 'an overwhelming and hallucinatory bouillon of arcane fact, mystic speculation and apparent outright fantasy.' In fact, it's more pot-au-feu than bouillon.

29

"Stop... that... train!"
The Dresser
(Ronald Harwood)

Our new home in Munich was close to the city centre, closer still to the Bürgerbräukeller (since demolished), where on 8 November 1939 a bomb exploded, killing eight people, shortly after Adolf Hitler quit the building eighteen minutes earlier than expected. This was not the only attempt on his life to be foiled by a last-minute change of schedule, encouraging some to suggest he had a sixth sense that alerted him to danger. He himself put it down to Providence. Clearly, whatever wartime magic Crowley and Gardner got up to in the woods, it faced stiff competition.

Adjoining our flat was a larger one owned by an elderly couple whose main home was over the border in Austria. ("This apartment is useful" the wife told me on our first meeting, "because it gives us somewhere to change for the opera.") Formal but never unfriendly, they turned out to be good neighbours, and the four of us got on well. So well that one evening we invited them to dinner, together with two other couples we'd by then got to know, each with at least one partner whose professional status, a retired judge and an eminent cardiologist, would meet with next door's approval. In addition, we brought out our best dinner service and our Georg Jensen silver, while the food and wine came from Käfer, the city's most prestigious grocer's, an establishment ten times more splendid than Uncle Davy's emporium in its heyday.

The evening went well, and two weeks later there came a return invitation. On the appointed day, Edward called me at work to report that for a good half hour a man had been carrying boxes into our neighbours' flat from a van parked outside in the street. As the vehicle bore Austrian number plates, he suspected it had travelled from their main home laden with china and silverware chosen to outrank our own. He was right, everything that evening was designed to impress, not just the Meissen tableware but the eight other guests, double our four, the funereal bowls of white peonies and cream-coloured roses, the unseen help in the kitchen and the couple hired to serve the food. Admittedly the enlarged company did not boast a judge (retired) or a heart specialist but the woman next to me was treated with such deference that I guessed she more than made up for it. Only half way through the meal did I learn she'd been a popular film actress in the 1930s and 1940s, someone who suffered death by drowning in so many films that she'd earned the nickname *Reichswassweleiche* or Drowned Corpse of the Reich.[54] For much of the meal she chatted to me not about films but about photography, revealing to my surprise that she knew Signor Resta's portrait of Madame Blavatsky: "Done on glass plates," she expertly informed me.

By the time the pudding arrived, and the umpteenth bottle of wine was uncorked, the atmosphere had grown more relaxed. Our neighbours were now pressing us to call them by their first names, the alliterative Hans and Hedda, but neglecting to specify if this entailed a switch to the familiar 'Du' form of address rather than the more formal 'Sie'. As Edward had yet to master the 'Du' verb endings, we played

---

54 Swedish by birth, Kristina Söderbaum (1912-2001) found fame in Nazi Germany, notably in the films of Veit Harlan, whom she married in 1939. Following his death in 1966, she became a photographer, while continuing to appear from time to time in films and on television.

safe and stuck to 'Sie'. Meanwhile keen to put our new friendship on the soundest of footings, our host who'd been a Luftwaffe pilot during the war, assured us that he'd never dropped a single bomb on England, although he did allow himself, emboldened by wine, to voice regret that the British had not joined forces with Germany in their fight against the Bolsheviks. He also disclosed that he was the holder of not one but two Knight's Crosses (*'Ich bin zweimal Ritterkreuzträger'*), the first earned after he was shot down over the Crimea.[55] He'd parachuted into a lake, breaking his nose on impact.

"In fact, I broke it twice," he disclosed. "That was the first time."

"And the second?" enquired someone.

It happened, he said, in bombed-out Hamburg shortly after the war ended. One day, in front of what remained of the city's railway station, he spotted a young German woman, by implication blonde and blue-eyed, sitting on the knee of an American soldier, a black American soldier. Was it for this, he asked himself, that he'd earned his two Knight's Crosses? On deciding it wasn't, he pulled the girl away and took a swipe at the soldier.

"But he hit back," he confessed, "and his arm was longer than mine."

From then on nothing could stem the flood of reminiscences that engulfed us, with the women, all of a certain age, describing the hardships they'd endured as hostilities drew to a close in 1945. One had made her way from Breslau, today in Poland, to Cologne to escape the advancing Russians, while another, after three happy years in Prague (home to Germany's oldest University, our host interjected for our benefit), found herself in Dresden on the very night British and American bombs turned the city into an inferno. Amidst all this reminiscing, Edward suddenly realised the woman on his right had made no contribution. Not wanting her to feel left out, he politely asked where she'd been when the guns fell silent in 1945.

---

55 Born in 1917, he was also holder of the Deutsche Kreuz in Gold, and among the last Luftwaffe pilots still flying Messerschmitts at the end of the war (see: John Manroe and Ron Pütz, *Bodenplatte: The Luftwaffe's Last Hope*, Stackpole Books, Mechanicsburg, PA, 2004, page 455 et seq.)

"In the Führerbunker," came the tart reply. "I was one of the typists."

The chance to question her further never arose, for our host picked that moment to tap the side of his glass and, assured of everyone's attention, inform the company that not only was I a high-ranking civil servant — the word *Beamter* never fails to impress Germans — but also the author of what he mendaciously called 'a best-selling book'. There were polite murmurs and my neighbour, the sometime film star, asked if the book was a novel.

"It's about the supernatural," replied Hans on my behalf. And with that he implored her to have another glass of schnapps, leaving everyone free once more to reminisce. I was not at all unhappy to be overlooked.

But not overlooked completely. An hour later as the company dispersed, I was shaking hands with a tall, white-haired man — who'd arrived unaccompanied but been paired with the sometime film star, clearly friends for they addressed each other as 'Du' — when he made a point of handing me his card. Saying that he, too, was interested in the paranormal, he suggested I might care to meet a man due to visit him shortly and an expert in the field. Which is how, on a Sunday afternoon two weeks later I found myself at his home in Grünwald, a leafy suburb of Munich, for *Kaffee und Kuchen*.

"I know you British normally drink tea with cake," he declared as his housekeeper came into the room with a tray, "but that's wrong. Only coffee goes with cake." Somehow, he managed to suggest we British got a lot of other things wrong as well.

"It's marble cake," the housekeeper explained for my benefit.

With us was the friend he'd mentioned at our first meeting, someone who in those days was Germany's best-known expert on the paranormal, his name familiar even to a foreigner like me.

Professor Dr Bender — his entitlement to call himself a doctor would later be challenged in the press — appeared regularly on television, looking avuncular but a touch self-satisfied, and rarely without his trademark pipe. He seemed to turn up whenever someone was needed to comment on a haunting or any other strange occurrence, with nothing too trivial to escape his scholarly attention. Over the years — he died in 1991 — I would hear him pontificate, never less than self-assured, on such curiosities as a mediumistic budgerigar (instead of "Hello Joey", the voices of the dead issued from its beak) and a hot-water tap from which similar noises emerged. It is said that the public lectures he delivered weekly in a darkened auditorium at the University of Frankfurt, his finely-hewn features illuminated by a single reading lamp, were every bit as spooky as anything Florence Cook or Mrs Duncan ever managed in their heyday.

His involvement in the supernatural went back to the 1930s. That his younger self suffered no disadvantage under the Nazis on that account was due in part to his timely decision to join the Party in 1933, but in part to the regime's ambivalent attitude towards the paranormal. In practice, this meant that despite its hostility to occultism[56] and those engaged in it (classified as 'political' offenders), the Nazi party's view of parapsychology was broadly sympathetic. In his book, *Fifty Years of Psychical Research*, published in 1939, Harry Price boasts of an official letter he'd received two years earlier inviting him to collaborate with a Professor Rothacker 'and his colleague Dr Hans Bender', the latter then just turned thirty, in establishing a Department of Parapsychology, the first of its kind anywhere, at the University of Bonn. Only the outbreak of war put paid to the idea.

By then, the rulers of Germany had already shown their intolerance of occultism. Organisations like the Theosophical and Anthroposophical Societies were automatically suspect because they evaded the control of the state and had an international membership, as of course did the Freemasons, although in their case the element of secrecy rendered them doubly suspect in the eyes of a totalitarian regime. The result was that measures introduced in 1935 to dissolve Masonic lodges throughout

---

56 Discussing astrology over dinner on 19 July 1942, Hitler denounced it as a swindle adding, perhaps with readers of Edward Lyndoe's column in mind, "one in which the Anglo-Saxons in particular have enormous faith."

Germany were extended to esoteric groups as well.[57] Only the so-called Waldorf schools, run on Anthroposophical lines, managed to survive, but even they began to close voluntarily over the next two years; an exception being the school in Dresden, which stayed open until 1941.

By contrast, Rudolf Steiner's recommendations concerning medicine and, more especially, agriculture were tolerated, even endorsed, by leading figures in the regime, although dismissed outright by others. Vegetables served at the Führer's table are said to have been cultivated along bio-dynamic lines, with times for planting and harvesting determined by the phases of the moon, as were the herbs grown commercially on land near several concentration camps, notably Dachau — where the man in charge was, reportedly, a former head gardener at Weleda, the large anthroposophical concern based in Schwäbisch-Gmünd and still flourishing today.[58] The quasi-magical character of its methods, requiring not only compliance with the lunar calendar but the use of special fertilisers, numbered 500 to 508 and each based on a particular, usually medicinal, plant[59] was similar — though I'd not known it at the time — to the methods favoured by Mr James. Quasi-magical or not, these methods are today, a good eighty years later, widely practised all over the world. (And, by the way, biodynamic wines are second to none.)

At the time I met him, Bender was preparing a study on so-called alien abductions, so without going into too much detail I told him of my encounter with the 'extra-terrestrial' Hubert in Brussels. He was

---

57 In a letter addressed directly to Hitler, Steiner's widow and two other members of Anthroposophy's governing body appealed for an exemption from the general ban, assuring him — and allowance should be made for the historical context — that the society had "no dealings of any kind with Freemasonic, Jewish, or pacifist groups, nor even any casual contact with them in any way", while "the Aryan line of descent of Rudolf Steiner was explicitly confirmed by the Reich's Office of Racial Politics in Berlin." The letter ends by stating that far from being "international in orientation" or at all subversive, the "Society... advocates German nationalism with the utmost loyalty."

58 See Staudenmaier, Peter, "Organic Farming in Nazi Germany: The Politics of Biodynamic Agriculture, 1933–1945, *Environmental History*, Volume 18, Issue 2, April 2013, Pages 383–411,

59 Two of the most popular are yarrow and oak bark. The first is stuffed into the bladder of a red deer and after six six months' exposure to the sun, is buried in the ground for a further half a year before being ready for use. The oak mixture goes inside the skull of any farm animal before undergoing a similar procedure.

less dismissive than I expected — I'd yet to hear about the talking tap and mediumistic budgie — and his explanation drew on quantum physics and the notion of relativity, two theories which were currently at odds, he declared, but soon to be reconciled, making distant galaxies, even alternative worlds, accessible at last. Time travel, too, might soon be feasible.

"To the past as well as the future?" I enquired.

The famous head nodded slowly. It was, he said, all down to wormholes, the name given to a hypothetical shortcut, famously described by Einstein as a bridge between two points in space-time, that might serve to link widely separated parts of the universe or indeed different universes. According to the theory of special relativity, if the particles at one end of a wormhole were accelerated to a high velocity, then anything passing through it would emerge from the other at a time prior to its moment of entry.

"Time dilation based on velocity," the speaker announced, as if that explained everything.

It was left to me to suggest that if a time traveller journeyed to the past and started out again, there was surely a risk that his or her subsequent history might end up differently from the one already experienced.

"You mean the Temporal Paradox?"

I could only suppose that I did.

"What you're thinking," continued the expert, "is that you might in theory kill one of your grandparents and so prevent yourself from being born. No problem. The time-line has a natural continuity so any event that's already happened, in your case your birth, cannot be rescinded. Somehow or other events will contrive to forestall it."

I was trying to make sense of it, when he made another observation. The afternoon was fast turning into a tutorial.

"We misunderstand Time because we think of it in terms of space. So did your eminent Mr Newton…"

"Sir," interjected our host, suddenly coming to life, "It's Sir Newton, not Mister."

"Isaac Newton," resumed the speaker, unused to correction, and dispensing with titles altogether, "considered time to be a dimension of space, an expanse across which events move in sequence. Even before Einstein came along, that was being called into question. What Einstein did was show how two observers moving at different speeds will register a different lapse of time for the same event. That's the principle governing wormholes. It's what may permit us one day to travel through time, as well as vast distances in space. Your Brussels friend may have done precisely that."

For me, unversed in physics, the flaw in Bender's approach sprang from the assumption that the traveller was bodily transported from one place to another, thereby implying that time, as Newton maintained, was itself an extension of space. After all something must travel through a wormhole for anything to emerge from the other end, even if physicists might try to wriggle out of it — the conundrum, that is, not the wormhole — by suggesting that this 'something' is composed of virtual particles, not the sort that you and I are made of.

It was at this point I remembered how Mr James had warned me once that Time is not a quasi-spatial dimension like length, breadth, or volume. If it gave the impression of being linear or, the word he used, 'sequential' (in Welsh *dilyniannol*), that's because we resemble someone seated in a moving train who looks out and sees a telegraph pole at, say, ten seconds to midday, another on the hour and a third ten seconds later. At noon the first pole already belongs to his past, the second to the here-and-now, while the third lies ahead in the future, yet were the same traveller to climb onto the carriage roof or, less perilous, stick his head out of the window, all three poles — past, present and future — would be experienced simultaneously.

At first this might seem to contain a Temporal Paradox of its own, for it suggests that, like the train, we are hurtling towards a pre-existent future, one we're powerless to change because we are already part of it. (That assumption is of course implicit in any attempts to predict the future, whether by resorting to horoscopes or tarot cards or those crystal balls — small, medium and large — peddled by the *Psychic News* bookshop.) If the future is already in place, then there goes our ability to determine what it will be. Anyone cherishing the notion of free will had better stay inside the train.

Well, not quite. For the absence of freedom is apparent only if we persist in thinking of time as a linear extension of space, with the future fully formed ahead of us. Once we accept that past, present, and future may be contemporaneous rather than sequential, we restore to our moral life, to each and every decision, the autonomy that a pre-arranged future would appear to preclude. This is because we are free (or at least as free as nature, nurture, and circumstances allow) to take a decision when offered a choice. And that choice determines a future which already takes that decision into account.

To help me make sense of it all, or at least as much sense as our position 'within' time allows, Mr James again suggested I imagine a railway carriage, this time with me inside it representing the present, and him, with his head stuck out of the window representing past, present, and future. I had then to imagine myself faced with two courses of action, a genuine choice in that the outcome was not predetermined. Now, despite the uncertainty he, from his vantage point, had necessarily to know what my decision and its outcome would be, both being contemporaneous. Yes, mine might be the freedom to decide but his was the privilege of knowing what decision I would take. Perhaps it's no coincidence therefore that some psychologists, Freud among them, suggest that the person each of us becomes in his or her lifetime, the product of choices freely made (more or less), is already present at our birth, although most stop short, quite rightly, of determinism. In that sense, the future, as much as the past, is again well and truly now.

Enough has happened in my life to make the notion plausible. It is arguable, for instance, that my adventure with Luca was foreshadowed by my obsession with circuses (not to mention the Staffordshire figure Mr James gave me several months before I met him) or that my childish invention of an extra-terrestrial civilization anticipated my encounter with Hubert in Brussels. Indeed, the Saturdays I spent in Tanrallt anticipated this book, and in no small way equipped me to write it. Throughout it, I have spoken of a reality beyond the here-and-now, yet one that accommodates both, a transcendent reality to which we may on occasion have access, as I discovered when I stayed overnight in Tanrallt.

The constituents of this reality form a single whole, referred to by medieval philosophers as the *unus mundus* or One World, and comparable to that ultimate reality, made up of abstract symmetries, which physicists have already glimpsed beyond the subatomic particles dancing on the edge of space and time. It is not far removed from Plato's proposition that the idea or 'form' of something matches our abstract notion of it but enjoys an existence beyond the space-time we're trapped in, neither mind nor matter but something partaking of both.

To sum up, therefore, behind the explicit or phenomenal world there exists an implicit reality, reminiscent of the one, indeed the One, that mystics throughout the ages have aspired to experience. Something Mr James never tired of reminding me is that the world about us, while real enough on its own terms, is illusory, its appearance and, possibly, behaviour determined by our perception of it. In Indian philosophy, this would give rise to the concept of maya, defined by Sarvepalli Radhakrishnan as 'the principle which accounts for the apparent conditioning of the unconditioned Absolute'. The challenge Mr James had set me was to resolve this ambiguity, by consciously reconciling the perceptible world with that imperceptible reality to which it essentially belongs. And, having done so, to feel at home in both.

To finish, let me describe an occasion when, while least expecting it, I was hauled onto the roof of our hypothetical railway carriage and shown all three telegraph poles at one and the same time. I never had the chance to tell Professor Bender about it, but you're welcome to join me up there before we change trains and go our separate ways.

It happened in Berlin shortly after the Wall had been breached but not yet demolished. The organisation I worked for in Munich had a sub-office in the city, and every month or so I would travel there on business, with Edward often joining me for the weekend.

One Saturday afternoon, the two of us were walking along the Kurfürstendamm when he, addicted to junk shops and flea markets, spotted a rather shabby arcade — next to the Komödie am Kurfürstendamm, I recall — with an even shabbier gallery on the first floor packed with stalls and small shops selling second-hand furniture, vintage clothing and assorted bric-a-brac. Naturally he insisted we go inside, he to search for bargains and me, with better German, to haggle over the price, should he discover anything he liked. By way of commission, he promised to buy me a beer — a traditional Berliner Weisse — at the Café Kranzler just across the road.

While he was rummaging about, I drifted over to a corner where rows of shelves were packed with second-hand books. Having seldom found anything of interest in such places, I was not too disappointed when this turned out again to be the case. About to wander off, I surprised myself by reaching up for a book, nondescript and virtually indistinguishable from the rest, on the topmost shelf. Only as I tried to wrest it from its neighbours — all were tightly wedged together — did I observe it was a manual of accounting practice, published in East Germany, its subject matter of no interest to me whatsoever. No sooner had I yanked it free than out from it fell several scraps of paper, by then yellowing with age.

My first thought was to retrieve them from the floor and put them, together with the book, back where they belonged on the shelf. Only as I stooped to pick them up did I see they were newspaper cuttings, one printed in old fashioned Gothic script, and that immediately aroused my curiosity. What I was holding turned out to be a cutting from the *Völkischer Beobachter*, the Nazi Party newspaper, but not until I turned it over did I find the article that whoever had cut it out had been so eager to preserve. With the by-line 'Prague, 16 May 1940', it reported the stir caused in that city by remarks made by David Lloyd George in London a week earlier. In a speech to the House of Commons, described by the reporter as 'scathing', the speaker had condemned the former Czech President, Edvard Beneš, for reneging on a promise made at Versailles in 1919 that Sudeten Germans would enjoy full autonomy within the newly created state of Czechoslovakia. Had that promise been kept, argued Lloyd George, and had similar rights been granted to ethnic minorities in Poland, the Second World War might well have been averted.

The second cutting was from the same newspaper, its print now switched to roman, this time dated simply 'March 1945'. On one side, it described fierce fighting taking place in the Rhineland and all along the Ruhr, a situation the German army, though heavily outnumbered, would soon get the better of, if only because it had to (*'Eine Lage... die gemeistert werden wird, weil sie gemeistert werden muss.'*). Again, only on turning the paper over did I see why it had been preserved. Here was a second piece about Lloyd George, this time by the paper's Stockholm correspondent, reporting the former statesman's death at the age of 82. Less sympathetic than the first, it claimed that history would hold him and other signatories to the Versailles Treaty accountable for the hostilities 'now about to reach their climax'. It even referred to him as *'der schlaue walisische Fuchs'* or 'the crafty Welsh fox'.

Who in Nazi Germany, I wondered, cared so much about Lloyd George that he or she cut out and preserved these two pieces, the second at a time when most people thought only of staying alive until the war came to an end? Suddenly I remembered Mrs Winkler, by then dead, who'd been such a steadfast admirer of Lloyd George, and never tired of telling the schoolboy me how much my voice reminded her of his. And that was before I'd even noticed the writing in the margin beside the text, done in pencil and by a hand I knew only too well.

Unwatched by whoever ran the bookstall — there was nobody in sight — I shoved the cuttings, together with a third scrap of paper inside my pocket and put the book, published in Leipzig in 1949, back on the shelf where I'd found it or where, possibly, the book had found me.

Coincidence it certainly was, an example of that synchronicity talked about by Jung and defined by him as 'a non-causal relationship which unites two unconnected events in a way so meaningful that the likelihood of chance is too remote to be taken seriously'. Where my experience that afternoon went beyond Jung is that the conjunction of events was tangible.[60] For in my pocket as I walked out into the sunlight and bustle of the Kurfürstendamm was evidence of a coincidence too improbable to be dismissed as accidental. Somehow the past had colluded with the future to create what Jung describes as 'a falling together in time, a kind of simultaneity' inside the present.

But how, asked a sceptical Edward, as we drank our beers, could I be certain it was my old teacher, Mrs Winkler, and not someone else who'd cut out and annotated the bits of paper now in my possession? The writing might well resemble hers and, yes, there was the Lloyd George connection, but she would not have been the only person in wartime Germany with a special interest in the former statesman. True, her husband worked for a bank and the cuttings were inside an East German treatise on finance, but umpteen other East Germans must have owned that particular book. (You may remember that he'd stayed there after the war, joining his family in Wales only in 1957.)

Fortunately, there was that third scrap of paper, the one I'd almost not bothered to pick up off the floor. No more than the corner of an old envelope, almost certainly used as a bookmark, it bore an East German postage stamp, commemorating the second winter sports championships at Oberhof. Visible, too, was the postmark, the date shown as '16.8.51' and above it 'Nordhausen', a town in what was then East Germany. A few weeks later I was told by Mrs Winkler's son, Eddie, that this was where his paternal grandparents had lived throughout the 1940s and 1950s. Inside the envelope must once have been a letter they had sent to his father.

---

60 Or perhaps not, given the famous occasion when a young female patient was describing to him a dream in which she'd been given a golden scarab brooch. Suddenly, according to Jung, he heard a tapping on the window behind him and saw through the glass a rose-chafer, the closest thing we have in Europe to a golden scarab, endeavouring to get inside the room — the darkened room, as he was careful to point out. Jung opened the window, caught the insect and handed it to his patient. It was, he admits, the only time he experienced something of this kind.

What the event shows is how fluid is the relationship between time past and time present, the latter the future so far as the former is concerned. In exceptional circumstances, as well as in dreams, all three may overlap, while on other occasions chunks of experience may be displaced and no longer occupy their 'rightful' position in time, much as Mr James had put it to me all those years ago.[61]

None of which will satisfy the sceptics. No amount of argument can do that. Only by ourselves transcending our three-dimensional environment and accessing the reality behind it can we grasp the former's true nature. Peculiar to the magician is an ability to experience this reality, not by losing oneself in it, as do the mystics, but by assimilating it in a way that makes it one's own.

Happily, this conscious integration with (and, in a sense, 'appropriation' of) the macrocosm does not mean that people who experience it then strut around persuaded they are God. True, every encounter with what some occultists like to call the 'Inner Planes' endows them with new confidence, necessary if they are to impose their will on the subtle forces recruited to foster a particular ambition, be they represented as gods and goddesses, angels, demons or puckish elementals, but this falls short, well short, of big-headedness. Remarkable, too, is that far from diminishing the everyday reality into which we are born, experience of something beyond it serves paradoxically to make our workaday world seem the more endearing.

All of which explains why, in making me aware of a transcendental reality, unfettered by time, by space and by causality, Mr James ensured that the reality it transcended, in this case the here-and-now of Tanrallt, was itself enhanced as a result. Here was a man who may have known other worlds but for now, quite rightly, this world was the one he loved best.

---

61 It is a phenomenon central to several plays by J. B. Priestley, notably *An Inspector Calls* and *Time and the Conways*, while Priestley himself wrote a popular study entitled *Man and Time*, based on the theories of J. W. Dunne, aeronautical engineer and inventor but nowadays best remembered for two books published in the nineteen-thirties, *An Experiment with Time* and its successor, *The Serial Universe*. His own dream experiences had persuaded the author that time is the progressive realisation of a pre-existing future.

Similarly, when I hoped all those years ago that Mr James would teach me magic, without having much idea of what magic was about, I did not seek a replacement for the everyday things which, like other boys of my age, I enjoyed getting up to. And at no time since, childish things put aside, has it distracted me from the everyday business of living. On the contrary it has helped me, as I've endeavoured to show, live life more fully, even when that life consisted of mundane things like college, disgruntled taxpayers, extraterrestrials and, best of all, lovers, the last of these with or without the forest bred lions.

It's odd that it never helped me find The Mousehole.

oOo

John Cowper Powys (right) and Louis Wilkinson at 12
Waterloo Cottages, the former's home in Blaenau Ffestiniog,
circa 1960. Wilkinson read from Aleister Crowley's work at
the latter's cremation (see below and Page 130)

Aleister Crowley Dies at Hastings

Mr. Edward Alexander (Aleister) Crowley, the writer and poet, who was well known for his interest in magic, died suddenly on Monday at Netherwood, The Ridge, Hastings, where he had been living for the past two years. He was 73 and a widower.

He published his latest book, "60 Years of Song," early this year. He had also done a number of futuristic paintings while at Netherwood, but, although people came to see him from all parts of the country, his interest in magic seemed to have waned and he seldom even mentioned the subject. On one occasion, however, he consented to give a lecture on the subject to a week-end conference at Netherwood.

Cremation was arranged to take place yesterday at Brighton.

The Daily Herald
(6 December 1947),
commenting on Wilkinson's
recitation of the Ode to Pan
at Crowley's cremation (see
Page 130), sniffily observed
that "any impressiveness the
passage possessed was only
gained by the speaker's fine
delivery and the sincerity
he put into his task."

Staffordshire pottery figure of the lion tamer
Isaac van Amburgh (1808-1865), given
to the author by Mr. James.

Cours Complémentaire (Secondary School),
Loudéac (Côtes-d'Armor) in the nineteen-sixties.

The "regulars" outside the Auberge de la Croix (with author back row, third left, and the proprietress, Madame Huby, front row, right. Missing is Monique, the Bardot look-alike.

School sports day in Loudéac: the author and colleagues. On his right is Thérèse "a woman so often crossed in love that the blame could only have been hers."

The author at 21

Luca Lambert
(without the "forest-bred" lions)

"Circus Days"
Pontivy, France.

Ronnie Herbert
"endowed with everything the skinny, full-faced,
mousy-haired me had coveted since old enough
to fret about such things"

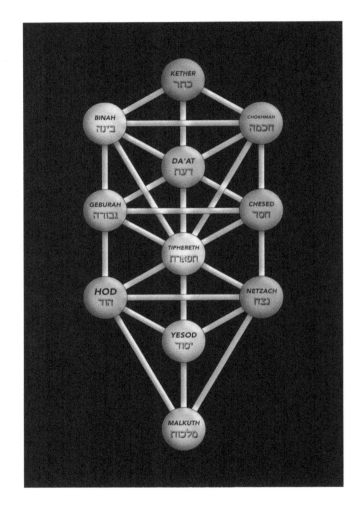

The Tree of Life

Edward Jones, looking untypically stern.

Balmoral
Edward Jones with the Queen's corgis (1967)

SPELLING IT OUT

DAVID CONWAY has been a civil servant for the past nine years. He has an office in Somerset House, and he's hot stuff on tax and Treasury problems. In his own time—and here's where you should take a deep breath—he's also pretty knowledgeable about astral projection, and love charms, and curses (although he says he's never cursed anyone). He can distil a draught that's said to guarantee eternal youth, and he can tell you how to divine the future.

In short, he's a magician, although he hates the word (" It's so rich in associations "), and he's very down on consorting with demons whose conjuration is likely to bring about more toil and trouble than even the Civil Service can handle. Talmudic tradition names over seven million of them, from Asmodeus to Valefar. But not one of them, says Conway, can be trusted. On the other hand, he adds, practising magic is a good deal safer than driving a car: "But you need care and skill to ensure safety."

It's a lot to swallow in one gulp, and Conway's not seeking converts. Cape have just published—at £5—his first book: Magic, An Occult Primer—which, they claim, is the first do-it-yourself manual on the subject. It's witty, informative, and very practical. "But," says Conway, "I have no intention of laying down the law. The last thing I want to do is make my mind up about anything. I prefer to remain sceptical, and that's how I hope the book will be read."

He means what he says, but lately there's been a boom in witchcraft (a fairly homespun kind of magic) which leads one to suppose that half the woods in the Home Counties are jampacked nightly with naked ladies prancing round bonfires on which cauldrons simmer. It's a busy little industry, says Conway, but they're not his people or his public. "In the first place, they're extremely gullible, and secondly they're interested in magic for very short-term rewards, mostly sexual. The trouble is that sex—which can be used legitimately as a means—becomes an end in itself.

"They're pathetic, really. I know one girl, a stripper, who was hired by one group to join in their rituals because they were all so unattractive, and they needed someone like her to turn them on, so to speak."

The only bonfire session that Conway attended was the result of his answering a small-ad in the New Statesman inviting followers of the Great White Goddess to contact a certain box number. He was interviewed by members of a witches' coven in Ealing (another would-be recruit was a West Indian who drove a number 11 bus), and eventually found himself in the boskage near Westerham, witnessing erotic tableaux which left him unmoved, and feeling distinctly chilly. He decided that witchcraft was not for him: "For one thing, the set-up was so artificial. For another, it was so damned cold."

Conway puts down the pretenders with finesse, but he is utterly serious about what he believes to be genuine magic. The rituals that he lists in his book are elaborate, and not without some trappings of hocus-pocus. But, he insists, they are not to be taken lightly. " Spells do work, and that's what worries me. If they didn't, then I could settle down and become a happy materialist."

He's not been that since he was five years old (he's thirty-two now), and he awoke one night to find two old ladies standing beside his bed. "Not for one moment did it occur to me that they were other than flesh and blood people. But when they disappeared—as I thought, into a wardrobe—I yelled for my mother. They came back the next night and one of them tickled me. When I yelled again they disappeared. But it went on until the family doctor was consulted." What finally transpired was that their descriptions tallied with those of two elderly sisters who had lived and died in the house thirty years previously. "Other members of my family had seen ghosts, and it was clear that I had inherited the psychic gift."

His parents ran a grocer's shop in a village near Aberystwyth, and Conway recalls a friend of his father who taught him the ABC of herbalism, "He could also put a hex on cattle, or take it off if he was spoken to nicely. He was a humble man—which is unusual for anyone connected with the occult."

He cast his first spell when he was twelve. "It was to help me through an examination, and it was a dismal failure. I'd have been much better occupied learning my French verbs." Subsequently, he treasured an old pair of socks which he had worn while taking—and passing—his school certificate exams. Darned and shrunken, they saw him through the rest of school and university (where he earned a double first in French and eighteenth-century French philosophy), until they finally fell apart during an unsuccessful driving test. "I doubt whether they possessed any special talismanic virtue," says Conway. "But I do know that my own confidence in them soothed my nerves, and improved my performance."

He's convinced that a good deal of magic is, quite literally, in the mind (" Beginning with telepathy "), and thinks it high time that occultists and physicists got together to examine the evidence. What's off-putting, he says, is that so many of the rituals are couched in medieval language. "But the fact that they are so elaborate teaches self-discipline. They are meant to discourage the dabblers."

He keeps at it, he says "Because I have this universal curiosity." Magic won't make him rich, or famous, and for one simple reason: "I'd much rather test my own ability." It sounds very Welsh, very puritanical but it can't be helped. "I come from a long line of non-conformists" explains Conway. "You can't get over a thing like that."

Frank Herrmann

INLAND REVENUE

The Sunday Times
"by then the worse for drink, I allowed myself to be photographed outside Somerset House . . . . with Inland Revenue clearly visible above my right shoulder."

Vogue March 15, 1972: "David, author of Magic: an Occult
Primer looks at past magicians and present revivals".

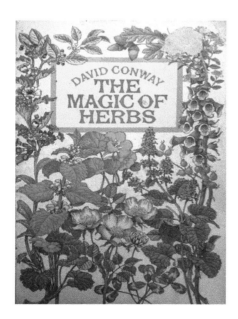

The Magic of Herbs, paperback edition by PANTHER (Granada),
originally published by Jonathan Cape, London, 1973.
(New edition: The Witches' Almanac, 2019)

Magic: An Occult Primer (original cover)
by M Mohan © Jonathan Cape Ltd 1971

**Helena Petrovna Blavatsky
(1831-1891)**

Photograph: Enrico Resta (1859-1942)

Éliphas Lévi Zahed

(Alphonse Louis Constant (1810 – 1875))

**Samuel Liddell
MacGregor Mathers
(1854 – 1918)**

**Edward Alexander
("Aleister") Crowley
(1875 – 1947)**

Hubert Wattiaux
"with long hair and a lumbering gait, he sometimes
reminded me of our caveman ancestors, having
the kind of broad, flattish face attributed to them."

The author and Maxine Sanders
at the author's home in Wales 2016

Passau 1989
With neighbours Hans and Hedda, the former a holder
of two Knight's Crosses, as well as survivor of two broken noses.

Vernichtende Feststellungen Lloyd Georges über die Kriegsschuld der Westmächte

„Versailler Vertrag von denen nicht eingehalten, die ihn diktierten"

1940

Prag, 16. Mai

Besonderes Aufsehen haben hier bekanntgewordene Einzelheiten aus der Unterhausdebatte vom 9. Mai erregt. Der konservative Abgeordnete Barter griff Lloyd George wegen einiger seiner früheren Kundgebungen und Artikeln an, die die britische Regierung in Verlegung gebracht hätten. Barter warf Lloyd George u. a. vor, daß er in der für die ehemalige Tschecho-Slowakei kritischen Zeit den „armen Benesch" kritisierte, von dem er sagte, daß er niemals das gegebene Wort gehalten habe.

Lloyd George unterbrach den Redner und erklärte, daß Benesch den vier Männern, die den Versailler Friedensvertrag redigiert hätten, versprochen habe, daß die Sudetendeutschen in der Tschecho-Slowakei die Autonomie erhalten würden. „Ich war einer der vier Männer", sagte Lloyd George. „Dieses Versprechen wurde nicht eingehalten, und ich glaube, daß diese Tatsache eine der Ursachen dafür war, was geschehen ist. Hätte Benesch das gegebene Wort gehalten, hätte Hitler niemals interveniert." „Der Versailler Vertrag", sagte Lloyd George weiter, „wurde von denen niemals eingehalten, die ihn diktiert hatten."

Weiter erklärte er: „Die Verpflichtung, nach der deutschen Abrüstung gleichfalls abzurüsten, wurde nicht erfüllt." Keine andere Regierung ist hierfür mehr verantwortlich als die britische Regierung, die im Jahre 1931 zur Macht gelangte. Amerika war damals ebenso wie Deutschland zur Abrüstung bereit, und zu dieser Zeit stand Reichskanzler Brüning an der Spitze der deutschen Regierung. England jedoch lehnte es ab, das gegebene Versprechen einzuhalten."

„Das gleiche Schicksal", fügte Lloyd George hinzu, „hatten die Versprechungen, die hinsichtlich der Minderheiten in der Tschecho-Slowakei, in Polen und anderen Ländern gegeben wurden. Versprechen, nach welchen ihnen die Autonomie zuerkannt werden sollte, und zwar nach Schweizer Muster. Der größte Teil des heutigen Elends wird durch die Tatsache verschuldet, daß die Sieger des Weltkrieges nicht die feierlich übernommenen Verpflichtungen der den Besiegten aufgezwungenen Friedensverträge eingehalten haben. Gelegenheit dazu war genug vorhanden. Der Geist, von dem die furchtbare Macht Deutschlands erfüllt ist, ist aus der Tatsache geboren, daß wir unsere Versprechen nicht eingehalten haben."

Lloyd George schloß mit den Worten: „Wir stehen nun der schrecklichen Antwort gegenüber, die je Menschen gegeben worden ist, welche das gegebene Wort nicht eingehalten und die Verträge verletzt haben."

Jede Bemerkung zu diesen Feststellungen Lloyd Georges, die die Schuld Beneschs und das Verbrechen der westlichen Staatsmänner eindeutig festlegen, also die Kriegsschuldfrage ein für allemal erledigen, würde ihre Wirkung abschwächen.

...lungen unseres ...jages in ... Holland durchgeführt wurden, besonders aus, ... daß sie neben dieser hohen Kriegsauszeichnung auch zum nächsten Dienstgrad befördert wurden.

Zwei weitere Auszeichnungen

Ritterkreuz für General von Kleist und Major Zwand

DNB Berlin, 16. Mai

Der Führer und Oberste Befehlshaber der Wehrmacht hat am 15. Mai 1940 dem General der Kavallerie Ewald von Kleist und dem Major Fritz Zwand das Ritterkreuz des Eisernen Kreuzes...

Major Zwand hat als Abteilungskommandeur eines Kavallerie-Schützenregiments im Polenfeldzug durch sein selbständiges Handeln und seine persönliche hervorragende Tapferkeit der 12. Armee den Weg zum siegreichen Vormarsch über den San erzwungen. In den Westkämpfen hat er sich erneut durch Tapferkeit beim Einzug in Holland hervorgetan.

Beschießung offener Städte wird sofort vergolten

Nach Beschießung Rastatts deutsches Feuer auf Hagenau

DNB Führerhauptquartier, 16. Mai

Französische Fernkampfartillerie beschießt seit 16. 5. ohne militärische Gründe die offene Stadt Rastatt. Deutsche schwere Flachfeuerbatterien haben daraufhin als Vergeltung das Feuer auf Hagenau eröffnet.

Britische Unverschämtheit in Südafrika

Kopenhagen, 16. Mai

Eine unverschämte Anmaßung von englandhörigen Soldaten ereignete sich in der Universität Potchefstroom in Südafrika. Diese ehrenwerten Soldaten warnten die Studenten der Universität, die „Vierkleur", die südafrikanische Landesflagge, zu hissen und versuchten, diese Flagge aus einem Studenten-Speisehaus zu entwenden...

Unsere Sold...

Links: Vorsichtig pirscht sich ein S... um die Lage zu klären. Die nachf... ein. Mitte: Der Einzug der deuts... grund das Rathaus. Rechts: Ein...

Foto: PK.-v. Estorff (Atlantic).

Völkischer Beobachter (Nazi Party newspaper), May 1940
Front and reverse of a cutting discovered by the author tucked
in a banking and accounting manual in a shabby arcade bookstall
in Berlin in 1990, referring to comments made by
David Lloyd George in the House of Commons

Lloyd George gestorben

Man or Mai 1945.

Von unserem Berichterstatter

Dr. Th. B. Stockholm, 27. März.

Im Alter von 82 Jahren ist David Lloyd George, zuletzt Earl of Dwyfor, gestorben. Als Mitverantwortlicher für das Diktat von Versailles und damit auch als Mitverantwortlicher für diesen Krieg, der jetzt seinem entscheidenden Höhepunkt entgegengeht, wird er in die Geschichte eingehen.

Der Mann, den seine Landsleute 1918 als Sieger feierten, erlebte den Ausbruch und die längste Zeit des Zweiten Weltkrieges, aber nicht sein Ende. Er wird diesem Ende, soviel wird man sagen können, mit einigem Bedenken entgegengesehen haben. Denn es bedarf kaum der Schlauheit dieses walisischen Fuchses, um zu erkennen, wohin die Politik seines alten Rivalen Churchill England in diesem Zweiten Weltkrieg geführt hat. Alles Triumphgeschrei, das jetzt jenseits des Kanals über die Schlacht um den Rhein angestimmt wird, kann nicht darüber hinwegtäuschen, daß die Politik der bedingungslosen Kapitulation und der Zustimmung zu allen sowjetischen Machtansprüchen England letzten Endes zum Verderben ausschlagen muß.

Lloyd George hatte diese Entwicklung kommen sehen. Seit 1938 erhob er seine warnende Stimme. Besonders kritisch beurteilte er die Blankovollmacht, die England 1939 den Polen gegeben hatte, diesen Polen, deren maßlose Gebietsansprüche ihm schon in Versailles auf die Nerven gegangen waren, weil er hier den Keim zu einem neuen Krieg erahnte. Er hat nach 1933 wiederholt Deutschland besucht und zeigte trotz seines Alters eine für einen Briten bemerkenswerte Aufgeschlossenheit für die Leistungen und Ziele des Nationalsozialismus. Aber er war ein Politiker ohne Anhang, seit er 1922 nach sechsjähriger Ministerpräsidentschaft durch die Carlton-Club-Revolte seiner konservativen Widersacher gestürzt worden und im Grunde ein gebrochener Mann war. Für die jüngere Generation in England, für Leute wie Eden, war er schon damals eine historische Mumie, reif für das Wachsfigurenkabinett der Madame Tussaud.

Ich sah ihn an einem Frühlingstag des Jahres 1937 müde und gebeugt vor dem Heldenmal der Stadt München stehen, vor jenem schlafenden Soldaten unter den großen Granitblöcken. Welche Gedanken mochten durch das Haupt mit den langen weißen Haaren gegangen sein? Daß sich überall in allen Ländern Europas, in jeder Stadt und in jedem Dorf Gefallenenehrenmale erheben, trug er an dieser Tatsache nicht auch Schuld, sogar schwere Schuld? Als im Sommer 1914 an ihn, den ehemals glühenden Pazifisten, die Frage herantrat, ob er dem Krieg gutheißen solle, da entschied er sich für den Krieg. Sein Nein hätte damals schwer in der Waagschale der Entscheidung gelegen. Aber Folgerichtigkeit ist niemals seine Stärke gewesen. Er war Pazifist, bekämpfte als solcher erbittert den Burenkrieg und gab 12 Jahre später die Parole „Hängt den Kaiser" und „Quetscht Deutschland aus, bis die Kerne quietschen" heraus. Er nahm als Finanzminister in den Jahren 1908 bis 1910 durch seine scharfe Steuergesetzgebung dem Oberhaus seine Machtstellung und ließ sich trotzdem zum Lord erheben.

VB. Berlin, 27. März.

Die Schlacht im Westen geht neuen Höhepunkten entgegen. Dem feindlichen Übermacht ist es gelungen, an verschiedenen Abschnitten in die Tiefe reichende Vorstöße zu führen und uns damit vor eine Lage zu stellen, die gemeistert werden wird, weil sie gemeistert werden muß. Schwache Völker mögen in solchen Tagen die Nerven verlieren und nicht mehr an ihren Stern glauben. Ein Volk wie das deutsche, das in schwerster Abwehr um Leben und Freiheit kämpft, das in diesem Krieg Übermenschliches vollbracht und einer Welt von Feinden unbeugsam die Stirn geboten hat, wird angesichts andrängender Gefahren erst recht in seiner Entschlossenheit wachsen, sich zu behaupten und das Schicksal mannhaft zu wenden. In dieser Haltung stellen wir uns der Entscheidung, um die jetzt gerungen wird. Festbleiben, harten Sinnes dem feindlichen Ansturm begegnen, in der Gewißheit leben, daß unsere Stunde wieder schlagen wird, das ist die Pflicht jedes Deutschen, der an sich, an sein Volk und den Führer glaubt und an die Gerechtigkeit der Sache, für die wir die Waffe führen. Nichts kann uns beugen, wenn wir in dieser Zuversicht den Wechselfällen des Tages die Stirn bieten — gläubig, stark und zu allem bereit!

Die Entwicklung der militärischen Lage im Westen zeigt in den letzten vierundzwanzig Stunden ähnliche sich durchkreuzende Linien wie in den Vortagen. An vielen Stellen wurde der Ansturm des Gegners aufgehalten; an anderen konnte er weiter vordringen. Die Aufgabe, die gegenwärtig vor Führung und Truppe steht, ist es, auch in den Gegenden des weitesten feindlichen Vordringens eine ähnliche geschlossene Front aufzubauen wie an den anderen Frontteilen, wo es gelungen ist, dem Vordringen des Feindes sich entgegenzustellen.

Dort, wo auf beiden Seiten die stärksten Kräfte ins Feld geführt werden, ist bezeichnenderweise dem Gegner das Vordringen bisher am wenigsten gelungen. Am Niederrhein wird im wesentlichen immer noch an der Bahn von Wesel nach Emmerich gekämpft. An der einzigen Stelle [...] amerikanische [...]

merns am Boden, sondern besonders in der Kraft der deutschen Gegenangriffe.

Auf dem rechten Flügel seiner großen Offensivbewegung, die die Westmächte gegenwärtig mit dem Ziel der Ausflankierung des Ruhrgebiets führen, nämlich in dem Brückenkopf, der zuerst bei Remagen gebildet wurde und sich jetzt von der Sieg bis zur Wied erstreckt, hat der Gegner nach Osten hin Fortschritte erzielen können. Die Front im Westerwald verläuft jetzt, roh gerechnet, von Eitorf über Altenkirchen bis westlich Montabaur. Dagegen vermochte er auch in den letzten vierundzwanzig Stunden die untere Sieg nicht zu überqueren. Im Zusammenhang mit diesen Angriffen stehen wohl Versuche, nördlich der unteren Sieg den Rhein zu überqueren. Auch dieser Versuch scheiterte aber. Dagegen konnten die [...] bei St. Goarshausen und Caub hin [...]

Völkischer Beobachter, May 1945

Front and reverse of the second cutting from the same newspaper that accompanied May, 1940 cutting discovered by the author, reporting the death of David Lloyd George.

INDEX